Throu

A NEW HIST...

IN 21 W...

Through Her Eyes

A NEW HISTORY OF IRELAND IN 21 WOMEN

Clodagh Finn

Gill Books

Gill Books
Hume Avenue
Park West
Dublin 12
www.gillbooks.ie
Gill Books is an imprint of M.H. Gill and Co.

Edited by Djinn von Noorden
Proofread by Esther Ní Dhonnacha
Printed in Scandbook, Sweden

A CIP catalogue record for this book is
available from the British Library.

5 4 3 2 1

The Author

Clodagh Finn is a journalist and the bestselling author of *A Time to Risk All*, a biography of Mary Elmes, the Irish Oskar Schindler. She has worked as a features writer, columnist and sub-editor for the *Irish Examiner*, the *Sunday Independent* and the *Irish Independent*. She has a degree in French and Archaeology from UCD and has a particular interest in history and archaeology.

The Illustrator

Holly Ingram is an illustrator and artist living in Dublin. She works primarily in her preferred medium of ballpoint biro. Holly graduated with a bachelor's degree in Fine Art from Dublin's National College of Art and Design in 2013. She is inspired by strong female subjects and protagonists, and is compelled to represent them and their stories in her work. www.hollyartist.com

For the O'Sullivan sisters, from left to right,
Breda, Kath, Una (my mother) and Pat

Acknowledgements

I could not have written about the 21 women in these pages without my own band of wonderful women. Heartfelt thanks to all of them, in particular, my sister Nuala Finn. There will be tea and sticky buns a-plenty to show my appreciation. That is not to say that there were not very many men who helped too. A huge thanks to them and to all the members of my very supportive family.

A big thank you to everyone at Gill Books, without whom there would be no book.

I can't say enough to thank the historians, archaeologists, researchers, academics and surviving relatives of the women featured. They were incredibly generous with their time and knowledge. Each one is thanked in the relevant chapters.

Finally, to the one who is ever-present and ever-encouraging, my husband Douglas Smith.

Contents

Author's Note   xiii

Woman of the Burren, one of Ireland's earliest
farmers (CIRCA 3600 BC)   1

Macha, the Celtic horse goddess of Ulster
(EARLY IRON AGE)   15

St Dahalin, early Irish saint and miracle worker
(CIRCA 500 AD)   31

Gormlaith, a queen to three kings
(DIED CIRCA 1030)   47

Aoife MacMurrough, countess and wife
of Strongbow (CIRCA 1153–1204)   63

Roesia de Verdun, castle-builder, landholder
and priory founder (CIRCA 1204–1247)   79

Margaret O'Carroll, medieval lady, patron of
the arts and negotiator (DIED 1451)   93

Katherine Fitzgerald, Countess of Desmond, who
reputedly lived to be 140 (CIRCA 1460s–1604)   107

Katherine Jones, Lady Ranelagh, intellectual,
woman of science, physician – and the brilliant
older sister of chemist Robert Boyle (1615–1691)   123

Ellen Hutchins, Ireland's first female botanist
(1785–1815)   139

Lady Sligo, landlady, style icon, humanitarian
and mother of 14 (1800-1878)   155

Jo Hiffernan, painter and muse to the artists
Whistler and Courbet (CIRCA 1843-1903)   173

Jennie Hodgers, a woman who fought as a male
soldier in the American Civil War (1843-1915)   189

Lizzie Le Blond, Alpine mountaineer and
photographer (1860-1934)   205

Clotilde Graves, acclaimed journalist, playwright
and bestselling novelist (1863-1932)   221

Sr Concepta Lynch, businesswoman, Dominican
sister and painter of a unique Celtic shrine (1874-1939) 237

The Overend sisters, farmers, charity workers
and motoring enthusiasts
(LETITIA OVEREND 1880-1977)
(NAOMI OVEREND 1900-1993)   255

Mabel Colhoun, pioneering archaeologist,
artist, photographer and teacher (1905-1992)   271

Rosemary Gibb, athlete, social worker, clown
and accomplished magician (1942-1997)   289

Jemma Redmond, groundbreaking
biotechnologist who printed living tissue
(1978-2016)   309

Bibliographical Notes   325

Author's Note

This is a book about possibilities – forgotten possibilities and overlooked ones. And it's a book about women. I have often wondered what kind of life I might have had if I lived in a different era. History books brought me some of the way. Archaeology opened up other perspectives, while myth and lore helped to flesh out the picture.

Drawing on all of them, I imagined myself into a real-life version of Doctor Who's fictional time machine, the Tardis, and touched down at several points throughout Irish history to 'meet' an Irish woman and force open a little aperture into her life and times.

I reported back to my niece Ciara Finn in an attempt to get a bit of perspective. She was born into a world more receptive than the one I experienced and, in turn, both of us enjoyed more opportunities than my mother and her three sisters – to whom this book is dedicated. But our shared experience of three generations did not prepare us for what we found. We were struck to discover that Irish women's lives were far more varied than you might ever know from reading conventional histories. To misquote the old rhyme, there were thinkers, toilers, soldiers, sailors and many more besides – pioneers and painters, scientists and writers, innovators and powerbrokers, yet few are widely known.

This collection of capsule biographies is an attempt to capture that heartening fact. It begins in the Burren in Co. Clare in 3600 BC, where we meet a 55-year-old woman whose partial remains were discovered under the prehistoric portal tomb at Poulnabrone. Her age alone makes her exceptional. Women in the early Neolithic were lucky to reach the end of their twenties. Now, thanks to revolutionary new technology, we also know what this early colonising farmer might have looked like – a modern-day Sardinian woman.

At the other end of the historical spectrum, Jemma Redmond brings the story right into the digital age. She was an award-winning biotechnologist who set out to 3D-print a better human being. She was also born intersex and campaigned on gender issues.

In the intervening millennia, there were women who had been forgotten and others who were cast as wily temptresses driving men into battle. One such woman, Gormlaith, a queen to three different kings, was said to have caused the Battle of Clontarf in 1014. While it is not always possible to rescue a complete version of women's lives from the existing records it is, at least, worth trying to tell the story from a female perspective.

In some cases, such as that of Queen Macha, the myth was inscribed on the landscape: the archaeological remains of the ancient capital of Ulster, where she once lived, are among the most important in Europe. In others, such as St Dahalin, the real woman was hard to find but her memory – or to be exact her miracle – endured with remarkable force. Thousands still visit Tobar na Súl, the Well of the Eyes, in Co. Kerry, where there are many recorded cures for eye complaints.

We've heard so much about Strongbow (Richard fitz Gilbert), but what of Aoife MacMurrough, the woman who played a central role in her father's political manoeuvres but was never allowed to take the stage herself? What might life in the twelfth century look like from her perspective? A century later, Anglo-Norman Roesia de Verdun became a successful landowner in her own right. After her husband died, she built Castleroche Castle in Co. Louth and was said to have successfully defended it against Irish raiders. How was life for her?

The fifteenth-century Margaret O'Carroll was 'the best woman of her time in Ireland' according to the *Annals of the Four Masters*, yet she does not feature prominently in the history books. Katherine FitzGerald, the old Countess of Desmond, is better known because her longevity has prompted several debates. She reportedly lived to be 140 years old, a feat that opens a window into health, ageing and the tried-and-tested methods of combating age in the sixteenth century. One of the best ways to stay young, it was said, was to rub salt butter on the body as if it were a seasoning, then to set yourself, naked, before a fire.

For some years I have been gathering the stories of people, who happen to be women, whose considerable contributions have been ignored, overlooked or forgotten. Why, for instance, has Lady Ranelagh, the older, brilliant sister of Robert Boyle, the father of chemistry, not made it into our history books or onto the national curriculum? She was one of the most prominent women of science and politics in seventeenth-century Ireland and England, yet she is largely unknown.

Ireland's first female botanist Ellen Hutchins is gaining more recognition, but what of Lady Sligo, a woman who spoke out against slavery with her husband in Jamaica and later helped her tenants in Mayo during the Famine of 1845? Or Jennie Hodgers, from Co. Louth, who fought as a male Union soldier during the American Civil War?

If the name Jo Hiffernan is familiar, it might be because she was thought to be the model for French realist painter Gustave Courbet's *L'Origine du monde* [the Origin of the World], the 1866 painting of a woman's genitals. But she was not. '*La Belle Irlandaise*', as she was known, had much to say in her own right and tried to make it as a painter in London after her family left Ireland to escape the Famine.

There are a number of firsts too – Clotilde Graves, dubbed the first female journalist by one of her contemporaries in 1880s London; Lizzie Le Blond, the trailblazing mountaineer elected first president of the Ladies' Alpine Club in 1907; Mabel Colhoun, a pioneering archaeologist and educationalist; and Rosemary Gibb, clown and magician, the first Irish woman to be admitted to the International Magic Circle in the 1990s.

The stories of women in war continue to emerge. The hundreds of women who participated in the 1916 Easter Rising have recently been remembered and acknowledged: here, we look at those who did much to help the often-forgotten Irish soldiers who fought in the Great War. Dublin sisters and motoring enthusiasts Letitia and Naomi Overend might not be best remembered for their humanitarian work, though both of them volunteered at the Irish War Hospital Depot in Dublin during World War I. When the war was over and public atten-tion shifted to the War of Independence, Sr Concepta Lynch and her community at the Dominican Convent in Dun Laoghaire, Co. Dublin, remembered the local boys who died on the Western Front by building a simple oratory on the convent grounds. Sr Concepta spent 16 years painting it in the magnificent Lynch Method of Celtic illumination she had learned from her father, Thomas J Lynch.

In 2020, it will be 100 years since she first took up her paintbrush. There is a certain symmetry about that date, which prompted me to write 20 chapters telling the stories of Irish women, from the Neolithic to the digital era. They are not, however, in any way designed to offer a complete history nor, sadly, are they representative: the women in this collection were often privileged and had opportunities unavailable to millions of others. Many come from the Church of Ireland tradition. For others, the Catholic Church offered opportunities that women otherwise might not have had.

What follows, then, is an attempt to offer 20 different ways of looking at what has gone before – but this time through *her* eyes.

Woman of the Burren

ONE OF IRELAND'S EARLIEST FARMERS (CIRCA 3600 BC)

As an elder, she would have been a source of knowledge that was highly regarded. She would have known the social and cultural environment, known where the best foraging grounds were and she would have remembered the lore and history of the past.

Dr Barra O'Donnabhain

If she were alive today, the Woman of the Burren – let's call her that after the place she was found – would look most like a woman from modern-day Sardinia. Analysis of her DNA tells us that. The same scientific data suggests that she wasn't very tall, genetically speaking, at least, but she was certainly strong and exceptionally healthy. Her bones confirm that she lived to be at least 55 years old, several decades more than the average woman could expect to survive in the fourth millennium BC.

This robust elder also had a remarkable story to tell because she was among the first wave of farmers who swept into Ireland almost 6000 years ago. They brought with them agricultural techniques and a tradition of building conspicuous monuments for their dead. Sometime after they arrived in Co. Clare, most likely from northern France or Britain, they built a tomb that still looks imposing in the dramatic landscape of the Burren.

Poulnabrone portal tomb is one of the most photographed archaeological sites in Ireland today – a symbol of an ancient past that is so often embroidered with myth and supposition. Yet we know what really happened at this singular place: it is now possible to capture a snapshot of Ireland's earliest farmers going about their daily business, thanks to the enlightening work of archaeologists and genetic researchers.

We can say, for example, that the Woman of the Burren looked nothing like the Irish population alive today. 'If you want an idea of what this person would have been like, look at modern-day Sardinians,' says Dr Lara Cassidy, a post-doctoral genetic researcher at Trinity College Dublin. '[They] are not completely the same, but genetically they are the most similar alive today.'

We can also say that this woman from the early Neolithic (or New Stone Age) was one of the first farmers who came in a mass migration of people into Ireland almost 6000 years ago. For decades, opinion was divided on how agriculture got here, but now there is evidence for significant movement into Ireland.

It's interesting to recall the earliest Irish origin legends that traced the history of Ireland back to a series of 'ancient invasions'. The word 'invasion' is too blunt, perhaps, as there is evidence that some of the newcomers mixed with those already here, yet there was conflict too, as excavations carried out under Dr Ann Lynch at Poulnabrone have shown.

Analysis of bones by archaeologists Dr Barra O'Donnabhain and Dr Mara Tesorieri (who, coincidentally, also has Sardinian connections) open an unrivalled window into life – and death – in the fourth millennium BC. One of those buried with the Woman of the Burren was struck from behind with such force that the tip of a projectile lodged in his or her hip. It's not possible to say if the victim was male or female but the weapon, made of chert, penetrated the bone. The person died shortly afterwards, although probably not from this injury.

In any case, a new understanding of those interactions – violent or otherwise – is now emerging thanks to pioneering technology that is coaxing information from ancient DNA in a way that was never thought possible. Dr Cassidy, with collaboration from Queen's University Belfast, the National Museum of Ireland and a number of Irish archaeologists, has succeeded in analysing DNA taken from prehistoric bones. In 2015, for instance, a study of a 5200-year-old female farmer from Ballynahatty, near Belfast, showed that her ancestors came from Anatolia, or modern-day Turkey, a centre of early agriculture and domestication.

It seems the ancestors of the people who arrived in Co. Clare around 3800 BC also made the same journey. They spread out from Turkey, all over Europe, and eventually settled in northern France. Some 6000 years ago, something happened to make them seek out new ground – a changing climate perhaps, or a growing population. They ventured north by sea, to England, Scandinavia and Ireland. When they arrived, one small group established itself in the Burren.

'It must have been a very dynamic time of colonisation – because that is what it is – with these people coming in who were adept at farming,' says Dr Cassidy:

They were establishing themselves and building these megaliths. One of the big questions I wanted to answer was whether the hunter gatherers already here had any input into these new farming communities, and indeed we are finding some evidence that there was small input from these groups.

There is evidence of violent interaction at Poulnabrone, though it's not possible to say whether the newly arrived farmers clashed with other new arrivals, or those already living in the Burren. In any event, they went on to build a structure that was visible and permanent. Standing 1.8 m high, it was their statement in limestone – their claim on the landscape perhaps, or a concrete expression of the community's shared identity.

When the Woman of the Burren was born some 200 years later, that monument would have been a constant in her life. And, as Dr Cassidy muses, she would have seen an awful lot of ceremonies centred around it in her 55 years: 'I wonder if she knew that she would end up there herself?'

The remains of only a select few survive. Over a period of six centuries, just 35 individuals (18 adults and 17 children) were interred there – a fraction of the general population. Or at least, only that number survive. Dr O'Donnabhain and Dr Tesorieri have suggested that this may have been a place of temporary burial and the remains may have been moved on elsewhere. We don't know how or why they were chosen, but we can at least strike certain criteria off the list. Age or gender didn't appear to be a factor, as archaeological excavations revealed in the mid-1980s. Men and women are equally represented – and there are children too, of all ages.

Blood ties didn't appear to matter either, with little evidence of genetic kinship between the individuals sampled from this house of the dead. That was one of the more surprising findings from a study of their DNA at Trinity College Dublin.

'It's hard to figure out why a group of unrelated people end up in this tomb,' says Dr Cassidy. 'Maybe they were spiritual ancestors or maybe they were chosen because of when they died – on a solstice, for example – or how they died? We can only guess.'

If they were members of some kind of social elite, it was an elite who led physically strenuous lives. There is significant wear and tear to their joints and many of the bones in the tomb bear the marks of degenerative arthritis in the upper spine. Like those buried with her, it's likely that the Woman of the Burren was accustomed to balancing heavy loads on her head and shoulders. Many of the community had arthritis in their upper limbs too, which was most severe in the wrists and hands. It was more pronounced on the left side, suggesting that many of these early farmers were left-handed.

It's astonishing to think that a detail, such as possible left-handedness, might be evident after five millennia, and so much more can be gleaned from the remains unearthed during conservation excavations in the eighties. The bones of this small farming community were intermingled and disarticulated so it is hard to establish individual narratives. Yet, the remains – fragmented and commingled as they were – force open a crack through which we can glimpse the very first farmers and how they lived over 5000 years ago.

Thanks to the artefacts they left behind, we can also imagine them at their daily work as potters, toolmakers, jewellers or craftworkers. We can say something about how they worshipped, conducted trade and even, at times, did battle: three adults bear the scars of injuries most likely inflicted in combat.

Life would have been difficult – and turbulent. The Woman of the Burren would have witnessed a lot in her lifetime. She lived at a time when sudden, unexpected death was a feature of everyday life. Hunger was common, disease too, and broken bones would have been an occupational hazard. One person had a compression fracture on the foot, probably caused by a heavy weight falling on it. It led to severe arthritis and deformity, yet this person must have been cared for in the community.

Others must have been nursed through their injuries. One young man who suffered a fractured skull lived to tell the tale. He was hit with a blunt object, possibly a stone from a sling, but the wound healed. Another suffered a fractured rib, maybe caused by a blow to the chest, but that injury healed too.

There was, however, one issue that didn't appear to trouble this community: dental health. The early farmers of the Burren had good teeth, a testament to an abrasive diet low in sugar and high in protein; a Paleo diet, Neolithic style! Of the 585 adult teeth found in the tomb, just one had tooth decay. Analysis of children's teeth, where they were found, also showed they were relatively healthy and suffered less physiological stress than medieval children in Ireland.

The rate of tooth loss was low too. The Woman of the Burren may well have had all, or most, of her own teeth when she died. She might, however, have used them as a tool to power-bite or crush various foodstuff or materials. Grooves in some of the teeth also suggest another activity – the regular threading of fibres through the teeth, perhaps to make string or fabric.

That fabric may have been used in clothing or as some kind

of bedding in houses that probably would have been more comfortable than the mud cabins of the poorest in the lead-up to the Great Famine of the nineteenth century, says archaeologist Dr Barra O'Donnabhain. Neolithic houses, he adds, were typically rectangular and made of timber; equivalent to a comfortable thatched cottage with a central hearth.

The Woman of the Burren possibly lived in a cluster of houses and although we don't know for sure what sort of clothing she wore, it would be wrong to think that her community were in any way primitive or brutish. As Dr O'Donnabhain explains, 'They were so skilled when it came to making clothes to suit their environment.' You need only look to the clothing worn by Ötzi, the so-called 'iceman' whose remains were preserved in the ice of the Tyrolean Alps for over 5000 years. His clothes would have been similar to what early Irish farmers wore, he says.

Ötzi's coat, leggings, loincloth, hat and shoes were all so well preserved that it was possible to see that they were made solely from leather, hide and braided grass. They were stitched together with fibres, animal sinews and tree bast (fibre made from bark) and even repaired several times. There were loops on the ends of his leggings that fastened to his shoes. The shoes themselves were made of several layers of material (tree-bast netting, deer hide and fur) and were stuffed with dry grass for insulation. Experiments with reconstructed shoes showed that they were warm and comfortable, even over long distances.

Ötzi also had a well-equipped tool kit complete with copper axe, longbow arrows and quiver, flint dagger, a retoucher to sharpen tools, along with material to start a fire and two pieces of birch fungus, probably kept for their antibiotic properties.

Like some of the people in Poulnabrone tomb, Ötzi was also the victim of an attack. He suffered a severe head injury but it was the arrow wound to his shoulder that caused his death.

Although no traces of clothing survive in the Burren, several pieces of what we might call jewellery do, including a finely crafted bone or antler pendant made by a specialised crafts-person using flint or quartz tools. He or she was working to a well-thought-out design, as evidenced by the incised outlines. Did the Woman of the Burren wear it? Did the polished beads, also found in the tomb, belong to her too? What of the honed antler toggles; did they once fasten a garment she wore?

The 26 stone tools that also survive give us a glimpse into daily life. They were made from local material and used to whittle and shave wood and plants (rushes or reeds), perhaps to make baskets, ropes or thatch. A study of the pattern of wear shows that those tools were not often used to scrape hides or cut meat. These early farmers did not eat much meat, even if they did keep cows, pigs and sheep or goats. 'Only pigs were native to Ireland,' says Dr O'Donnabhain. 'The rest had to be introduced by the earliest generations of farmers by whatever flimsy boats they had. So, in those first years of agriculture, animals like cattle and sheep would have been new and prob-ably a bit wonder-inducing for the local Mesolithic [8000 BC to about 4000 BC] population.'

The animal remains that survive were of young animals and their bones don't show any sign of butchering, further evidence that the community in the Burren did not eat much meat (there is little sign of animal protein in their bone collagen) although they did drink animal milk. They supplemented this with whole grains, fruits such as berries and crab apples, nuts and maybe vegetables. Surprisingly, these early farmers did not make use of the sea and its bounty of fish, seabirds and shellfish at nearby Ballyvaughan Bay. Theirs was a wholly terrestrial diet.

Yet they did trade with people overseas. A polished stone axe and a fragment of another were made of dacite, a volcanic rock that is not local. Perhaps it was a gift used to forge relationships between two distant communities, as archaeologist Gabriel Cooney suggested about similar objects from the period. It certainly seems to have been a treasured object as great effort was taken to polish it. Two quartz crystals, also found in the tomb, seem to be imbued with a deeper, though unknown, significance.

The Woman of the Burren would have known their meaning – and much more besides. Her advanced age meant she would have been a keeper of stories, a guardian of community history. As Dr O'Donnabhain explains, most traditional societies value age and in a society where child mortality was high and parents typically didn't live beyond their thirties, the wider community – and its elders – assumed a great importance:

> It really did take a village to raise a child. They depended on the wider community to survive so the community becomes much more important and, within that, the elder is a very important person, one who is central to knowledge and skills. As an elder, she [the Woman of the Burren] would have been a source of knowledge that was highly regarded. She would have known the social and cultural environment, known where the best foraging grounds were and she would have remembered the lore and history of the past.

Dr Cassidy suggests that her knowledge of the past probably extended to how her ancestors came from France or Britain and established themselves for the first time in Ireland.

She also probably told stories about the building of the tomb itself, a feat that demanded skill, organisation and considerable collective effort to quarry and transport the stone, possibly using timber rollers and ropes, to the site. The archaeologists who excavated it evocatively described what that process might have been like:

> The positioning of the large slab-like capstone must have been a nerve-racking but exciting operation, especially as the dramatic profile began to take shape. A ramp, presumably of stone and clay, must have been constructed against the back of the chamber to allow the capstone to be manoeuvred into place.

The Woman of the Burren, however, would have been able to explain why they chose this particular spot in a landscape that was then heavily wooded with pine, oak, elm and hazel. There were only pockets of exposed limestone here and there when the first settlers cleared scrub by setting fires. They picked a place along a routeway into the Burren and one that was near water.

Perhaps that was just a practical consideration but portal tombs, with their covered chambers and enormous capstones, are often found near water. 'Water', as the Poulnabrone excavation report explains, 'tends to be an intrinsic part of most spiritual beliefs. The fact that this particular source is a spring where the water bubbles from the ground and creates a pond when the water table is high might suggest a symbolic association with birth.'

The tomb's entrance is also aligned with the entrance to a ravine, which leads to an amphitheatre-like space that is now covered in hazel scrub. We can't say how – or if – these people used this natural enclosure as a public space but its existence opens up an intriguing possibility of a community gathering to entertain, perform, maybe pray.

The burial of the dead was a highly complex process that involved extensive manipulation of skeletal remains. Bodies were first left to decompose, but not outside. Some bones were burned or deliberately broken and then moved in and out of the tomb. Some body parts – feet and skulls – seem to have been lined up along the edges of the burial chamber while other bones were jammed into crevices, such as the fragment of mandible (lower jawbone) that tells us the Woman of the Burren lived to such a great age.

The funerary rituals were deeply significant to the people carrying them out, says Dr O'Donnabhain. There is evidence of the dead being treated in a very similar way at a Neolithic burial site in a cave in Annagh, Co. Limerick. 'The bones may have been considered treasured ancestral "relics" to be passed among the community. Maybe they were moving between tombs. Is that how they forged alliances?' he wonders. Others have suggested that such complex burials were a way of emphasising the solidarity of the group at times of social change.

And it was a time of immense social change. As Dr Cassidy explains, Europe was shaped by two major episodes in prehistory – the advent of agriculture and, later, the introduction of metalworking. Both innovations brought profound cultural change and genetic change, which is now beginning to be charted. She adds:

> Now we have this immense power to look at how populations are related to one another … We have Irish genomes from all time periods from the Mesolithic [8000 BC to 4000 BC] to modern times. With that data, we propose to plot a demographic scaffold for the island.

Genetic research at Trinity College has identified three distinct Irish populations and two mass migrations. The earliest people, the hunter-gatherer or Mesolithic population, were very similar to Cheddar Man, the famous human male skeleton found in England whose DNA revealed that he had blue eyes, curly hair and dark skin. Researchers at Trinity College Dublin and the National Museum of Ireland found similar results in Ireland. Dan Bradley, Professor of Population Genetics at Trinity College Dublin, said the team analysed two people from about 6000 years ago whose ancestors came here at the end of the last Ice Age.

'There is nobody like them alive today,' Dr Cassidy explains.

The first migration were the early farmers who swelled the country's population tenfold to an estimated 100,000 people. Some 1500 years after that, the second wave – and the foundation for the modern Irish population – arrived in the Copper and Early Bronze Age. A huge influx of people moved in from the steppe above the Black Sea in Russia, bringing with them oxen and a society that appears to have been hierarchical, male-driven and probably violent. They also brought with them the so-called 'Celtic curse', haemochromatosis. One of the Early Bronze Age men studied at Trinity College Dublin and Queen's University Belfast was a carrier for the iron overload disorder that is particularly prevalent in Ireland.

Over time, there were other movements into Ireland. The Vikings made their mark as did the Anglo-Normans, but nothing on the same scale as the influxes that took place in the Stone Age and early Bronze Age. The Woman of the Burren was not one of the very first farmers to come to Ireland but she probably knew the stories – or possibly earliest legends – about those who did.

Macha

THE CELTIC HORSE GODDESS OF ULSTER (EARLY IRON AGE)

Macha was, and still is, the Horse Goddess because her female spirit was akin to that of an unbroken horse. Wild, free and strong. She could run fast and never became prey to the dominant male power of the day.

Kate Fitzpatrick, myth-writer and
teacher of Celtic spirituality

Macha is a goddess with many different faces. This powerful, otherworldly woman gave her name to the city of Armagh (Ard Mhaca, meaning Macha's height) and to the ancient capital of Ulster, Emain Macha (anglicised as Navan Fort). But she also assumed human form and it is the story of her traumatic experience as a mother-to-be that is, perhaps, the most poignant.

While heavily pregnant, she was forced to race against the ancient King of Ulster's prized horses to prove a point. She pleaded with him to wait until her child was born, but the king was not for turning. Macha's husband Cruinniuc had let it slip that his wife could outrun the royal steed and the king, incensed, threatened to put him to death if the race did not go ahead.

To save him, Macha went to the starting line, her swollen belly visible to the crowd assembled at Emain Macha. The chariot led by the king's horses drew alongside her. A mark was set in the sand and the race began. The horses' long manes straightened in the wind as they galloped on the track. But next to them Macha was an arrow. She had emerged from the otherworld like lightning on a stream and now she sped past the horses with the grace and lightness of the wind. She passed the finish line with seven lengths to spare.

The exertion of the race, however, took an immediate and terrible toll. She fell to the dusty ground and went into labour. Writhing in agony, she cried out for help as she gave birth to twins. 'A mother bore each of you, help me now, please ... help me,' she implored the onlookers, but nobody came forward to help her. Not one. Instead, they jeered and mocked, afraid that any assistance would be seen as an insult to the king.

Macha must have had an inkling of what was to come. Earlier, she had warned her husband not to say anything of their life together when they were invited to enjoy the king's fair day with its feasting and music. Cruinniuc promised he would not. Life had improved beyond measure since Macha came to live with him at his remote hilltop home. He was a widower with four children when Macha arrived, suddenly, from a place beyond the waves and began to care for them all. Now she was pregnant herself and the family was happy and content.

Despite the warning, Cruinniuc forgot himself during the merriment of the feast and boasted of Macha's supernatural speed. He could not take it back now and watched in horror as his wife, alone and humiliated, gathered up her babies – a boy and a girl – and returned to the otherworld. Before she went, she told the men of Ulster they would pay dearly for disrespecting a woman in her condition. She condemned them to feel the pain of labour for five nights and four days whenever they needed their strength in battle most. The curse would afflict every warrior of Ulster – with the exception of Cú Chulainn – for nine generations.

And, finally, she said: 'This place will bear my name and that of my children.'

This place, Emain Macha (meaning the twins of Macha), still bears her name as it has done for centuries. The name – or an earlier version of it – appeared on the first known map of Ireland created by Ptolemy around 140 AD. And the famous goddess continues to influence: a new Irish-language cultural centre called Aonach Mhacha (the Assembly of Macha) is due to open in autumn 2019.

Her name has been stitched into the landscape over millennia, but there is more to the place names than legend. Emain Macha (or Navan Centre, as it is now called) was at the centre of the heroic sagas of the Ulster Cycle but it was also a very real ancient capital. In the same way that archaeologists unearthed a real-life version of the legendary city of Troy depicted in Homer's *Iliad*, Irish archaeologists have found the physical remains of the place so evocatively described in the ancient Cycle.

'We have a real place to situate the myth,' says Damien Houlahan, a guide at Navan Centre, as he climbs a drumlin where a grassy mound covers the tangible remains of a vast temple built in Macha's time. 'It is very rare in mythology that you get a block of stories and a place as well. There is a Troy, and there is an Emain Macha. The Ulster Cycle is Ireland's *Iliad*; he explains.

Macha's story marks the beginning of a cycle that has brought the exploits of Cú Chulainn and Medb, the warrior queen of Connacht, among others, into the fabric of many an Irish childhood. While Macha, Cú Chulainn and his Homeric counterpart Achilles are mythical figures, the descriptions of chariots, feasting and weaponry have real-life counterparts in the Irish Iron age when Emain Macha was experiencing something of a golden age.

In 95 BC – we know the precise date – the hill on this singular site was a hive of activity. Visitors to the centre today are invited to turn back the clock and imagine the scene: 'Something remarkable is happening,' they are told. 'There is a tangible excitement in the air. From all over, people arrive with earth to pack into the growing walls of a massive temple, 45 metres in diameter, now in the last stages of construction.'

What they were building was a great circular temple of wood that has no parallel in Ireland.

'Its true purpose,' continues the narrative, 'remains a mystery, but it was no mere burial ground or ritual sacrifice site. The Celts were in retreat in Britain, pushed to the fringes of England and Wales by the Romans and under threat in Scotland. But in Ireland their society and pagan religion still dominated. And Emain Macha … is a vital part of that society.'

When excavations began at Navan Fort in the 1960s, archaeologists expected to find the remains of an Iron Age royal site; glimpses perhaps of the court presided over by King Conor Mac Nessa. His palace is described in the *Tochmarc Emire* (The Wooing of Emer) as a place of state, rank and plenty with 'fruits and fatness and harvest of the sea'. The king's chamber, it was said, had carvings of red yew and a ceiling made of silver. Its bronze pillars stood 30 feet tall; each one inset with glittering gold so that it was bright by day and by night. The site did yield some tantalising real-life echoes of King Conor's palace. In 1992, for instance, archaeologist Chris Lynn found a structure that was similar to the description of Conor's great hall.

The hilltop complex has seen many waves of people over the centuries, but it assumed particular importance around 400 BC. During that time, it may have been a royal centre with visitors coming from as far away as North Africa or Gibraltar – or so it seems, as the skull of a Barbary ape was found in one of the high-status round houses. Was this a valuable gift from a visiting dignitary? Or maybe even an exotic pet? Some classical references suggest exotic animals were traded as pets, although only the animal's skull was found. In any event, it travelled a very long way to get here. The astonishing discovery shows the incredible reach of those early communities – they had contact with countries very far away.

And, despite the name Navan Fort, the ancient people who lived here were not trying to keep those visitors out. It was never a fort and has no fortifying defences. Instead, it was surrounded by an immense earthen bank with a ditch inside it. (Forts have the ditch on the outside to make access difficult.) As Damien Houlahan explains: 'So instead of trying to keep something out, in many ways they are trying to keep something in. The ditch goes the full circumference of the whole drumlin and it's man-made, built around 94 BC.'

A year later, the enormous freestanding temple was complete. Inside, timber posts were laid out in a series of circles that would have looked like a giant spoked wheel from above. The interior was also divided into 34 sections, perhaps a reference to the 34 tribes mentioned in the sagas. In any case, it was a significant feat of architectural engineering. 'Try dividing an apple into 34,' says Damien, to illustrate the point. 'It would have taken a huge effort to build this and the effect would have been visible for miles around.'

It may have been roofed but if not, the thicket of timber posts would have resembled a forest of oak trees – and perhaps that was the intention. Was this a sacred oak grove, or a sanctified wood dedicated to Macha, as archaeologist John Waddell has suggested? If so, are we looking at the archaeological imprint of a people who honoured Macha, the goddess and queen of the supernatural race, the Tuatha Dé Danann?

The possibility that Navan Fort is the physical expression of myth in the landscape prompted Chris Lynn to describe it as one of the most important archaeological monuments in Europe. The archaeologist, who directed excavations there, believes it possible that some of the legends survive from a time when they were a part of everyday life and religion:

In the myths and legends of the Ulaidh (the Ulstermen), Emain is portrayed as a royal headquarters, the capital of a warlike aristocracy and a place of assembly for the people occupying the northern quarter of Ireland. Early Irish myth and legend are of great interest because they preserve elements of a prehistoric tradition that have not survived elsewhere.

Back on the hilltop, the view is all-encompassing. If the elite assembled here to conduct their ceremonies, they would have been visible for miles around. Damien Houlahan sketches a tentative picture: a procession of dignitaries and the Red Branch warriors are on the outer bank while the royal elite gather in the temple. There are huge fires – and eventually there will be one that burns the shrine to the ground.

There is fanfare, bustle, colour – and noise. Loud noise. We can say that with a degree of certainty as four magnificent trumpets, each nearly 2m long, were retrieved from a nearby lake called Loughnashade (or Place of the Jewels). Three are now lost, but the remaining one – a thing of immense beauty on view at the National Museum of Ireland in Dublin – has allowed experts to unlock its secrets.

When played, the Loughnashade trumpet was capable of producing a sound at least as loud as the terrifying din said to have been made by the Celts' trumpeters and horn blowers as they ran naked into war. The ancient writers wrote of the chilling sound of their instruments, their war cries, yells, leaping and hideous songs, all of which were designed to confuse the enemy. The trumpet found at Loughnashade is more likely to have been used in ceremonies, but it would have been just as loud.

'It could deafen a listener if played in an enclosed place, and in the open air the sound would carry for miles,' according to Simon Dwyer of Ancient Music Ireland. The composer and specialist in ancient instruments has played an exact replica of the trumpet, made by Scottish silversmith John Creed using Iron Age techniques.

The first surprising thing is its weight – this imposing-looking instrument weighs just a single kilo. It could easily be held aloft, giving its player the appearance of a tall, long-necked creature from a distance. Simon Dwyer imagines the effect:

There were four trumpets found together at Loughnashade … Thus, an exciting scene can be imagined of a line of trumpets high in the air leading an Iron Age army with much fanfare. In Irish mythology, the *Táin Bó Froích* tells of how music made by [Queen Medb's husband] Ailill's horn players was so wonderful that 30 of his men died of rapture.

The trumpet also shows the immense skill of Iron Age metal-workers who produced a very finely crafted instrument from riveted sheets of hammered bronze. They were also skilled musicians with a deep understanding of sound. The circular disc at the end of the trumpet was first thought to be a visual flourish but experiments show it has sound properties that allow for harmonies. It also increases the volume, which led didgeridoo player Philip Conyngham to suggest it was an early loudspeaker.

The design of the trumpet tells another important story. The same disc is beautifully decorated with a lotus bud in a style of art known as La Tène, or high Celtic art: this shows that the people living in the area around 95 BC were Celtic, even if it is not fully understood how a Celtic language and culture took hold in Ireland.

It is not understood either why the temple built to honour Macha – or perhaps other gods and goddesses – was burned down relatively shortly after its completion. Having been briefly used for ceremonies, it was then torched and covered by the mound that is still there today. 'They were definitely trying to create something that stood the test of time,' guide Damien says. They succeeded in that – the mound is the centrepiece of a complex that has more than 80 sites of archaeological significance.

We have a trumpet, a temple and a mythical tale all dating to the same period, the first century BC. But what of the ordinary people; the men and women who attended or watched the ceremonies take place on the sacred hill? They probably lived nearby, says Damien, though the area has not been excavated.

Instead, a house of a slightly later date has been reconstructed to allow visitors to meet the people of the Iron Age. Inside, Finn, a man wearing a *léine* (linen tunic) over colourful plaid trousers, takes on the role with relish. 'Come,' he says, 'sit by the fire.' Hospitality is a very important part of the culture, he explains, as is cleanliness. Before entering the house, visitors are expected to go to the stream to wash and then rub sheep fat and herbs on their skin.

Then, they are invited to sit around a central hearth, which casts a warm glow around a circular, spacious interior. During winter, meat hangs from the roof to be smoked but it's late spring, a lean time in the Iron Age calendar. 'We're down to the grains,' says Finn. They have oats for porridge, honey and milk. They grind the oats by hand on a stone quern, or grinder – but the result is coarse and gritty, which wears down their teeth. Finn is hoping his ground-down set will hold out until he dies: 'I'll be here until I'm about 33 if the gods are good to me.'

The gods are invoked regularly and it is clear that there is little separation between the sacred and profane in daily life. Macha and the stories of the Cycle would have been part of the everyday here, told around the fire in houses like this one built in the first century AD. In modern times, we tend to think of stories as frivolous or entertaining; in ancient times, they were anything but. 'Myth is deadly serious,' as Jaan Puhvel put it. They tell people about their place in the world and how to understand it. They explain their beginnings and, often, plot out the way ahead.

The stories of the Ulster Cycle that have echoed down the centuries also tell us something about the people who told them. They offer fleeting glimpses of the thoughts, values and beliefs of an ancient people who immortalised Macha by naming two places of immense importance after her. It's not unreasonable to assume, then, that the story of her difficult passage through this world served as some kind of reminder to early peoples to value women and motherhood.

Macha is also known as a mother goddess and at a time when childbirth was so dangerous, it made sense to tell a story that instilled respect for women, pregnancy and childbirth. A child did well to make it past its first summer in the first century BC. Childhood itself was difficult as young children worked on the family holding and were prone to accidents, not to mention disease and hunger.

Life for women in the Iron Age was difficult too, as it was for everybody. But women and men were not equal, although there is a modern tendency to see the laws that governed them, the Brehon laws, as progressive and woman-friendly. Women were under the protection of a male – their fathers, brothers, husbands or sons – and the legal system was designed more to protect the family and its inheritance rather than the rights of any individual.

Famously, the Brehon laws allowed for divorce. A husband had several grounds to leave his wife: if she was unfaithful, brought shame on his honour or smothered her child, to mention just some of them. On the other hand, a woman could divorce her husband if he spread false rumours about her, was unfaithful, impotent – or even obese.

More infamously, the laws also permitted polygamy. Finn, however, has no desire for a second wife, he says. His wife has the same status as he does because she came to the marriage with equal wealth. If he decided to take a second wife, his first wife could choose her. 'Then, she is allowed to beat her for three days and three nights so that she knows who is boss,' he says, matter-of-factly.

Everybody in the household – children, parents, relatives – slept in the same bed, a slightly raised ledge of bedding made of ferns and heather. Daily life would have been a busy, bustling, loud and rather pungent affair with geese, dogs and pigs wandering around the enclosure. A weaver (probably male, as weaving was considered men's work) might have been at work outside. In another part of the enclosure, there might have been bread baking in an oven, or a cauldron with berries, stale urine and plants bubbling on a fire to dye the colourful clothes so popular among Iron Age communities.

Cattle was their wealth and, in summer, they went cattle raiding in a practice that dominates the most famous story of the Ulster Cycle, 'Táin Bó Cúailnge' (The Cattle Raid of Cooley). In it, the warrior queen of Connacht Medb and her husband Ailill prepare a raid on Ulster to steal its prized brown bull, Donn Cúailnge. A poetess of Connacht, Feidelm, warns them against it: 'I see it bloody, I see it red,' she says, although they fail to heed her warning.

The description of Feidelm in the saga is detailed and vivid and it gives us a fascinating picture of what an idealised woman in the Iron Age might have looked like:

She wore a vari-coloured cloak with a golden pin in it and a hooded tunic with red embroidery. She had shoes with golden fastenings. Her face was oval, narrow below, broad above. Her eyebrows were dark and black. Her beautiful black eyelashes cast a shadow on to the middle of her cheeks … Her teeth were like a shower of pearls between her lips. She had three plaits of hair: two plaits wound around her head, the third hanging down her back, touching her calves behind. In her hand she carried a weaver's beam of white bronze, with golden inlay. There were three pupils in each of her eyes. The maiden was armed and her chariot was drawn by two black horses.

Macha, too, must have taken on a very real aspect when she was conjured up by a people famous for their storytelling. Julius Caesar said of the Celts: 'It is said that they memorise immense amounts of poetry, and so some of them continue their studies for 20 years. They consider it improper to commit their studies to writing.'

In the Irish version of those studies and poems, women are portrayed in many different ways – poetess, warrior queen, mother goddess, to name but a few. And they had power. Macha's rage at her treatment is felt for nine generations. It was as if she raced against the king's horses for the sake of all women: to send a strong message to the male rulers of the time that there were dire consequences for mistreating women. We can't say how the story was interpreted in the past but, from a modern perspective, it demands respect for the female members of a community.

We can't really say how gendered Iron Age society was either, but it would have placed a much bigger emphasis on the community than the individual, says Damien Houlahan. They needed to, to survive. 'It would have been barbaric too and hard with disease and hunger. It would have been very hard for both men and women. But one thing is for sure, ancient people had a respect for the environment and the landscape and there was a balance and we have totally lost that.'

Today, at the place named after Macha, the Irish Iron Age is brought back to life with an evocative combination of archaeology, living history and myth. But there is something else here too that is not visible – spirituality. Yet that is not quite true because, a few miles away, Armagh's Christian past is very evident. St Patrick built his first stone church there in the fifth century and the city is the ecclesiastical capital of Ireland with two cathedrals – one Catholic, one Church of Ireland – both bearing his name.

Now, however, there is a growing interest in an older, sacred feminine past to counterbalance the traditionally male nature of the Christian Church. In the past decade, staff at Navan Centre recognised that the spiritual side of the site resonated with its modern visitors. To respond to that, they introduced a series of very well-attended Celtic mindfulness workshops, which grew out of a talk given in 2012 by Kate Fitzpatrick, a woman who has spent almost three decades studying and teaching the spirituality within Celtic myth.

She grew up in Northern Ireland in the 1960s, '70s and '80s, at the height of the Troubles, and draws on Macha's story to introduce the idea of healing and transformation for the counties of Ulster. 'Macha is in the air here,' Kate says:

I believe she is a guide for women, giving them strength, tenacity and courage; bringing in a wave of healing to the

Northern counties. She was, and still is, the Horse Goddess because her female spirit was akin to that of an unbroken horse. Wild, free and strong. She could run fast and never became prey to the dominant male power of the day.

Kate tells the story of her own spiritual journey in *Macha's Twins*, a book that is in such demand at Navan Centre that staff can't keep it on the shelves. 'The journey took me back to the myths of the Ulster Cycle and a call to heal my own Catholic roots within the Northern Irish story.'

Her message has struck a note. For the last eight years, she has been giving talks and running workshops and retreats at Navan Centre. 'There is a huge wave of interest. In a deep and urgent way, Macha's story is looking for resolution of the wounding of women over centuries. She is a source of transformation in the lives of women. Macha is still important to the site – and to people today.'

St Dahalin

EARLY IRISH SAINT AND MIRACLE WORKER (CIRCA 500 AD)

People have great regard for Dahalin's well. They still go and put water on their eyes and there are cures associated with it. I know of people who said they were cured of minor eye problems.

Joe Slattery, Kerry Head

L et us, for a moment, imagine the fear that took hold in the convent on Kerry Head when Dahalin and her community of nuns realised that a band of raiders was fast approaching. Some say they were Vikings; those fearsome seafarers, 'with the tumult of the ocean in their blood, who desecrated churches, plundered monasteries and burned homes in every sea-washed country in Europe', to quote one nineteenth-century account. It is more likely, however, that they were not Vikings, as Dahalin is likely to have lived at least two centuries before the Norsemen made their first incursions on Irish soil in the eighth century.

In any event, the threat was real and imminent when Dahalin pulled on her woollen cloak – her name means bright mantle or cloak – and went out into the night to face the marauders. As they made their way towards her convent, she struck them blind. They wandered around like drunken revellers, stretching their arms out in front of them to feel their way over the bumps and hollows of the uneven terrain on this spectacular headland.

Once the enormity of what had befallen them hit home, they fell to their knees and begged Dahalin (or Daithlionn/Daithle) to restore their sight. She took pity on them and, after making them swear to abandon their plundering ways, led them to a well and told them to wash their eyes. They did so and, after their sight was restored, they left in peace.

Some 15 centuries after Dahalin's miracle, people still come to her well seeking cures for a variety of eye complaints. We can't know if – or indeed when – this early church leader supposedly blinded the would-be intruders, but it is a simple fact that the memory of it, passed down through the generations, continues to inspire and soothe more than a millennium later. Tobar na Súl, with its sweeping views of the mouth of the Shannon and Loop Head, attracts hundreds of visitors every year. Pilgrims follow the ancient tradition of bathing their eyes in the water and paying rounds – circling the well three times, while saying a decade of the rosary with each rotation.

Visit it today and you might see the pair of broken spectacles cast off and left behind in an earthen flowerpot beside the well, evoking the biblical story of the lame man who threw away his crutches when Christ restored his ability to walk. In the townland of Glendahalin, or the glen of Dahalin, in north Kerry, there are many anecdotal accounts of contemporary cures, or at least partial ones, and just as many stories of modern pilgrims. One man whose sight was affected in an accident visits regularly and reports an improvement, while many others report cures.

Local farmer Joe Slattery says people have been coming to the well for as long as he can remember. His mother before him also witnessed a steady stream of visitors and she even saw the trout reputed to live in the well. It was said that anyone who saw the trout would be cured: 'People have great regard for the well. They still go and put water on their eyes and there are cures associated with it. I know of people who said they were cured of minor eye problems.'

Another local man, Billy Gentleman, also speaks of cures among the faithful and recalls one woman who visited the glen on the advice of her aunt. 'She was married, but there were no babies. She came to the well and had twins afterwards. She called one of them Mary St Dahalin. It is a well for eyes, but I've heard of cures for other complaints. A lot of people have great faith in the well and we have heard of people who have been cured.'

Local historian and author Bryan MacMahon, who was born in nearby Ballyheigue, is one of them. He was brought there as a very young boy and was always told that the well water cured him of conjunctivitis:

For local people, the secluded setting with views across the lordly Shannon estuary to Co. Clare has always made it an attractive place to spend some quiet time. People can connect with their ancestors, and remember that they walked the same paths in times of trouble and times of celebration. Dahalin is distinctively local and all the more intriguing because of the veil of mystery about her and her small community here. For some people, the spiritual and historic dimensions of the location are appealing, being simpler and more immediate than other religious rituals and structures.

That immediacy is palpable at the open-air Mass held annually on 4 June on Dahalin's feast day. It is often better attended than weekly Mass and draws scores of people from far and wide. One year, a visiting Swiss choir accompanied by Alpine horns even sang in this secluded spot.

For decades, the well was overgrown and hard to find, but pilgrims still sought it out. Now it is much more accessible thanks to the work of local priest Fr Jerry Kirby. He was among the first to record his memories of it and he is the one responsible for how the place looks today, complete with a stone memorial, plaques and benches. When he retired to his native Ballyheigue from Illinois in the 1980s, he formed a local committee and, with help from many local people, restored the well on land donated and still maintained by Sean and Betty Foran.

This early Irish saint was credited with a single miracle in her lifetime, yet the memory of it has not merely survived but thrived, making it unscathed into the cynical digital age. Dahalin may have lived in early medieval Ireland, but her spiritual potency endured because it was woven into the fabric of local lore down through the centuries.

The salutary story of 'Láimhín' Crosbie, for instance, shows that it was only the foolhardy who dismissed the traditions associated with the region. Crosbie, one of the well-heeled worthies associated with the local castle in the nineteenth century, apparently scoffed at the miraculous powers of the well, dismissing them as mere superstitions. When he allowed his Kerry Blue terrier to splash about in its water, Dahalin took swift and decisive action – more than a millennium after her death. The dog became rabid and bit its owner who, in turn, descended into madness and was seen standing on a wall barking like a dog. The 'curse' even followed him into the afterlife; there were apparent sightings of his ghost wandering through the night, barking as it went.

Another version of the story has it that Crosbie's intentions were more wholesome. He was simply looking for a cure for his dog, but Dahalin considered this blasphemous and withered his hand as revenge; hence the nickname Láimhín, meaning little hand.

Dahalin, however, was not a vindictive woman. There is another account of a local woman who went to the well to fill a pot for her stove. When the water failed to boil, she returned it to the well, perhaps realising her mistake, and went unpunished.

But what of the living, breathing woman behind the miracles? Early Irish saints, and in particular female ones, are often elusive. Even details of the life of Brigit of Kildare, Ireland's most famous female saint, are sketchy and contradictory. Little wonder then that there are few written texts about a lesser-known provincial saint and her community of early Irish nuns. We know they were there, however, because the real-life Dahalin left behind concrete evidence of her influence in early medieval Ireland.

The ruins of her church, said to be the oldest in north Kerry, stand on a height overlooking her well. Known locally as Teampall Daithleann (Dahalin's church) or simply *séipéilín* (little chapel), it's a small rectangular building that is just 5.5 metres long. Little remains of it now, but enough to make out a nave, a lintelled doorway of chiselled sandstone and parts of the walls, which were almost a metre thick. A survey completed in 1841 contains a sketch of an east-gable window, but that has since crumbled and fallen away.

Archaeologist Caroline Toal dates the church to around the eighth century and confirms that it was named after Dahalin. She also suggests that Dahalin and Bishop Earc (or Erc) were brother and sister, a connection that Bryan MacMahon also makes.

Those associations open a fascinating peephole into the rich ecclesiastical landscape of early medieval north Kerry. To start, Dahalin's link to Bishop Earc catapults her lifetime back a number of centuries into the late fifth to early sixth century. It puts her into possible contact with St Brendan the navigator and also even St Brigit herself who, some sources tell us, visited Munster to spend time in the pastoral care of Bishop Earc.

One anonymous account of her life in Latin, *Vita Prima Sanctae Brigitae*, says St Brigit lived in close proximity to Earc which, in turn, places her close to Dahalin. It is tantalising to think that the Kerry holy woman met Brigit in her lifetime, a saint whose 'outstanding and innumerable miracles' were greeted with 'the tumultuous applause of the multitude'.

One of those 'marvellous feats', her biographer Cogitosus tells us, was miraculously ending a woman's pregnancy to restore her to 'health and penance'. The saint apparently met a woman who had taken a vow of virginity but had lapsed 'into youthful desire of pleasure, and her womb swelled with child'. Brigit blessed her and 'exercising the most potent strength of her ineffable faith ... caused what had been conceived to disappear'.

She was not the only Irish saint who forgave wayward sisters by making their pregnancies disappear, but it would be misleading to think of it as evidence of some sort of early feminism. The rights and wrongs of terminating a pregnancy in sixth-century Ireland are perhaps best understood by the need for religious women to preserve their virginity at all costs. Virginity was power, as Dr Elva Johnston explains: 'There was a belief in the early church that women could be freed from a defective femaleness through virginity ... Some of the Church fathers believed that ascetic virgins could transcend the feminine state and be transformed, in a spiritual sense, into men.'

Some of Ireland's female saints took extreme action to avoid marriage and, by extension, keep their virginity intact. Dahalin's decision to enter the church – if indeed she made it – was unlikely to have been opposed as her brother was a bishop. Other women, however, were forced to resort to desperate measures to keep would-be husbands at bay. Even St Brigit herself took the extreme step of gouging out an eye to stop her marriage to an aristocratic suitor, we are told in *Bethu Brigte*, another anonymous account of her life. When her brother, incensed by the loss of financial gain, criticised her, his eyes burst apart in his head – and his descendants were cursed for ever.

That story has a certain resonance at Tobar na Súl, where people come to heal eye complaints. Miracles associated with sight had a particular currency in the early church. Of the 400-plus ways that saints meted out punishment, deliberate blinding was the second most common. Often the blinding was temporary, but sometimes it did not go according to plan. Take the experience of Cork saint Cranat of Fermoy who, following Brigit's example, took out both eyeballs to avoid marriage.

However, as Dr Elva Johnston describes in a fascinating account of this lesser-known female saint, the miracle back-fired in gruesome fashion when one of her eyeballs got lost. It was eventually retrieved from a tree but a piece of bark was lodged in it so that when Cranat put it back into her eye socket, she was left with a fierce, piercing gaze.

How are we to understand this rather graphic account? Is it a mischievous story designed to warn us that women's miracu-lous powers were somehow less potent than those of their male counterparts? Perhaps not, but whatever about the challenges faced by women in the spiritual realm, there were real and calculable struggles in the profane everyday.

Women, for example, faced an uphill struggle when it came to acquiring land to build monasteries, but in this – as in many things – Dahalin had an advantage. As Earc's sister, she would almost certainly have been a literate and educated woman, skills vital to run a convent in the early church. She would also have been, to use a modern phrase, very well connected: her brother was said to be the 'soul-friend' of St Brendan's father, Fionnlagh. Indeed, Earc foretold the birth of the great Brendan the navigator. When he heard that Cara, Fionnlagh's wife, dreamt that her bosom was full of gold and her breasts shone as bright as snow, he interpreted it as a sign that a glorious birth was on the way. And it was. Brendan (or Bréannainn) was born in 483 AD and Earc baptised him at Wether's Well (Tobar na Molt) near Ardfert, not far from the headland where he and his sister ran their respective reli-gious communities.

Earc's church, Ceall Mhic an Deagha (or church of the son of Daigh), was on the south side of Kerry Head at Keel, Glenderry, with a commanding view across the bay to Brandon mountain and the Dingle peninsula. It's possible, even likely, that he helped Dahalin to acquire land on the north side of Kerry Head.

It was not unusual for women of the church to draw on the support of brothers who had entered before them. There is even a written example of one religious sister buying property and raising money for herself. *The Book of Armagh* tells the story of Cummen, a nun who used what would have been her dowry to buy half an estate in Armagh. She later bought out the other half through clever trading. We're told she made an elaborate mantle and sold it for a brown horse which, in turn, she sold for a *cumal* of silver, equivalent in value to three cows.

How Dahalin established herself on the north side of Kerry Head is lost to us, but at the beginning of the sixth century she was at the heart of an area that had deep religious significance. Although it seems isolated now, an ancient pathway called the Red Ditch (or Cladh Ruadh) ran from the glen in Kerry Head all the way to the Cork–Limerick border. The path is thought to date to the Early Iron Age, which opens the possibility that Dahalin's well was once a pagan shrine whose origins were conveniently forgotten, or perhaps rededicated to the local saint.

It is not entirely clear how Christianity took hold but we know that in 431 AD there were enough Christians in Ireland for Pope Celestine to send a specially appointed bishop, Palladius. Local saints also played an important role in spreading the word and, by the end of the fifth to early sixth century, it seems the new religion was well established around north Kerry.

Dahalin – the protector and healer – was on the north of the headland while her brother – pastoral leader, educator and prophet – ran a monastery to the south. Ardfert, one of the places associated with St Brendan, was just a few short miles away. It would later become a major ecclesiastical centre with a magnificent cathedral.

In Dahalin's time, however, religious architecture was much less grand. It's unlikely that she ever prayed in the stone church still visible today, rather in an earlier version made of timber or wattle and daub. That little house of prayer would have been at the sacred centre of a monastic enclosure bound by a fence or ditch. Without excavation we don't know what it looked like, but we can sketch an evocative outline thanks to archaeological evidence from other medieval church sites.

If we were to step inside the boundary fence of Dahalin's sixth-century monastery, we might find a noisy, bustling place with dogs, cats and clucking hens running around the western perimeter. Fowl were valued for their eggs and meat, and the nuns might have supplemented that with barley or oats as well as vegetables and herbs grown in a garden. They might have had a pig or a few sheep or goats. A cow too, perhaps, and an area where they churned butter. It's unlikely they had a horse, though, as they were mostly associated with men – and men of rank at that.

The nuns would have been involved in agriculture, although not directly. Unlike monks, nuns did not farm their own land, but we can imagine Dahalin adopting the role of farm manager, reaching out to the local community to engage them as labourers, herders, craftsmen and metalsmiths. Running a convent, however small, demanded worldly skills as well as spiritual ones, so any abbess of the time would have been a competent administrator, employer and businesswoman.

She would also have had to deal with seasonal food scarcities made worse by periods of bad weather, particularly in spring when stocks were running low. The nuns may have salted or smoked meat to preserve it, but there would have been times of the year when fasting might have been done for practical as well as spiritual reasons. There would have been times of plenty too, with communal feasting – with butter, salted meat and the honey so valued in the Brehon laws – and celebrations of saints' days, Christmas, Easter and baptisms, marriages and funerals.

The threat of intruders, so vividly recounted in the lore, was real. While Dahalin is portrayed as valiant and fearless – and she may well have been – in early medieval Ireland, the most potent source of power any religious woman could have was her piety. It is interesting that several accounts from the 1930s claim it was Dahalin's prayers, rather than her own miracle, that saved the community. In February 1938, local man Michael Godley wrote: 'One certain stormy night a party of pirates sailed from the little bay nearby and attacked the Convent. The Community begged for mercy but the invaders were deaf to their pleading. The Abbess prayed to God to spare them and as an answer to her prayer the party were struck blind.'

Away from the daily hubbub, prayer was at the centre of daily life for nuns and monks of the early church. Dahalin and her sisters would have led austere rule-bound lives, character-ised by strict obedience, fasting and prayer. The holy part of the monastery would have been separate from the domestic zones and it most likely included a cemetery. We can't say how local people interacted with the convent, but they may well have visited for spiritual guidance and pastoral care and to receive the sacraments.

At the time, Kerry, like other counties, was made up of several small kingdoms. North Kerry was part of the prominent Ciarraige Lúachra kingdom and the landscape outside the convent enclosure was still very rural. It would have been dotted with raths or cashels, the circular enclosures we commonly call ringforts.

Archaeology opens a window on those early settlements with their houses, workshops, food stores, cobbled pathways and rubbish heaps. The people living in them were related, but the notion of family or *muintir* was far more extended than we understand it today. Several generations of a single family lived together, along with a foster family and servants and slaves. There are several references to slaves in the annals and the early Irish law tracts.

We can only guess what Dahalin meant to the people, and in particular to the women living around Kerry Head at the time. Though she faced daily difficulties, she would have enjoyed a standing that ordinary women did not. While women of wealth might have been better off than those further down the social scale, in general, a woman's status was less than that of her husband or father. News of the curative powers of the well would have circulated among the community, and surviving artefacts from early medieval Ireland give us an insight into how important religious relics were in the daily lives of women.

The beautifully crafted Moylough belt shrine, for instance, was supposedly put around the waists of pregnant women to safeguard their babies at a time when the infant mortality rate was very high. The belt, with its exquisite bronze, silver foil and enamel decoration, was certainly worn, as proven by a study of wear patterns on its metal circumference. While it dates to the eighth century, the status of sacred belts and girdles dates to St Brigit's time. Her own belt, for example, was said to cure any illness or ailment. Sacred belts were even used as otherworldly lie detectors. St Mobhi's belt would not close on any individual, fat or thin, if they were not telling the truth.

Meanwhile, the Well of the Eyes on Kerry Head was dedicated to conditions affecting sight, but it was part of a complex ecclesiastical landscape richly embroidered with beliefs. Many of those are irretrievable, but there are echoes of a distant past in some of the legends and traditions that survive. For instance, on the other side of the headland, people and their animals were promised a cure for all ailments by the healing power of a rounded stone called a 'bulley' or 'bauley', which fitted snugly into the top of a pillar with a cross etched into it. When the stone was moistened in the nearby well, it had healing properties – although its curative powers were exclusively reserved for blood members of the local Corridon family. A replica stone sits on the pillar in the Corridon graveyard to this day.

Nevertheless, the story shows how sacred places – wells, shrines and graveyards – continue to command respect as part of a tradition that has its roots in early Christian and probably even pagan times. Stories of cures would certainly have circulated to the early members of the faithful and there would have been stories associated with the local saints, who played a pivotal role in spreading Christianity.

Dahalin's achievements, however distorted by time, are still remembered, but when she was alive it's likely there were many other accounts of local saints, women among them, who have since been forgotten. One such woman, recently brought back into the light by Dr Elva Johnston, is the remarkable Canir, a sixth-century saint who walked on water in an attempt to get onto Scattery Island, an extensive monastic settlement in the Shannon estuary not far from Dahalin's convent.

Canir had a vision that she wanted to die and be buried there but, when she arrived, St Senán refused her entry, telling her that 'women do not come to this island'. She challenged him and the exchange is recorded in fascinating detail in *Lives of Saints from the Book of Lismore*. She boldly countered:

> Where did you get that arrangement? Christ … came to redeem women no less than to redeem men. He did not suffer less for the sake of women than for the sake of men. Women have given humble service and ministration to Christ and to his apostles. Women then, no less than men, enter into the Kingdom of Heaven. Why, then, would you not take women to you onto your island?

His response? 'You are stubborn.' All the same, he allowed Canir onto the island and she was granted her wish to die and be buried there.

We don't often hear the voice of local female saints, but here is evidence of one who spoke eloquently and convincingly for women in a male-dominated church. Not only that, her speech took place near the convent of Dahalin, another female church leader whose 'voice' must have offered hope, healing and encouragement to early medieval women.

It's extraordinary to think that Dahalin's voice, or at least a version of it, still resonates with pilgrims today. Her life story is composed of a familiar blend of legend, tradition, faith and something very tangible; the remains of a stone church bearing her name. You could, if you had a mind to, tug at the strands of the story until it unravelled; or almost unravelled, because no matter how much you try to unpick it, one undeniable fact remains: hundreds of people visit St Dahalin's well every year. The numbers are even likely to rise as two modern routes – the Wild Atlantic Way and the North Kerry Way walking trail – now pass near it.

Like so many early Irish women, St Dahalin is a shadowy figure. It's possible to rescue only the barest outline of her from the past, yet she lives on. Her legacy has proven to be real, relevant – and lasting.

Gormlaith

She was endowed with great beauty ... but it was said that in all characteristics for which she herself was responsible, she was utterly wicked.

The Icelandic Brennu-Njáls saga

Gormlaith, the Princess of Leinster, so we're told, made a buck-leap into the marriage beds of three of the most powerful kings in medieval Ireland. She leapt into Dublin to marry the Norse king, Olaf. When he was defeated, she took another mighty leap into Tara and married its king, Máel Sechnaill. After that, she leapt into Cashel to marry his bitter rival, the famous Brian Boru.

She was, some said, a key player in a real-life game of thrones. For others, she was the femme fatale responsible for the Battle of Clontarf. Another account paints her as the beautiful but vindictive woman who plotted to murder her third and by then ex-husband Brian Boru. While early accounts of her role differ, they all have one thing in common – Gormlaith (pronounced Gorm-la) was a woman at the centre of things.

Yet today, this woman – daughter, wife and mother of kings – hardly figures in the history of royalty or battle in eleventh-century Ireland. This is in spite of the fact that she was well-acquainted with both, and she had a unique perspective. She was closely connected to all the main players on both sides of the battlefield at Clontarf in 1014. Her husband fought against her brother while one of her sons took the 'Irish' side against another on the 'Viking' side.

Gormlaith, just like the battle itself, reflected the complex mix of political allegiances at play. What better person to cast light on the true nature of a battle that is too often seen as the triumph of the Christian Gael over the heathen foreigner? If only we could stand in her shoes and see the famous conflict – and life in medieval Ireland – from her perspective. At first glance, it seems we can. She figures prominently in many of the surviving sources, although most of them cast her in a bad light. In the twelfth-century text, *Cogadh Gáedhel re Gallaibh* (*The War of the Irish With the Foreigners*), she is blamed for causing the war although it has been suggested the story was misinterpreted.

There is little room for misinterpretation in a poem written a century later. It references her infamous 'three leaps', or her succession of royal marriages, with a heavy tone of disapproval. Yet it was not at all unusual for a woman, particularly an aristocratic one, to marry several times in a lifetime – or indeed to divorce. Brian himself had four wives and it is possible he took one of them while still married to Gormlaith.

No matter, more scorn was to come. The Icelandic sagas vilified her, conjuring up an image of a beautiful but wicked sorcerer bent on evil: 'She was endowed with great beauty ... but it was said that in all characteristics for which she herself was responsible, she was utterly wicked,' the thirteenth-century *Brennu Njáls* saga said. No room for misunderstanding there: Gormlaith was a malign, though powerful, force.

As the years went by, she would become the dark foil to Brian Boru's ever-brightening depiction as the man who saved the Irish from Viking oppression. As he became more pious, his wife was portrayed as ever more pagan; a warning of the threat posed by women who had relationships with enemies and foreign men.

The Book of Leinster was alone in praising Gormlaith for her three marriage alliances which, it said, had served the province of Leinster well. That was, perhaps, a more honest appraisal because the Irish elite often had many spouses. It was an effective way of maximising political alliances and furthering the reach of family influence. To give one extreme and later example, Pilib Mag Uidhir, Lord of Fermanagh, had 20 sons by eight mothers. Women had multiple partners too: the names of two women who each had five husbands are recorded in the *Banshenchas*, a medieval text on the lore of women. Irish marriage practices, however, were very much at odds with Church teaching, and Pope Gregory VII said so in no uncertain terms in the eleventh century. He had even heard rumours, he wrote, that Irish men were guilty of deserting their wives and sometimes even selling them.

The real Gormlaith was born into a society with many definitions – and categories – of marriage. It's not entirely surprising, then, to find there is no trace of her mother's name. We know Gormlaith was born in Naas to the King of Leinster Murchad mac Finn, so she had royal blood in her veins. One source says her mother was from a dynasty in Connacht, but there is also a piece of intriguing evidence that opens up the possibility that Gormlaith was born to a Viking slave concubine of the king.

Her mother is recorded as a *scirrdech banamas* in a twelfth-century genealogies text, an old Norse term that academic Dr Muireann Ní Bhrolcháin has translated as 'baptised slave'. Could the woman who married three kings have been born to a slave? When Dr Ní Bhrolcháin uncovered the possibility, she said she was about to throw a bomb into early Irish history. But it made sense too, she added: Gormlaith's possible Norse heritage explained why, in her mid-teens, she married Olaf (or Amlaíb Cuarán), the influential Hiberno-Norse king of Dublin. She wrote:

> Apart from the cold historical facts, there is a quiet human drama here. If Gormlaith's mother was a Viking servant or slave, probably taken by an Irish raiding party and perhaps forcibly baptised, it would explain Gormlaith's marriage to Olaf despite the age gap. Both had a similar background and were probably bilingual. He might see her Viking, albeit slave, pedigree as a disadvantage. On the other hand, perhaps her father felt that it would be difficult to arrange a marriage for a daughter with such parentage? Her mother's ancestry is probably lost forever, a *banamas* [slave] in Ireland, she could have been anyone, even of royal descent at home.

Whether she was of Norse descent or not, we can walk alongside Gormlaith as she went to live in Viking Dublin around 970. It was a noisy, jostling, smelly place that was home to about 3000 people. It minted its own coins and, ironically, was at the centre of a booming slave trade. The surviving neck manacles and chains, now on view at the National Museum of Ireland, are a chilling testament to our Viking – and Irish – ancestors who bought and sold people.

Excavations at Wood Quay in Dublin city in the 1970s laid bare part of the town that Gormlaith would have known. The wattle-and-daub houses of the people who lived there more than a thousand years ago were wonderfully preserved, along with their boundary fences, latrines, rubbish pits, cooking utensils, combs, games, toys and even ice skates. It was likely that Gormlaith lived nearby at Christchurch Place or perhaps even where Dublin Castle is today.

She would have known a busy international port with the constant toing and froing of ships and the bustle of markets selling gold, silver and spices. We don't know much about her life with Olaf, other than the fact that the couple had at least one son, Sitric Silkenbeard. As a young mother, she may well have found herself isolated in the royal court as her husband continued to make many military forays into Leinster.

Olaf's influence extended beyond the east of Ireland into York and Northumbria in England. 'The Danish yoke lay heavy not on Ireland alone, but on England also,' as the *History of Ireland* rather poetically put it in 1908. The Danes exacted taxes so punitive that 'none of the men of Erin had power to give even the milk of his cow, nor as much as the clutch of eggs of one hen ... to an aged man, or a friend'. For a people who placed such a high value on offering hospitality that was a particular blow.

But then, the Danes, like Gormlaith herself, suffered a good deal of bad press. In more recent years, the image of the wild, plundering barbarians has been redrawn thanks to archaeological finds, which reveal a people who were also artistic, sophisticated and well groomed. Gormlaith's husband, for instance, would most likely have been a man who trimmed his beard and paid attention to his appearance. In fact, the Vikings were so particular that Irish and English women often preferred them to native men. That didn't go down too well with the locals, a point John of Wallingford of England made very strongly when he complained about those dapper interlopers who combed their hair, changed their clothes often, bathed on Saturdays and had many 'frivolous devices' about their person.

The frivolous devices were likely to have been combs, tweezers, whetstones to sharpen blades and even ear spoons, used to scoop wax from their ears. Vanity kits and caskets were also common and, as a royal Viking woman, Gormlaith would not only have been well groomed but well dressed. We can even say she probably had the luxury of having her clothes pressed, or 'ironed', as evidenced by a type of linen press found in the grave of a Viking woman of the period. Excavations at Finglas in Dublin uncovered a beautifully carved piece of whalebone that was thought to have been used as a proto ironing board. It was found with a glass ball, which would have been covered in leather and used to smooth fabric just like an iron.

As well as a wrinkle-free dress, Gormlaith might have worn amber glass beads around her neck and a pair of oval brooches that held up a pinafore-style dress. Many of these brooches were gilded with gold and silver and would have been quite splendid. There would have been much to dazzle in the royal court of Viking Dublin, to judge from a Norse saga about a merchant called Gunnlaug who is welcomed by Gormlaith's son Sitric when he later became king.

When Gunnlaug recited a poem, the king suggested rewarding him by giving him a couple of merchant ships.

'That's too much my lord,' said the [court] treasurer. 'As rewards for poems, other kings give valuable treasures, fine swords or gold bracelets.'

The king then gave him his own clothes made of new and precious cloth, an embroidered tunic, a cloak lined with precious furs and a gold bracelet weighing half a pound, we're told in the Norse saga of Gunnlaug Serpent-Tongue.

The story might not reflect the reality of Gormlaith's royal court but it gives some idea of the wealth and luxury one might have expected to find there. In any case, it was all soon to come to an end. In 980 Olaf led a disastrous campaign in Tara and was roundly defeated by the new High King of Ireland, Máel Sechnaill. The victorious high king besieged Dublin for three days and nights and, according to the annals, released many Irish hostages and slaves and also made off with plunder and jewels.

Could Gormlaith have been among his spoils of war; a trophy wife to underline a great victory?

It is possible that Gormlaith was used as a political pawn in the bigger game of power and control of territory. She may have been taken by Máel Sechnaill, although she could have been a widow by then. Some even question if the marriage took place at all, but there is little doubt that she married his rival, Brian Boru, the famous King of Munster. It's not clear how the couple came together but at a time when Brian was flexing his political muscle in Leinster, in the 980s and 990s, she would have been seen as a good catch. Marrying a Princess of Leinster would bolster his influence in that province, as Professor Máire Ní Mhaonaigh has suggested.

As we know from history, Brian's political ambitions didn't quite go according to plan, although he was elevated to mythical status after his death at the Battle of Clontarf. Gormlaith, on the other hand, was demonised as the woman who caused the battle and, worse still, was said to have plotted to kill her saintly husband.

Did she? Let us try to pick a path through the myth and the hyperbole to see the role played by Gormlaith – and other women – in that most famous of battles.

The taunting and goading started the night before the great clash on the battlefield.

'No man in Ireland can fight me,' Plait, 'a brave champion of the foreigners', boasted loudly. Domhnall, son of Emhin, snapped back with a retort in seconds. He would stand against this bragging warrior, he said. The next day, at sunrise, Plait came forward and called for his challenger of the night before.

'Where is Domhnall?' he shouted three times.

'Here, thou reptile,' Domhnall said, as he stepped forward.

A terrible fight ensued until both men fell dead at the same moment, 'the sword of each through the heart of the other, and the hair of each in the clenched hand of the other ... And the combat of these two was the first combat of the battle.'

That is how the famous twelfth-century account *Cogadh Gáedhel re Gallaibh* (the *Cogadh*) reports the opening blows of the Battle of Clontarf in April 1014. It went on to describe, in the most vivid detail, how the 'fearful, murderous, hard-hearted Danmarkians' fought the 'fine, intelligent, gifted and renowned' Irish side with the valorous Brian Boru at its head.

The battle raged from sunrise to sundown. It was so furious and bloody, wrote the chronicler, that it was like 'a heavy sparkling show of flaming stars' or the clashing of four opposing winds. The Danmarkians had 'thrice-riveted' armour and both sides fought with bright axes and hard, straight swords. They were evenly matched at first, but towards evening the Viking side flagged and retreated to the sea. Their ships, however, had been carried off on a rising tide and many of the men drowned; others shouted their cries for mercy.

Brian Boru's grandson Toirdelbach chased his enemies into the sea but was hit by a wave and drowned. His father, Murchad, was killed shortly afterwards. The famous leader of the Dál Cais dynasty, Brian, would not survive the battle either. He was famously kneeling at prayer in a tent when he was put to death by Brodir, the fearsome Viking leader of the Isle of Man fighters.

There were heavy casualties on both sides; tens of thousands, the chronicler said, though the number, like the language used, is fanciful and overblown. Without doubt, it was a very significant battle but it was not what the medieval propagandists claimed it to be – an Irish triumph over the so-called 'foreigners'. It was more a battle between a Munster army, under Brian Boru, against a Leinster army. Vikings fought on both sides and they were not all expelled when the fighting was over. Ironically, Brian Boru's own Viking son-in-law Sitric Silkenbeard would go on to rule as King of Dublin, post battle.

But what of his mother, Gormlaith? Did she cause the battle in the first place and, if so, whose side was she on?

If Gormlaith was as scheming as some of the chroniclers suggest, then she must also have been a very powerful behind-the-scenes player; a woman who was well versed in the political intrigue of the day.

The same text that brought us the Battle of Clontarf in various hues of bloody crimson (the *Cogadh*) also recounted the root of Gormlaith's treachery – essentially, it stemmed from her refusal to sew in a button. Gormlaith's husband Brian Boru had given her brother, the King of Leinster, a gift of a tunic with silver buttons. When one of them fell off, Gormlaith's brother, Máel Mórda, asked her to repair it. Instead, she threw the tunic on to the fire and reproached her brother for accepting the gift as it showed he submitted to Brian's power.

Her act was heavy with symbolism: a wife who was siding with her origins in Leinster rather than with her husband.

This, however, is not what finally turned Máel Mórda against Brian Boru – that came a little later, when Máel Mórda had a row with Brian Boru's son over a game of chess. He left the house in a fit of pique and later attacked the messenger Brian sent after him. When Gormlaith's brother arrived back in Leinster he spoke of his dishonour and turned against Brian Boru. The stage for conflict was set.

Later, Gormlaith's role would be considerably inflated. The Icelandic sagas claimed she was furious that her son with Brian Boru, Donnchadh, was not going to inherit the kingdom. Spiteful and seeking revenge, she incited her brother and her son Sitric to rebel against Brian. To ensure his defeat, she encouraged them to recruit outside help. That was how Brodir, the ferocious Viking who eventually murdered Brian, came into the picture. It was even said that Brodir was promised Gormlaith's hand in marriage as a reward. She was being set up, yet again, as a war prize, but this time as a woman in her fifties. As one modern-day wag commented: 'She must have been some babe.' Or very powerful. Or both.

Gormlaith, we're told, watched the fighting from the battlements of Dublin with her son Sitric and his wife Sláine. Sitric was on the so-called 'Viking' side but, to complicate matters further, Sláine was Brian Boru's daughter, but by another wife. Marriage as political strategy was a common reality, which meant that often both sides on a battlefield were closely related, if not by blood, then by marriage. That led to conflicting allegiances, as happened quite pointedly in Dublin in 1014: when Sláine saw the Vikings retreat into the sea, she quipped that they were going back to where they belonged.

Then, as the *Cogadh* tells it, Sitric said, 'What meanest thou, O woman?'

'The foreigners are going into the sea, their natural inheritance …' replied Sláine. Sitric 'became angered and gave her a blow'.

Striking a different kind of blow, another Irish woman was said to have used her magical powers in an attempt to safeguard her son in the battle. Eithne had woven a special raven banner for her son, Sigurd, Jarl of Orkney, before he set sail for Dublin. The banner would bring victory to the side who brought it into battle – but, alas, death to the bearer. As it turned out, Sigurd the bearer died in the battle, but his side suffered defeat too.

The supernatural featured prominently in accounts of the battle. The Vikings were said to have anointed their arrows with the blood of toads and dragons and there were many otherworldly omens of the deaths to come. Meanwhile, witches and demons vied with birds of prey to claim the dead on the battlefield.

It's interesting to note that Eithne was referred to as a 'clever' woman which, in her case, meant that she had powers of the occult. Gormlaith was also referred to as 'clever', though it's not clear what that might have meant in the eleventh century.

'Some Irish women were educated,' explains Dr Catherine Swift. The life of St Rícenn, for example, is interesting on this, she adds: a seven-year-old girl was fostered by a priest but then went to the nuns to learn to read. In the Brehon laws, education for girls often entailed learning to embroider or how to become 'delightful' wives, but in this case, a royal daughter was being taught how to read and then was apparently given the freedom to choose whether she wanted to become a nun or marry. She decided to marry, became a mother and was also a patron of church foundations.

It's not entirely clear what happened to Gormlaith after the Battle of Clontarf, though she may have married Máel Sechnaill at this point. 'If she did, she was indeed clever,' says Dr Swift, as he became the strongest king in Ireland after Clontarf, where Brian and his eldest son both died.

Meanwhile, Gormlaith's son with Brian, Donnchadh, went on to inherit from his father and to describe himself as 'King of Ireland', while Gormlaith's first son, Sitric, would remain in power in Dublin until 1046. When she died, around 1030, Gormlaith was the wife of a king and the mother of two kings.

After that, as scholar Gwyn Jones wrote, 'Clontarf was too important to be left to the historians, so passed into the legend-maker's hand.'

If the medieval myth-makers were unkind to Gormlaith, so too were the historians of the twentieth century. One of them, John Ryan, was particularly virulent in his assessment of Gormlaith's role. He argued that the men of Leinster might not have risen against Brian 'were they not nagged into irresponsible fury by a woman's tongue'. He wrote: 'It is Ireland's misfortune that at such a moment this sharp, able and irreconcilable woman was in a position to do untold mischief.'

One of the few exceptions is the portrayal of Gormlaith as 'a lady of rather remarkable character' by Sister Mary Francis Clare (or Margaret Anna Cusack), herself a rather remarkable lady who stood up to the Catholic hierarchy and spoke out against landlords in the nineteenth century.

The Nun of Kenmare, as she was also known, wrote more than 30 books. In her *Illustrated History of Ireland*, she celebrated Gormlaith's strength, referring to the 'wonderful accounts of her zeal and efforts in collecting forces'. Sr Mary Francis also recounted how Gormlaith dispatched her son, Sitric, to Orkney to recruit forces to fight Brian. When Sitric promised the Earl of Orkney his mother's hand in marriage in exchange for assistance, his mother was having none of it. And she said so in no uncertain terms. Later, Sitric promised Brodir his mother's hand in marriage but told him to keep the agreement secret, so that the Earl of Orkney might not hear of it. It's not clear what his mother thought about that.

In the centuries following the Battle of Clontarf, Gormlaith was recalled as a central and powerful though malign figure. It was, as Dr Swift says, a kind of medieval rendering of the 'Eve in the Garden of Eden' story – the fate of many women in the period. 'In the nationalist version of Clontarf since [the translation of *Cogadh Gáedhel re Gallaibh* in 1867], it was all about armies and military insurrection and also Catholicism,' she says.

Looking at Gormlaith's life from this remove, Dr Swift thinks that she was a woman using whatever power she had: if she was still married to Brian at the time of the battle, she would have been quite isolated; perhaps she was plotting her son Donnchadh's career rather than her own. 'I do get a sense she is more than a pawn but maybe that's because so few women are depicted in our sources in this period,' she says.

Pawn, mother with ambitions for her sons, behind-the-scenes mistress of manoeuvres: there is a case to be made for all of them – as well as one to restore Gormlaith to her rightful place in the history of eleventh-century Ireland.

Aoife MacMurrough

COUNTESS AND WIFE OF STRONGBOW
(CIRCA 1153–1204)

Aoife was never a victim. It speaks to the self-confidence of the Irish aristocratic class that she was able to hold off King Henry II and stop her [inherited] estates being asset-stripped.

Dr Linda Doran, historian

I f we want to get to know the real Aoife MacMurrough, we might think of her not as Strongbow's famous bride, but as his widow. It is only then that the woman herself comes into focus. In sharp contrast to the image of the compliant bride that lingers in the public imagination, the widowed Aoife was a countess with power and influence. She had an income; she had the king's favour, and she was exploiting her late husband's considerable estates in England and Wales. She may even have acted as a military commander at her strategically placed castle in Wales when it was threatened with rebellion.

Her name appears several times in the royal records after her husband's death in 1176 – just six years after they were married. She called herself Countess of Strigoil or Countess Eva, heir of King Diarmait, and signed at least two charters. She never remarried, perhaps deciding to maintain her own independence instead. Surviving records give us a glimpse of a woman very different from the submissive young girl depicted in *The Marriage of Strongbow and Aoife*, the nineteenth-century painting by Daniel Maclise, which is on view at the National Gallery of Ireland in Dublin. Yet that is the image that lives on – the cowed and fearful Aoife standing among the smouldering ruins of a defeated Waterford city.

If Maclise's image of the fall of an Irish Viking town draws heavily on artistic licence, it also captures something of the post-battle horror in Waterford. To get an idea of what it was really like, take a moment to study the fearsome twelfth-century arrowheads that are preserved in a glass case at Reginald's Tower in the city today. They were found outside the town walls and may date to that fateful August in 1170 when the Normans with their chainmail, superior weaponry and archers stormed the town where, contemporary chronicler Gerald of Wales wrote, 'they slaughtered the citizens in heaps along the streets' to gain a bloody victory. They also put two Viking leaders to the sword in Reginald's Tower, an earlier building than the one standing today, and the very place where Aoife was said to have been first introduced to Richard fitz Gilbert – also known as 'Strongbow'.

We can only guess how the 17-year-old Aoife felt when she arrived to be married, amid the stench and chaos of recent conflict, to a man more than 20 years her senior. Even if Gerald of Wales exaggerated the extent of the damage to Waterford, Strongbow was still in battle dress preparing to march on Dublin. From his perspective, the marriage sealed a political alliance that promised large swathes of land and, ultimately, control of Leinster. For Dermot MacMurrough, Aoife's father, the arrival of outside military aid offered a real opportunity to regain the Kingdom of Leinster. He might have made promises to Strongbow that were not within his power to deliver under Irish law, but that did not stop him.

The marriage, with its long-lasting political implications, has been told from both men's perspectives for centuries. But what of Aoife MacMurrough, the Princess of Leinster? The story has seldom – if ever – been examined from her point of view. We know what the union promised to deliver for her father and her soon-to-be husband, but what did Aoife herself stand to gain by marrying Strongbow?

On the face of it, not very much. Richard fitz Gilbert might have had a great name, but there was little behind it, or so Gerald of Wales claimed. He said the nobleman came with ancestral prestige rather than any real possessions. Though biased and at times unreliable, Gerald of Wales was not wrong: Strongbow was somewhat down on his luck in 1170. To start with, he was out of favour with the king. While King Henry II recognised his right to inherit certain estates in England and Wales, he withheld many others. Strongbow had been denied lordship of his estates in Normandy as well as the earldom of Pembroke and he did not have permission to use a title.

That was only part of the story. Strongbow was heavily in debt. He had, according to twelfth-century historian William de Newburgh, wasted most of his inheritance and he wanted to get away from his creditors. Exchequer records confirm that he was in debt to at least one moneylender to the tune of 80 marks.

Did Aoife's father know this? What of Aoife herself? Or perhaps, as the historian Professor Marie Therese Flanagan suggests, they may have discussed the potential gain for Aoife in the proposed alliance. If Strongbow stood to inherit in Ireland – whatever the difficulties with Irish law – Aoife was also likely to inherit estates in England, Wales and Normandy. Under feudal law, a widow was entitled to the profits of one-third of her husband's estates. Strongbow's wealth and position might not have been considered substantial in 1170, but he was, after all, a man with prospects.

If Dermot MacMurrough and Strongbow plotted about how they would regain the kingdom of Leinster, they must at least have talked about recovering Strongbow's inheritance and titles too. They may well have discussed possible trading opportunities between the two countries. Strongbow's estates in Wales were ideally placed to trade with Dublin and the east coast of Ireland. It's possible too that the husband-to-be agreed to designate dower lands – the inheritance due to a widow under feudal law – to Aoife.

Did Dermot present the match in those terms to his eldest daughter, outlining the potential wealth and prestige that lay ahead for her and her children? Or did he even feel the need to consider her thoughts at all?

He loved his eldest daughter – or so we are told in *The Deeds of the English in Ireland*, a twelfth-century Anglo-Norman poem – but the deposed King of Leinster was not a sentimental man. Gerald of Wales described his 'warlike spirit' and said his voice was hoarse from the din of the battle. Dermot was, he wrote, 'one who preferred to be feared rather than to be loved, who put down the nobles and exalted the lowly, who was obnoxious to his own people and an object of hatred to strangers. His hand was against every man, and every man's hand against his.'

Even if there is only a grain of truth in the description, it is unlikely that Aoife felt she could protest. Irish marriage law did allow women to divorce, but it was still weighted in favour of men. Men were allowed more than one wife and Dermot had married two women; Sadb and Aoife's mother Mór. In 1152 he also notoriously kidnapped the lady Derbforgaill, the wife of a rival king, O'Rourke of Breifne. He 'kept her for a long space to satisfie his insatiable, carnall and adulterous lust', according to the *Annals of Clonmacnoise*.

Other versions of the story portray Derbforgaill as a Helen of Troy figure who eloped, aged 40-plus, with Dermot, bringing her cattle and furniture along with her. A year later she went back to her husband – with her cattle and furniture intact. Later again, she used her personal wealth to rebuild the beautiful nuns' church at Clonmacnoise, reputedly to atone for her sins. The story, in whatever form, is interesting because it casts a twelfth-century woman in a number of possible roles – temptress, pawn in a political manoeuvre and/or penitent. Yet, repentant or not, Derbforgaill was still blamed for Dermot's expulsion from Ireland and, ultimately, the arrival of the Normans.

We can't say what, or if, Aoife knew of those earlier events, but the young Irish princess would certainly have been keenly aware of what was expected of her. She would also have known of the political implications of her match – and perhaps she even welcomed the marriage. It's entirely possible she saw Strongbow as a good catch; a man who would secure her father's kingdom and pave the way for any children they might have.

Whatever was going through her mind in August 1170, it is unlikely that the marriage ceremony looked like the scene so memorably depicted in Daniel Maclise's painting. While there was a Romanesque stone church on the site of Christ Church Cathedral, a public ceremony was not necessary to validate a marriage, Eamonn McEneaney, director of Waterford Treasures museum, explains: 'All that was needed was a witness and, given the circumstances, it was more likely to have been a swift affair even if it did take place in the church.'

If Aoife did dress in wedding finery, it would have been something that was considered the height of fashion in twelfth-century Ireland, if not Europe. 'She would have been very sophisticated,' McEneaney explains:

> There was significant trade between Ireland and Europe and anything she wore was likely to have been influenced by European trends. She was a member of the ruling class and that would have been reflected in how she dressed. You wanted to create an aura of importance around yourself to underline your role in society.

There may also have been a particular dress code for princesses. The sons of provincial kings, for instance, were allowed to wear gold brooches, but the sons of lesser kings wore silver ones, according to *Cáin Iarraith*, a twelfth-century law tract. Cloaks and brooches were also considered suitable royal gifts, we're told in *Lebor na Cert*, a text on the rights of kings. There may well have been a 'what to wear' guide for royal brides too.

In any case, not long after the wedding in August, Aoife's new husband and his knights were on their way to Dublin.

They took control of that city and soon much of the south-east was in their hands. Some accounts have it that Aoife led armies on Strongbow's behalf, although there isn't any evidence for it. That is not to say that she didn't play a role – and perhaps even a significant one – in her husband's affairs.

Dermot MacMurrough died in 1171, just a year after his daughter's marriage. In his absence, Strongbow must have relied on his wife's knowledge of Irish life and customs. In turn, it's possible that she had an influence on him. One little piece of evidence, outlined by Professor Flanagan, suggests that might have been so. Aoife's father had founded at least three nunneries in Leinster and it's interesting to see that Strongbow founded a Benedictine nunnery in Usk in Wales in 1173. Was it at Aoife's prompting? Perhaps. She supported the Benedictine nuns in her own right much later when she signed a charter granting them a mill in Cambridgeshire.

If we know a little about Aoife the widow, we know next to nothing about her life as a wife and mother. In the six years she was married to Strongbow, he was busy with mili-tary campaigns in Ireland and France and frequent visits to England. It's possible she travelled with him as her daughter Isabella would later do with her husband, William Marshal. It was more likely, though, that she kept an eye on affairs at Ferns in Wexford, her father's patrimonial land of Uí Chennselaig.

It made sense to stay put as she was also a new mother to Isabella, who was born in 1172, and Gilbert a year later. The couple had two children at a time when it was difficult to raise a child beyond the age of five. It was considered an achieve-ment for a couple just to reproduce themselves. While Aoife and Strongbow succeeded in doing that, disease and infection made life precarious. The couple's son did not make it to adult-hood. He died in his mid-teens. His father Strongbow also died prematurely – and unexpectedly – in 1176 from an injury to his foot.

While his marriage to Aoife had been a political alliance, it's possible the couple came to respect, if not love, each other. Gerald of Wales painted a picture of Strongbow as a biddable man when he was not on the battlefield: 'What he could not accomplish by force he would effect by gentle speech. As a private individual he was more disposed to be led than to lead. In time of peace he had more the air of an ordinary soldier than of a commander.' He provided a physical description too: he was a tall man 'with reddish hair, freckled skin, grey eyes, feminine features, thin voice and short neck'.

He was also so successful as a military commander that King Henry II felt it necessary to come to Ireland personally to keep him in check. Henry's expedition to Ireland in 1171–2 set a precedent that would have long-lasting implications: the king established himself as overlord of Leinster, bringing Ireland under English royal lordship for the first time.

The king also took control of Dublin, Waterford and Wexford from Strongbow and later tested Strongbow's loyalty by sending him to Normandy to quash a rebellion. When Strongbow was successful, King Henry rewarded him by giving him back control of Wexford. Later, he was appointed as Henry's agent in Ireland. At the same time, he was also winning concessions from the king in relation to his estates in England, Wales and Normandy. It's interesting to speculate how much Aoife knew of her husband's military and political affairs. Given how efficiently she appeared to cope in England after his death, it is reasonable to assume she had more than a passing knowledge of the workings of twelfth-century politics on both sides of the Irish Sea.

Richard fitz Gilbert came to Ireland as a man in debt with a name but no title. When he died, six short years later, he had gained widespread respect as a man of wealth and influence. Dermot MacMurrough's gamble, it seemed, had paid off.

Or had it?

Strongbow's estates were technically held by the grace of the king, which meant the monarch was not obliged to pass them on to Aoife and her children. And, as Professor Flanagan has pointed out, the king was also quite capable of ignoring the inheritance rights of his subjects even when succession was more straightforward. Yet Aoife and her children were clearly recognised by the king. She first appears in the royal records as the Countess of Strigoil (modern-day Chepstow Castle in Wales) in 1176–7 and, it is noted, she received an inheritance payment of 60 shillings.

What is not noted, however, is how a young widow with two small children in tow managed to travel to an unfamiliar country and royal court to secure an inheritance for herself and her children. Dr Linda Doran imagines that she must have been a very good negotiator to have been able to hold her own in the predatory court of Henry II: 'She negotiated that extremely well. She must have been really clever – and charming. She was never a victim. It speaks to the self-confidence of the Irish aristocratic class that she was able to hold off King Henry II and stop her estates being asset-stripped.'

Aoife MacMurrough would have been a well-educated woman. She spoke Irish and probably Latin, most likely learned under the system of fosterage where children were fostered out to learn a range of skills from horse riding and board games for boys to sewing and embroidery for girls. It's likely that children of Aoife's status would have had a special chaplain responsible for their education, Dr Doran explains. That education would have had a spiritual side but it was likely to have included practical aspects too, such as reading and writing and learning Latin. Aoife probably spoke French too, to converse with her Norman-French-speaking husband.

That must have stood to her when she arrived in England shortly after his death. Her son Gilbert, the male heir, was not yet old enough to inherit so the Crown took over the administration of his lands. Yet Aoife, as Strongbow's widow, was entitled to a third of the income from her late husband's estates. And it appears that she received her due – or at least part of it. We can pick up traces of her life from the records, which show she got payments from her manors in Essex and Hertfordshire and also estates in Cambridgeshire.

Another payment, an advance of £20 from the king in 1183–4, opens up the possibility that Aoife was not only living at Strigoil Castle in Wales, but also defending it.

'The sum of 20 pounds suggests that [Aoife] was, in fact, being assigned the responsibilities of a military commander in this region for 20 pounds was precisely the figure paid to Ralph Bloet from 1184–5 onwards for his custody of Strigoil,' writes Professor Flanagan. The castle was strategically placed on a cliff in the Welsh marches, along the border between England and Wales, and the Crown feared it was under threat from a Welsh rebellion. The money was spent on repairs, restocking and seed.

We can't say what life inside the castle was like but the remains of the two-storey great tower at Chepstow Castle still stand. There was a great hall on its first floor which, explains archaeologist and architectural historian Ben Murtagh, would have been used for ceremonies and meeting important people: 'It is likely that Aoife would have been quite familiar with this building. Close by, there would have been other important buildings in timber within the then castle – one of which would have been occupied by Aoife and her household, when in residence in Chepstow.'

Without excavations of the earlier phase of Chepstow Castle, we can't really know what Aoife's living quarters were like, but it would have been a fairly comfortable place, he adds.

The degree of opulence possible in a medieval palace is evident at Dover Castle where Henry II's Great Tower has been reconstructed with lavish tapestries and sumptuous furnishings and decorated in rich, bold colours that would probably look gaudy to a modern palate. Aoife, of course, did not have the same means at her disposal, but Dr Doran speculates that there would have been some very comfortable rooms in her castle: 'There would have been a really decent fireplace, furs, rugs, soft fabrics to make the place warm. She would also probably have had books, and maybe a business area with a desk.'

One of the reasons we know so little about Aoife's life is because the role of women was so often downplayed, says Ben Murtagh. 'She – like her daughter after her – would have been fairly powerful people in their own right. Women were fairly powerful but they had to act through the man. Also we hear about them through the prism of men where the role of women is often downplayed.'

For all of that, Aoife MacMurrough's strength of character shines through the fragmentary records about her life. As Professor Flanagan writes, it was very unusual for a young widow, whose marriage was in the gift of the king, not to remarry: 'That she had not been remarried … and had issued her own charters in which she described herself as her father's heir suggests that she may have been a strong personality in her own right.'

She also had to cope with the loss of her son, Gilbert, who died at some point between 1185 and 1186 before he was old enough to inherit. The focus of attention then turned to Aoife's daughter, Isabella, who was a ward of the Crown. We know a lot more about her; she comes across as a strong-minded, independent woman who earned the respect of her husband, William Marshal. William became one of the wealthiest men in the realm when he married Isabella. And he never forgot it: there's a record of him acknowledging that he owed every-thing he had to his wife. Later, he spoke about seeking his wife's consent and counsel, which is quoted in one of Kilkenny's oldest books, the *Liber Primus Kilkenniensis*.

We can only speculate on the influence Aoife had on her daughter. Like her mother, Isabella was educated and spoke Irish, French and Latin. She may even have had a knowledge of Welsh or English in order to converse with her servants. She was described as good, fair and wise and a courteous lady of high degree. It's interesting to note that Isabella also raised strong daughters who became political players in their own right.

We don't know if, or how often, Aoife visited Ireland during her years in England. Professor Flanagan noted that the only evidence of her presence in Leinster after her husband died was a charter she issued to the Archbishop of Dublin, John Cumin. While there are several references to her in the royal records in England, she fades from view around 1189 when her daughter married and the newlyweds inherited Strongbow's estates.

The date of her death is often given as 1189 although it seems too much of a coincidence that she would die in the same year her daughter and son-in-law inherited her castle. Historian Paul Martin Remfry believes she may have moved to Goodrich Castle in Herefordshire around this time. There is a tower in the castle called the 'Mac-Mac' tower which, Remfry suggests, could be a contraction of MacMurrough. While that is not certain, it's likely that Aoife, Strongbow and their children visited the castle and stayed there because the tower is thought to have been built by Strongbow's father. In any case, in 1204 the castle went to Aoife's son-in-law Marshal, which could mean that she was alive until then. If so, she would have been 51 when she died.

Meanwhile, Isabella and William went on to become something of a medieval power couple, to give it a modern tag line. In Wales, they extended their castles at Pembroke and Chepstow and in Ireland, they restored Kilkenny Castle and established New Ross. Isabella appears to have been her husband's close political adviser, but she emerges as a strong, capable leader too. She also travelled regularly with her husband, which was not as uncomfortable as it might seem given that the nobility travelled with a large entourage and much of their furniture: everything from tapestries to collapsible beds.

William Marshal went on to regain Strongbow's lost title and became Earl of Pembroke. He was also Lord of Leinster and later regent of England. When he died in 1219, he was the richest man in the British Isles. In essence, he and his wife had amassed the titles, the power and the estates that Dermot MacMurrough and Strongbow might once have talked about securing all those decades ago.

Could any of that have happened without Aoife, the Irish countess who paved the way for a new generation? While the traces of her influence and power are scant, they are there. Perhaps it is time to bring them into the foreground and honour Aoife the strong and capable widow as well as Aoife the shy and submissive bride.

Roesia de Verdun

CASTLE-BUILDER, LANDHOLDER AND PRIORY FOUNDER (CIRCA 1204–1247)

There can be no doubt that in order to successfully erect and maintain castles in thirteenth-century Ireland required a woman of remarkable vision and perhaps ruthlessness.

Dr Gillian Kenny

Roesia de Verdun debunks many of our preconceived ideas about women in the past. She was a wife, mother and widow, but this thirteenth-century noblewoman was also the only woman ever to build a castle in Ireland. Even in her day, she was considered exceptional. When, in 1236, she erected an impressive fortress in Co. Louth, it was noted that she had done something 'none of her ancestors was able to do'.

But that was not all. Roesia, or Rose, rented land, took adversaries to court – the Abbot of Mellifont among them – and paid a heavy duty to the English king to allow her to remain single after her husband died in 1230. Under the law, she was a *femme sole* – an unmarried woman who had the right to own property and make contracts in her own name. And it appears she wanted to stay that way.

The remains of her castle, so dramatically situated on top of a rock north-west of Dundalk, still impress today. If we could see the spectacular ruin from a main road, like the Rock of Cashel, it would be one of Ireland's best-known monuments, Professor of Archaeology Tadhg O'Keeffe has suggested. The extraordinary woman who built it might be better known too.

Instead, the castle is more likely to be known for its legend rather than its exceptional design, although one has much to do with the other. The story goes that Roesia killed her master mason when he had finished his work. What better way to ensure that his castle design, so important as a symbol of power and dominance, was not repeated elsewhere?

Another version of the legend has it that a recently widowed Roesia moved to Co. Louth to manage her lands and immediately set about building fortifications. Her reputation as a quick-tempered woman preceded her, however, and the local masons and architects avoided the commission. To entice them, she offered to marry any man who built the castle to her specifications.

The name of the mason/husband-to-be who stepped forward is not preserved, but after their wedding banquet, Roesia called him over to the window of their sumptuous bedroom to admire the view of what was now their joint lands. Then she pushed him out of the window to his death, keeping the castle design safe and her estate intact. Others say she simply got jealous of her husband and pushed him while he was looking out the window of the banqueting hall. Either way, the formidable Roesia went on to take centre stage, managing and defending her castle. It was even said that she led her men in battle, riding out fully armoured, to take on her Gaelic enemies in an area that would have been on the borderlands between the Gaelic and English populations.

Locally, one of the castle's windows is known as the 'murder window' to commemorate her crime. In the centuries that followed, the memory of 'Rose of the rock', as she was sometimes known, was used to scare children. She was depicted as a sort of female bogeyman who would come to get you if you didn't behave.

Yet to succeed, as Roesia de Verdun did, would have taken remarkable strength, self-belief and determination. As historian Dr Gillian Kenny puts it:

> She is largely portrayed as a powerful and sometimes malicious figure, who often behaved like a man and had few scruples. There can be no doubt that in order to successfully erect and maintain castles in thirteenth-century Ireland required a woman of remarkable vision and perhaps ruthlessness.

She was also well connected and personally known to the English king, Henry III. When she proposed building another castle by the sea, the king commanded she be given the use of his men in Meath and Uriel (Drogheda) for 40 days. That castle was never built but Roesia still had much to occupy her time. She wouldn't have been alone in that. Lordly noblewomen had a degree of influence, which they exerted in many different ways: they managed property, supported military action, resolved disputes, provided diplomacy and signed charters, to mention but a few. Their power, however, as historian Susan

Johns writes, was constructed around their role in the family – as wife or widow – as opposed to that of men, which was rooted in owning land.

It's not surprising, then, that the first reference to Roesia de Verdun is when she married Theobald Butler in 1225. Interestingly, she kept her own name and, more unusual still, passed it on to her male children. Dr Kenny suggests her decision was testament to her family's prestigious background and her own strength of character. She was also Theobald's second wife so she was ensuring her children would inherit under the de Verdun name, rather than as Butlers who were heirs to the Ormond lands in Munster.

The de Verdun inheritance was significant. Roesia's grandfather Bertram de Verdun had influence and wealth. He had substantial estates in Staffordshire in England and had been granted large swathes of land in Co. Louth as well as the town charter of Dundalk. He left his fortune to his son Nicholas who, in turn, left it to his only surviving child, Roesia.

It was the beginning of a new era of urbanisation and castle-building in Ireland. The Anglo-Normans who, in 1169, had been invited by Dermot MacMurrough to help him reclaim the kingdom of Leinster now settled in the country where they built castles, manors, churches and established towns with streets, markets, walls and burgage plots [a house and strip of land] that were rented to tenants.

Some have suggested that Roesia herself did not come to Ireland – many noblewomen did not. The country was still an unsettled place where conflict with the uprooted Gaelic elite was frequent and unpredictable. The weapons that survive from that time – spears, mace heads, daggers, axes, billhooks

– open a window into a society where violence was a constant threat. Gerald of Wales wrote of the Irish as a people who carried an axe as if it were a walking stick, ready to inflict a mortal blow if necessary: 'From the axe there is always anxiety. If you think you are free from anxiety, you are not free from the axe,' he wrote at the end of the twelfth century.

Yet Roesia is mentioned several times in the record in connection with Ireland: building a castle, then actively defending her property and taking legal action against anyone who encroached on her territory. It's possible she did that from her base in Staffordshire in England, where she was born in 1204, but not entirely likely.

Her husband Theobald Butler spent a lot of his career in Ireland and given that Roesia had five children during the five years of their marriage, it's reasonable to suggest that she spent some time here too. On the subject of frequent pregnancies, Dr Kenny has found that peasant women of the time, in contrast, had children every other year. Unlike noblewomen who gave their children to wet nurses, peasants breastfed their own children, which was likely to have played a role in spacing out their pregnancies.

Aristocratic women may have had nurses and servants, yet they were also expected to take a hands-on approach to everything from their children's discipline to their education, according to Christine de Pizan, one of the few medieval women authors. In her book of instructions for women, she carefully spelled out the duties of the lady of the castle. Her manual appeared a little after Roesia's lifetime, but the instructions still give us an insight into what would have been expected of women in the thirteenth century.

Mothers should introduce their children to God, it said, and help them to learn to read and to understand something of Latin. A woman should also watch over her children's upbringing diligently. 'She will want her children to be brought to her often. She will consider their appearance, actions and speech and she will correct them severely if they misbehave,' Christine de Pizan advised in *The Treasure of the City of Ladies*.

Roesia had five young children when her husband was summoned to Brittany on royal service in October 1229. In his absence, she would have been expected to step into his shoes. Women were expected to be able to replace their husbands – knights, esquires and gentlemen – when they went off on journeys, or to follow wars. The supposedly apocryphal tale that puts Roesia at the head of her men riding into battle seems less fanciful when you read what Christine de Pizan had to say about a women's role in defence:

> We have also said that she ought to have the heart of a man, that is, she ought to know how to use weapons and be familiar with everything that pertains to them, so that she may be ready to command her men if the need arises. She should know how to launch an attack or to defend against one, if the situation calls for it. She should take care that her fortresses are well garrisoned.

Isabella Marshal, Aoife MacMurrough's daughter, famously defended Kilkenny Castle against attack in 1207–8 when it came under siege while her husband William Marshal was away. She was heavily pregnant at the time and was said to have lowered a man down over the battlements to send news of the attack to another castle while she maintained the garrison. It has been suggested the attempted siege was a tall tale told by King John to Marshal to upset him; even so, the king would not have told it if he didn't think it plausible that a woman could respond like that to the crisis. Regardless of whether it happened exactly as the story suggests, Isabella was credited with quashing an attempted rebellion in Kilkenny and taking hostages.

We tend to think of medieval women in the same way as we think of Victorian ones, sequestered, demure and removed from the action but, as Dr Kenny has said, they were anything but: 'They were used to the privations of life in a colony that was often under attack. They were used to hearing orders bellowed and they were used to seeing men-at-arms clash.'

For Roesia, however, her husband did not return from his journey. He died in France in July 1230 and his body was brought back to Ireland to be buried, either in Limerick or at Arklow. While her children would not inherit the Butler lands, as a widow she was entitled to a third of her late husband's estate for her lifetime. Just a year into her widowhood, her father also died, so she was now entitled to apply for the inheritance she was due under the de Verdun name. It was granted by King Henry III in 1233.

Roesia de Verdun was now a very wealthy woman who had no intention of marrying again. To make sure she wouldn't be obliged to do so, she paid the customary heavy fine of 700 marks to King Henry III who, less than a decade earlier, had been the one who purportedly made an 'urgent recommendation' that she marry Theobald. Roesia was ensuring that he wasn't going to make further recommendations, urgent or otherwise. The sum she paid underlined her determination –

it was a vast amount in the thirteenth century. Did she then, as the legend suggests, come to Ireland in 1233 to oversee the building of her castle in Co. Louth?

If, as the royal records suggest, the castle was complete by 1236, that would have been remarkably quick by the standards of the day. The construction would have been an enormous undertaking involving carpenters, blacksmiths, tile-makers, stonemasons, woodcutters and rope-makers. Treadmills would have hoisted stones up to the top of the enormous walls, a task made all the more complicated by its hilltop location.

It was arduous and very labour-intensive work, with each member of the sizeable team dependent on the others. For instance, a carpenter depended on a woodcutter to fell a tree but before a carpenter could, say, make a door, a blacksmith was needed to forge nails, brackets and hinges. Blacksmiths, in turn, had to be on hand to sharpen the stonemasons' tools, which were blunted every three days or so, or work might completely grind to a halt.

While Roesia de Verdun may not have managed the detail of the building process, the king congratulated her when it was complete. The legends all make much of the castle's singular design, and there is something in that. As Professor O'Keeffe has said, medievalists today view the castle with renewed awe at every visit though, like its builder, it is relatively little-studied. It is, he suggests, a building-complex of apparent contradictions. To mention two of them: the immense defensive curtain wall gives the impression that the castle is impregnable, yet there is virtually nothing on the inside that can't be seen from the outside. Also, the gatehouse tower leads you to believe the castle was entirely military, yet it would also have offered 'fairly high-grade accommodation', as Professor O'Keeffe puts it.

We can't say if Roesia de Verdun ever made use of that deluxe accommodation, but the English conquest brought with it a degree of luxury that had not been seen before. Trade increased, along with the trappings of an aristocratic culture that had its roots in France. Pheasants and rabbits were imported to satisfy hunting enthusiasts. New deer parks were established. Hawking, or falconry, was popular: a pastime that was also enjoyed by women.

Food, entertainment and hospitality, already very important in Ireland, continued as a means of strengthening bonds between lord and vassal. If Roesia sat down to a lordly table at Castleroche, it would have been laid with knives and spoons (forks came a few centuries later), glazed pottery from Bristol or Northern France, glasses, bowls, tankards, perhaps a ewer for handwashing and an array of jugs decorated with little figurines of animals such as monkeys. Some of them may even have been puzzle jugs, with the spout filled in so that the guest would be 'puzzled' when they went to pour the wine but nothing came out. A prank, thirteenth-century style.

If they laughed and teased, they may have done so in Norman French. 'For a couple of centuries after the conquest, French was the polite language, the language of commence and civic government,' writes Professor Edward Curtis. The first acts of parliament in Ireland in 1310 were in French. The 'conquerors' themselves were a very motley crew; they came from South Wales and had Flemish roots although neither Welsh nor Flemish took root here. The three languages vying for supremacy were Norman French, Irish and English. Latin was used in law and education.

Meanwhile, the documents that survive in English give us glimpses into Roesia's affairs. There were a number of legal cases but she also solved a long-running dispute with Hugh de Lacy, Earl of Ulster, in 1235. She was granted a lease on the king's manor in Louth in 1241 and, in 1244, she was given extra time by the king to settle her waste lands in Ireland.

Although, relatively speaking, we know a lot about Roesia de Verdun, we know little of her daily life and if – or when – she spent time in Co. Louth. That is so often the case with women in the past. As Dr Kenny puts it: 'When you talk about women in medieval Ireland there are a lot of ifs, buts and maybes.' Yet Dr Kenny has succeeded in piecing together a vivid picture of the women who lived in Co. Louth at the same time as Roesia and in the centuries that followed.

She has traced the single girls, married matrons and venerable dowagers who left behind traces of their lives in accounts of their lawsuits, feuds, gossip, love affairs and working lives:

Burghers' wives and daughters, maid servants, thieves, prostitutes and a myriad other manifestations of medieval womanhood all existed in the busy and crowded towns and villages of Louth. Some lead exceptional lives, most do not, but what they all provide are invaluable insights into the lives and activities of these generations of daughters, wives, mothers and sisters as they went about the struggle of their daily lives.

If building a castle set Roesia de Verdun apart from other women not only in Ireland but in Europe, she was far from being the only woman in medieval Ireland who showed a bent for business. In Co. Louth, Dr Kenny has found several striking examples of single women who had an entrepreneurial streak. The Blund family of Dundalk, for example, had several female heirs who were active in the town's economic affairs. Three daughters from the family were granted land by their father around 1326.

Likewise, the women of the Carter family, also from Dundalk, were involved in land deals. Alice Carter and her three daughters were landholders. One of them, Eva, started acquiring land with what Dr Kenny describes as 'entrepreneurial zeal':

> In 1316 Alice granted lands to her daughter Eva and from then until 1346 Eva systematically set about acquiring land in and around Dundalk … Eva Carter may be an example of a single woman who never married but who worked and expanded her holdings in Dundalk during her lifetime instead of pursuing the usual route of wife and mother.

Eva's property dealings took place several decades after Roesia de Verdun managed her lands in the same county but, again, it puts paid to the misconception that women were not involved in economic life.

Roesia de Verdun, however, was an exceptional woman. While many noblewomen found themselves in possession or in charge of castles because of early widowhood, they rarely built them. She was then, to use Professor O'Keeffe's term, in that 'very exclusive club of castle-building women'. Yet she is remembered as the scheming woman who killed her mason/ husband, he writes:

Roesia's portrayal in local folklore as a murderess, whatever its origin … may well reflect a deep-rooted social belief – a sexist belief, in today's thinking – that any woman capable of building a castle, an instrument of social violence, was in touch with her masculine side and was capable of violence herself.

It is also possible, Professor O'Keeffe adds, that the story is simply a retelling of an earlier story, recorded by English chronicler Orderic Vitalis, about Aubrey, Countess of Bayeux, who had her master mason beheaded after he built the tower of Ivry-la-Bataille castle in Normandy to prevent him reproducing the design.

But Roesia's story does not end there. Instead of simply retiring to a nunnery, as some medieval women did, Roesia went on to found her own. In 1239 or 1240 she established the Augustinian priory of Grace Dieu in Belton in Leicestershire. She retired there in 1242, but initially faced opposition. There was some anxiety about the spiritual state and the material possessions of the new foundation – not enough of the former and too much of the latter, perhaps.

Roesia and her nuns, however, had the support of the Franciscan theologian Adam Marsh who wrote to the Bishop of Lincoln to appeal for compassion for the 'new plantation' at Belton. 'It is very desirable that there should be no delay here,' he wrote. Compassion, it seems, was forthcoming and Roesia spent the last five years of her life at Belton and died there in her mid-forties. She was buried at Grace Dieu and her son John went on to inherit her estate in 1247.

The priory ceased to exist in 1538 when Henry VIII dissolved the monasteries. At the time, local villagers removed Roesia de

Verdun's body and reburied it in St John the Baptist's church at Belton. In the UK, it seems, she is remembered as the pious founder of the Grace Dieu priory – in stark contrast to how she is remembered in Ireland.

At least, though, she is remembered – and perhaps as time goes on, the stories we tell about Roesia de Verdun will encompass all the elements of her life as a noblewoman, wife, mother, widow, castle-builder, landholder, estate manager and founder.

Margaret O'Carroll

MEDIEVAL LADY, PATRON OF THE ARTS AND NEGOTIATOR (DIED 1451)

*She was the only woman that has made most of preparing high-
ways, and erecting bridges, churches, and mass-books, and of
all manner of things profitable to serve God and her soul.*
Scribe Dubhaltach Mac Fhirbhisigh

On 26 March 1433 Margaret O'Carroll, clad in a cloth
of gold, welcomed thousands of guests to a lavish
feast in Killeigh, Co. Offaly. She stood high on the
battlements of the town's great church while her husband,
circling on horseback below, directed the 2700 assembled
guests to eat and drink their fill at a magnificent banquet that
would be remembered for centuries. There was 'both meat
… and all manner of gifts', and Margaret recorded everyone's name on a roll – the chieftains, brehons (judges), bards,
musicians, gamesters and the poor – to make sure nobody
was forgotten.

Earlier that day, Margaret (or Mairghréag) offered two chal-
ices of gold to the church and took two young orphans into her

care for the good of her soul. Margaret the Hospitable, as she was known, was benevolent but also deeply pious.

There was nothing to compare to the glory of that day, the chroniclers said, but Margaret threw a second, equally spectacular banquet in the autumn of that same year. Again, general invitations were sent to thousands to attend a feast at the other end of her kingdom in Rathangan, Co. Kildare. Again, they came in great numbers; the men of learning, the harpers, the storytellers, the minstrels, the poets. All were accommodated in a temporary town of wattle huts built especially for the occasion – or at least that is how they had coped with the crowds invited to a bardic school a few decades earlier, according to the poet Gofraidh Fionn Ó Dálaigh. Each profession was lodged on a separate street: 'Wide avenues were laid out with lines of conical roofed houses of timber and wickerwork: a street for the poets, one for the musicians, one for the chroniclers and genealogists.'

The atmosphere may well have had something of a modern-day music festival about it with its 'pop-up' accommodation, bustle, performers, music, a collective sense of excitement and the promise of entertainment to come. There was also food and a gratuity for each guest, both very welcome in 1433, a year recorded as one of food shortages and famine.

The bards, harpers and their followers played to the guests who, Richard Stanihurst wrote of a later feast, sat and lay upon pallets of straw. 'The company must be whist, or else he chafeth like a cutpurse,' he wrote. Even those who wrote critically of the Irish and their wild, uncivilised ways were admirers of their music. They spoke in glowing terms of the harpers who were present at every occasion from feast and royal banquet to wakes and ale-house gatherings. The harp, it was said, could produce three strains of music, one that brought on sleep, another that produced laughter and yet another that reduced the listener to tears.

There were other instruments too – the *timpán*, a small stringed instrument, and various types of horns, pipes and whistles. A professional musician in the fifteenth century was likely to have been relatively well paid and highly regarded. The deaths of famous musicians went down in the annals and some decades before, in 1405, the death of the chief composer of Ireland, Cerbhall Ua Dálaigh, who wrote the still-famous song 'Eibhlín a Rúin', was noted with sadness. The same annals noted that Margaret's father, Tadhg O'Carroll, was a great patron of musicians. His daughter followed in his footsteps.

Hospitality was at the heart of Gaelic life. Under the Brehon laws, it was even considered a right for certain people: travellers (which included poets, historians, lawyers and doctors), lords and a king and his servants were entitled to demand hospitality in Irish homes. Of all the groups, the poet was the most feared as he – although there were some female poets in medieval Ireland – had the power to immortalise a perceived lack of hospitality in a stinging poem.

The fear a hungry poet could instil in a potential host is vividly captured in the *Life of Saint Lasair*, which recounts the terror felt by the saint when 'nine hungry poets and men of learning' came looking for hospitality at a time when food was scarce. 'O woman-saint, noble and honoured,' they said, 'this poet-company has come seeking thee, for nor food nor drink has passed their lips for a long weary space of time'. St Lasair 'blushed deep' and went to the chapel to pray fervently and ardently for something to give 'that harsh insensate band'. Her prayers were answered when she saw a nun coming towards her laden down with food and drink.

A poet was a very powerful figure in fifteenth-century Ireland. The annals even recorded that three sudden deaths were caused by a poet's 'miracle' during the century. A particularly biting satire might also inflict death by shame. The unrestrained verse of Aithirne, the intemperate poet of the Ulster Cycle of sagas, was so potent that it left three blotches on one woman's cheek: shame, blemish and disgrace. The woman later died of shame and bashfulness.

Myth that may be, but the power of poets and bards was real and it's clear from the laudatory verse they penned with great enthusiasm about Margaret O'Carroll that she lived up to her reputation as a patron of the arts. The poet Seithfín Mór, for example, wrote about her in glowing terms as a woman with a bountiful and pious heart. While she gave feasts, she never forsook her prayers: 'A woman who lives by rule. She protects herself against our art, her words are on our side,' he wrote.

Several poems survive, all of them listing the virtues of the day – piety, generosity, hospitality – and ascribing them to Margaret O'Carroll. There is no reason to disbelieve them, but other surviving records help us to build a more three-dimensional picture of Margaret O'Carroll not only as a benevolent and holy noblewoman but also a politically aware and independent one. She kept her maiden name when she married, she built bridges and churches, she negotiated the release of hostages without asking her husband's permission and she made an arduous journey to Spain to venerate the relics of St James at Santiago de Compostela.

We know little of her childhood other than that she was born into privilege. Her father Tadhg O'Carroll (Ó Cearbhaill) was a powerful lord of Éile, a kingdom that corresponds to modern-day Offaly. He had five children by three wives and it is thought Margaret's mother was a woman called Mór. Margaret doesn't appear in the record herself until she married An Calbhach O'Connor Faly sometime before 1417. An Calbhach was head of a neighbouring lordship that encompassed east Offaly and west Kildare and his marriage to Margaret was a strategic alliance most likely intended to strengthen Gaelic power in a region that was close to the English Pale.

It succeeded. Within five years, An Calbhach was lord of Offaly. In the years that followed he became one of the most powerful men in west Leinster. He had military skill and political nous, which he used to gain ground in raids against his Anglo-Irish neighbours in Meath and Kildare. Margaret's banquets, held at opposite ends of her husband's kingdom, must also have been intended to underline those territorial gains. The hosts were making another point too: the bards and musicians and harpers were reasserting Gaelic culture at a time when the Irish were rallying against the Anglo-Irish.

If there was a revival in Gaelic culture in the fifteenth century, there was also an upsurge in interest in pilgrimage. There was something of a boom in the numbers of Gaelic-Irish pilgrims going to Santiago de Compostela in Spain. Margaret, a deeply pious woman, may have been influenced by that but there was also a family tradition of pilgrimage. Her father Tadhg had gone on pilgrimage to Rome in 1396. He spoke about seeing the ruins of ancient Rome and stopping off at several centres of pilgrimage en route. His daughter may well have been inspired by him; she certainly looked beyond Ireland when it came to her faith. In 1441 she and her husband were granted a papal plenary indulgence, forgiving them of their sins.

In 1445 Margaret decided she wanted to do more and prepared to make the long, difficult and dangerous pilgrimage not to Rome but to Spain. Santiago de Compostela was favoured over Rome for two reasons, explains Dr Bernadette Cunningham. It was easier to get to by sea and it was easier to get forgiveness for sins there because jubilee years – when indulgences were generously given – were much more frequent in Spain.

The journey began at home with a series of practical and spiritual preparations. Before travelling, pilgrims visited the local church to be blessed and to have psalms said over them. Psalm 91, which asked for God's protection, foreshadowed some of the dangers that lay ahead. It called on God to keep plague and harm away from your tent; to protect you if injured and to protect you against treading on a snake. All of those were real risks – and medieval Irish pilgrims faced many more, as Dr Cunningham writes:

> We should not underestimate the magnitude of the undertaking entered into by those from Ireland who went on pilgrimage to Santiago in the centuries after 1200. It involved leaving family and property unprotected for a prolonged period, expending a considerable sum on travel and enduring personal hardship in lands where the language and lifestyle were unfamiliar.

Travelling by sea was also fraught. Most pilgrims experienced seasickness and storms but, if they were lucky, they escaped the pirates and thieves who targeted them. Then there was the difficulty of getting food and water at sea – or worse, in a strange and unfamiliar land. The deaths of nine Scottish and English pilgrims were recorded, some decades later, in northern Spain on their way home from pilgrimage. They died after eating local fruit and drinking water from a stream, even though they had been warned not to.

At least Margaret O'Carroll was not travelling alone. She was part of a large entourage that included Gaelic-Irish and Anglo-Irish lords and 'many more noble and ignoble persons' as the *Annals of Lecan* pointedly put it in 1445. She would also have had her own servants and – though it is not recorded – there must have been great anticipation when the party left Offaly for such a challenging but rewarding trip.

It was a spiritual as well as a physical journey. Margaret had already been praised for her devotion. That in itself was reason enough to go; there was no better way of expressing devotion than by undertaking a pilgrimage. She had also shown she was keen to safeguard her soul in the afterlife by applying to the pope for indulgences. Now she was on her way to gain further indulgences, for herself or perhaps for others.

An English pilgrim, William Wey, gave a fascinating account of the indulgences that were on offer in Santiago at that time. It reads like a shopping list with very clearly defined relation-ships between the time, effort and money spent by the pilgrim and the rewards guaranteed. For instance, a person could be forgiven a third of their sins if they went on pilgrimage to the church of St James in Santiago. If they joined the church's procession on a Sunday, they gained 40 days of indulgence, that is 40 days off the punishment time for sins committed.

On a feast day, that number went up to 300 and doubled if a
pilgrim visited the church of St James on the feast of the dedication to the church.

A preoccupation with death and, by implication, the
need to be in good spiritual condition for the afterlife was a
common preoccupation in medieval Ireland. However, as Dr
Cunningham suggests, it was particularly acute in the fifteenth
century because the horror of the Black Death was still a relatively recent memory. For Margaret it had particular resonance: her father's first wife, Joan Butler, died of the plague
in 1383.

When the Black Death first arrived in Ireland in 1348, it
claimed tens of thousands of lives and, in some areas, the population fell by up to 50 per cent. There were several outbreaks
later in the century, including one in 1383, which Margaret
must have known about so well. We can't say how it was
spoken about among her relatives, but a famous account by the
fourteenth-century friar and chronicler John Clyn of Kilkenny
gives us a chilling insight into the suffering of a community
rendered powerless by an infectious disease. He wrote:

The plague was so contagious that those touching the dead
or even the sick were immediately infected and died, and
the one confessing and the confessor were together led to
the grave. And because of fear and horror, men scarcely
ventured to discharge works of piety and mercy, namely
visiting the sick and burying the dead ... the pestilence
gathered strength in Kilkenny during Lent, for between
Christmas Day and March 6th eight Friars Preachers
(Dominicans) died. There was scarcely a house in which

only one died but commonly man and wife with their children and family going one way, namely crossing to death.

He said he was setting down on paper what he had witnessed to act as a faithful account of what happened. Then, poignantly, he added his final words: 'I am leaving parchment for the work to continue if, by chance, in the future a man should remain surviving, and anyone of the race of Adam should be able to escape this plague and (live) to continue this work I have commenced.'

The next entry, written by another scribe, reads: 'Here it seems the author died.'

Those who could, responded to plague with prayer or by going on pilgrimage as Margaret O'Carroll was doing now. The outbreak of plague in the late 1300s had personally affected her family but she would also have been aware of how it affected others. In her own time, the dangers of widespread plague might have passed, but disease, illness and regular food shortages made life precarious. We can't pinpoint her reasons for going on pilgrimage but the daily reminders of sudden death – and the implied need to be prepared for the afterlife – were very likely to have played a part in her decision.

Once she had completed her spiritual preparations, Margaret O'Carroll turned her attention to practical ones. She is likely to have travelled with her own servants but her luggage may well have been minimal, for practical reasons but also for spiritual ones. Many medieval travellers used the pilgrimage as an opportunity to turn away from the world with its ungodly trappings to focus, instead, on an inner spiritual journey. She probably did pack her prayer and psalm books though because, as Dr Kenny has noted, at this time the number of laywomen readers had increased dramatically. Women were also buying books, even though they were expensive.

If Margaret O'Carroll and her fellow pilgrims pared down their personal belongings, they were not in a position to scrimp on money. The journey itself was costly – there wouldn't have been any change from the entire annual income of a prosperous knight, according to one estimate. Then money was needed to make donations once pilgrims arrived at their destination. Thieves, pirates and other miscreants were all too aware of this and targeted pilgrims at sea and later as they made their way by road to Santiago.

Each sea vessel had a lookout who kept watch for enemy ships and pirates as the passengers tried to make themselves comfortable on the decks below. The bigger ships had several decks and might have had a cabin but Margaret O'Carroll may well have endured a very uncomfortable five to ten days at sea before landing in the port city of A Coruña in north-west Spain. In the harbour, pilgrim William Wey, who was travelling around the same time, counted 84 ships. Some 32 were English but there were also ships from Ireland and France. It must have been a terrific sight; a forest of ship masts and sails flapping in the wind as several hundred pilgrims prepared to disembark.

The journey to Santiago took about four days on foot or two on horseback. It must have been a busy, crowded route where pilgrims interacted and mixed with other. Perhaps they shared pious thoughts or forged new contacts, which would be exploited later. Some commentators have even suggested that this was the first age of the overseas package tour.

Once there, there was a well-established format that involved visiting the cathedral, looking at the relics of St James and finally making an offering – only cash and jewellery were accepted – in exchange for indulgences. Margaret may have stayed for three or four days but it was not without incident. Two of her travelling party died in Spain, Gerott, one of the Geraldines (or Fitzgerald dynasty) and Evilin, 'mother to the sons of Piers Dalton'. The *Annals of Lecan* also recorded another fatality: O'Driscoll, a man from West Cork, died at sea on the journey home.

The loss of life, however, did not appear to deter pilgrims. Margaret's husband, who did not accompany her on her recent trip, followed in her footsteps several years later. For now, though, the couple's attention was elsewhere. Margaret returned from Spain to find her husband at 'greate warr', as the annals put it, with the English de Berminghams. Both sides had taken hostages, a practice that was common between warring factions. What was less common, however, was what happened next: without consulting her husband, Margaret negotiated the release of several Irish prisoners with the Anglo-Irish government. One of them was the son of a man she had recently joined on pilgrimage.

Margaret was later praised in the annals for her actions, although they were sketched in only the barest of detail. It must have taken a woman of considerable character to do what she did. How did she go about initiating the hostage exchange? We don't know if she spoke English, but she was clearly diplomatic and skilled in negotiation. The fact that she did all of that without telling her husband, much less consulting him, shows she was very independent-minded. Meanwhile, she continued to show her devotion by commissioning the construction of a number of new churches, roads and bridges. As the annals trumpeted: 'She was the only woman that has made most of preparing highways, and erecting bridges, churches, and mass-books, and of all manner of things profitable to serve God and her soul.'

And, of course, she was a mother too. She and An Calbhach had seven children, five sons and two daughters. Two of her sons predeceased her and two more died shortly after her, a reality at a time when life expectancy was low and unpredictable. Margaret died of breast cancer in 1451 and her son Feidhlim died a few months later, probably of leprosy.

Yet her contribution as a patron of the arts and devout woman lived on after her, particularly through her daughter Fionnghuala (or Finola) who was spoken about in the same glowing terms as her mother. One tribute went:

> Fionnghuala's splendour is so great that no woman
> can be set above her
> From her girlhood – high praise! – her mother's nature
> shows in her; 'ere she came to a husband she was pregnant
> with generosity

Many centuries after her death, Margaret herself would inspire more poetry. In the nineteenth century, politician, journalist and poet Thomas D'Arcy McGee wrote two poems that were perhaps even more flowery than those written by the bards several hundred years before. In one, simply called *Margaret O'Carroll*, he wrote:

> Of bards and beadsmen far and near here was the name of
> names –

The lady fair of Offally – the flower of Leinster dames –
And she had joined the pilgrim host for the citie of St James.

The poem is quoted in its entirety in *Illustrious Irishwomen* by Irish author Elizabeth Owens Blackburne, who also writes of Margaret O'Carroll: 'She must have been a woman of remarkable spirit and capacity; and when to these were united the virtue, benevolence, and piety which all chroniclers agree in ascribing to her, it is no wonder that they felt a pride in recording her good deeds.'

Looking at her legacy today, Dr Cunningham says:

You can read between the lines of the surviving sources to see that she was an influential, wealthy, independent-minded woman, who relished her prominent position within the lordship. Her patronage role was not unusual for the wives of Gaelic lords, and the fact that we know so much about her is probably a reflection of her good relationship with the poets and historians who benefited from her lavish hospitality.

There is a moving epilogue to Margaret O'Carroll's remarkable story. In the early part of the last century, the remains of a woman were found in a wall space at the cemetery at Killeigh, Co. Offaly, alongside a Spanish-style cross. Was it Margaret O'Carroll? She was certainly buried there but so too were many others who, like her, had visited Santiago de Compostela. All the same, the artefact and its associated remains remind us of a woman who was a patron of the arts, a negotiator, a pilgrim, a mother and a beloved figure not only in her own time but in the centuries that followed. In short, as the annals summed up: 'She was the best woman of her time in Ireland.'

Katherine Fitzgerald, Countess of Desmond

WHO REPUTEDLY LIVED TO BE 140
(CIRCA 1460s–1604)

They say for certain that within these few years the Countess of Desmond lived to her 140th year, and cast her teeth three times.

Francis Bacon, 1623

The Old Countess of Desmond lived to be 140 years old – a fact confirmed by no less a person than Sir Walter Raleigh, the Elizabethan explorer and mayor of Youghal, Co. Cork. He claimed to have known the woman personally and to have proof of her advanced years. She was a well-known figure in Youghal town too, walking the five or so miles from her castle in Inchiquin every week when she was well over 100. But that was nothing compared to the journey she made to seek redress from Queen Elizabeth I some time later, supposedly walking all the way from Bristol to London, dragging her 'decrepit' daughter of 90-plus in a cart after her.

She never did divulge the secret of her longevity, but it was reported she had grown at least three sets of teeth in her lifetime. She might still be going strong had she not fallen from a cherry tree when she was 140 years old. Some even said she was 162. There is no reason to hold back when creating the stuff of legend.

Katherine Fitzgerald's exceptionally long life has certainly assumed the quality of legend; enduring, as it has, over the centuries to be debated and dissected with each new telling. It's easy to see the appeal. Given our preoccupation with mortality, how reassuring to hear of a woman who outwitted death for so long. She is important in the narrative of sixteenth-century history too, not least because she purportedly witnessed all of it. Here was a venerated elder holding strong as the House of Desmond crumbled all around her. From her castle at Inchiquin, she represented the last survivor of a way of life that would soon give way to a new social and political order with the English colonisation of Munster.

But was she real? Scratch the surface of her life story and, before long, you encounter a 'tissue of deepening improbabilities', as Richard Sainthill put it in 1861. Yet the Old Countess was indeed a real person. More than that, the story of her life – incomplete as the real version is – offers a starting point for the exploration of the reality of Irish women's lives during a century of rebellion, conflict and social upheaval.

Let's start with her age, which was the countess's singular achievement at a time when the average life expectancy was less than 30 for men and 34 for women. A quarter of babies died before their first birthday and death was a frequent visitor in daily life. Famine, disease, warfare and bad weather all took a toll. In the 1500s there are at least five references to outbreaks of plague. In 1575 alone, it claimed the lives of 3000 people in Dublin.

In a world where life was so precarious, it's not surprising that a woman who defied the odds would be celebrated, although she was not alone: some people did live long, healthy lives. There's a record of two fifteenth-century bishops – Miler Magrath of Cashel and Eugene O'Harte of Achonry – who lived to be 100.

But then the Irish as a race were particularly long-lived, as English philosopher and writer Francis Bacon noted in 1623. He even revealed the elixir of youth:

> The Irish, particularly those who live in the country, even now, are very long lived. They say for certain that within these few years the Countess of Desmond lived to her 140th year, and cast her teeth three times. But it is a custom with the Irish, placing themselves naked before a fire, to rub – and as it were season – their bodies with old salt butter.

In the nineteenth century, Richard Sainthill even suggested scientifically testing the salted-butter-in-front-of-the-fire technique. If it was found not to prolong life, at least the tests would do wonders for the sale of butter, he reasoned.

In another account, we're told the countess owed her longevity to Old Thomas Parr, the apothecary:

> This extraordinary woman lived to the amazing age of 145 years, and preserved her faculties to within a short period of her death. Many years previous to her departure from life the Countess became acquainted with Old Thomas Parr, of Salop; and it is generally thought that Parr gave her a supply of the herbal medicine by the aid of which he maintained his vigour to such an extreme period of life – viz., 152 years.

The article, published in *Old Parr's Almanack* in 1861, went on to describe how Parr's Pills helped restore weak and shattered constitutions:

> They completely renovate the system. A very short trial is sufficient to prove their efficacy. To women they are invaluable. They correct all the irregularities to which the sex is liable, and, by assisting the secretions, give such an healthy action to the organs as to give the colour of the rose to the complexion, and tone and vigour to the whole frame.

Thomas Parr developed the miraculous cure and lived at least as long as the countess. His own physician attributed his long, healthy life to a diet of sub-rancid cheese and milk, coarse and hard bread and a small drink of sour whey.

Sixteenth-century medicine, however, was not dependent on a fireside basting in butter or Parr's Pills. Medical knowledge and scientific thinking were at least as advanced in Ireland as elsewhere in Europe. Physicians in Ireland were academically well trained, explains Dr Aoibheann Nic Dhonnchadha, medical manuscripts expert and Assistant Professor at the Dublin Institute for Advanced Studies.

Some 16,000 pages from medical texts written in Irish survive. They tell a story of an Irish medical profession that kept up to date with recent academic developments in their field. The practice of medicine was hereditary and those who went to medical school would have studied a curriculum that was on a par with those offered in Europe or England, says Dr Nic Dhonnchadha:

It is clear from the textbooks that treatments were basically the same as elsewhere in Europe, i.e. firstly phlebotomy (bloodletting), which was both therapeutic and prophylactic; herbal treatment (adapted to local conditions); cupping [a cup was applied to the skin to create suction]; cautery [burning a part of the body to remove or seal it]; diet and exercise (just as highly rated in medieval times as today). Medical texts voice a general reluctance to engage in surgery: it was largely regarded as a last resort.

If Katherine Fitzgerald sought medical help during her lifetime, she would have been treated by a physician who believed men and women had very different anatomical features and constitutions. So-called 'women's conditions', however, were extensively covered in the medical manuscripts, which had references to menstruation, fertility, the principles of obstetrics and the rules for neonatal care, to mention a few.

Textbooks were based on the writings of ancient physicians such as Hippocrates and Galen, but there were others. The work of Persian physician Avicenna was studied along with the medieval writings on gynaecology attributed to Trotula. One of the most popular medical treatises in Ireland was the *Lilium Medicinae* written by Bernard of Gordon, a professor of medicine in Montpellier in France who systematically listed all the diseases of the body from head to toe along with causes, treatment and prognosis.

Bernard of Gordon covered women's health in detail. To quote one example, he considered menstruation to be a natural process and a cause of concern if it stopped. The reasons for loss of periods, he wrote, included 'too much exercise, hunger, emotions, obesity, fever, dropsy, vaginal scarring and similar observable factors'. He warned against prescribing too powerful a remedy to treat the problem as some substances had contraceptive or abortifacient properties. In other cases, though, it was the contraceptive properties that were sought as they might 'protect public women', or prostitutes, as physician Gilbert the Englishman pointed out.

There are few references to patients' ailments in the Irish manuscripts although one sixteenth-century physician, Corc Óg Ó Cadhla, does mention treating female patients. Corc explained that he finished transcribing a medical manuscript on 22 March 1578 while he was in Graiguenamanagh, Co. Kilkenny, where he treated the two daughters of Brian Caomhánach, chief of his sept, for menstrual irregularity. He didn't outline his treatment.

We can't say anything about Katherine Fitzgerald's experience of medicine in her lifetime other than the fact that she lived for an unusually long time. She didn't make it to 140, but historian Clodagh Tait thinks the real countess probably lived well into her nineties. That, in itself, was enough to earn the title the 'Old Countess'. Also, as Dr Tait points out: 'In that period, people often embroidered their ages, adding years to gain venerability at a time when they were losing power and losing authority.'

There was another factor at play. Calculating age was often a very approximate business as people were not numerate. They remembered their birthdays in unspecific ways. Dr Tait gives an example: 'A person might have been told that they were born in spring after such an event happened and then it mightn't be clear which year the event itself took place.'

The date of Katherine Fitzgerald's birth is given as some time in the 1460s. That is only plausible if we believe Sir Raleigh's claim that she danced in the court of King Richard III, who ruled until 1485. The young Katherine was even supposed to have said the king was the 'handsomest man in the room' – except for his brother Edward – and 'very well made'. We know that because her 'testimony' was later quoted by those objecting to William Shakespeare's portrayal of the king as 'crooked-back Richard' in a play a century later.

While the date of Katherine's birth is uncertain, we know she was born into privilege at Dromana Castle in Co. Waterford, the seat of the Fitzgeralds, Lords of the Decies. Her parents were Sir John Fitzgerald, Second Lord of Decies, and Ellen, daughter of John Fitzgibbon, the White Knight.

'Her birthplace no doubt was a princely castle … on the banks of the Blackwater,' the *Cork Constitution* rather fancifully wrote in a series of articles on the Old Countess in 1885. It went on to describe how grand it must have been with its turret, tower, ornamental windows and castellated appearance, all set in the 'superb and romantic scenery' of the Blackwater, or 'the Irish Rhine', as the writer called it.

The medieval castle of Dromana was indeed spectacularly situated, built on high ground overlooking the Blackwater River. We can only speculate about Katherine's life there. Her story comes down to us through a handful of documents: a marriage settlement, a few deeds, a lease. We know she married an Earl of Desmond at some point between 1505 and 1529. It's not even certain which one, but it's thought to have been Thomas 'the bald' Fitzgerald. The couple had one daughter before Katherine was widowed in 1534. After that she lived the rest of her famously long life at Inchiquin Castle until her death, supposedly aged 140, in 1604.

Inchiquin was an outpost of the Desmond kingdom, which extended over most of Munster. The dynasty had dominated political and social life in the south of Ireland for centuries, but that was about to come to an end. Even if we shave several decades off Katherine's life, she would have been alive to see the catastrophic aftermath of the Desmond rebellions in the later sixteenth century. The defeat of the House of Desmond opened the way for the Munster plantation but it also laid waste to the south of Ireland.

Contemporary writers wrote of a place left 'unpeopled' by war. Disease and famine claimed many more lives and it was estimated that the population of Munster fell by a third between 1569 and 1583. As the *Annals of the Four Masters* vividly put it: 'It was commonly said that the lowing of a cow, or the whistle of the ploughboy would scarcely be heard from Dunquinn to Cashel in Munster.'

The English poet Edmund Spenser described a province devoid of man or beast and the pitiful state of those affected by famine and illness: 'Out of every corner of the wood and glens they came creeping forth upon their hands, for their legs could not bear them; they looked Anatomies [of] death, they spoke like ghosts crying out of their graves; they did eat of the carrions, happy where they could find them …'

Katherine Fitzgerald, in Inchiquin, was at a remove from the worst of the violence. There was a garrison nearby and she would have had some interaction with the soldiers. She was probably there to keep an eye on things and to send back messages reporting on what was happening, Dr Tait suggests:

These are war-like societies but they are not necessarily consistently violent. The men were trained for war and people were prepared for war but the wars were often small scale. They were skirmishes and raids, not necessarily these dramatic set pieces. Earlier in her life, the Countess was probably familiar with these periodic enmities between these semi-autonomous leaders in their own territories. She would have understood the ins and out of that.

The most violent thing that happened in the vicinity during Katherine's tenure was the sack of Youghal. Gerald, Earl of Desmond, was spurred into rebellion by an English breach of faith, the annals tell us. They also describe what happened in Youghal in November 1579:

The Geraldines [the Fitzgerald dynasty] seized upon all the riches they found in this town, excepting such gold and silver as the merchants and burgesses had sent away in ships before the town was taken. Many a poor, indigent person became rich and affluent by the spoils of this town. The Geraldines levelled the wall of the town, and broke down its courts and castles, and its buildings of stone and wood, so that it was not habitable for some time afterwards.

Katherine Fitzgerald may not have walked into Youghal as a centenarian, as the legend suggests, but she certainly had a connection with the town. The Earls of Desmond had a house there and she would have known of the destruction and its aftershock. The sacking of the town was a very dramatic event: it is one of only two times during the sixteenth century when an

Irish town fell to attackers; the second time was Kinsale in 1601.

We don't know how the sack of Youghal affected Katherine, but we're told she later found the wherewithal to walk to London to petition Queen Elizabeth I when she lost her castle. That is not at all as fanciful as it seems because another Countess of Desmond did just that, though not when she was 140 years old, and not on foot. In 1567 Countess Eleanor Butler begged the queen to pardon her husband, the so-called 'Rebel Earl', Gerald Fitzgerald, when he was imprisoned in the Tower of London. She even went to live with him there for a time before they were both released.

She later went on the run with him when he led the second Desmond rebellion in 1579, living in cabins, woods and caves – in stark contrast to the luxury she would have enjoyed at their castle in Askeaton, Co. Limerick, with its servants, banquet hall, gardens and fishponds. Her husband was eventually caught and killed, and their castle destroyed.

After the rebellion, the countess was destitute. She wrote to Lord Burghley, Queen Elizabeth's adviser, to outline her plight. She, who once owned gowns of cloth of gold, widespread domains and princely castles, now found herself with no meat, no clothes and no dwelling: 'Myself and my poor children were almost famished, whereupon, the Lord Deputy sent us a dish of meat from his own table,' she wrote.

In 1587 she travelled to England, again seeking an audience with the queen; again, she succeeded and Queen Elizabeth granted her an annual pension of £200. It was paid out of compassion for her unhappy and miserable situation, which had been caused by her husband's disloyalty rather than her own, the queen later wrote.

Countess Eleanor was probably known to Countess Katherine, although they may never have met. Ironically, Eleanor could also be called the 'Old Countess' as she lived into her nineties. Longevity, it seemed, was a feature of the Desmond countesses, but they were not the only women who moved outside the private sphere into the political in the sixteenth century.

Others also successfully negotiated deals at the English royal court. In 1533 Mairgréag, the daughter of an Offaly chieftain, went to London and negotiated the return of her chieftain father Ó Conchobhair Failghe. She was sent because she could speak English, the annals noted. In 1593 and 1595, Grace O'Malley (or Granuaile), the so-called 'Pirate Queen', petitioned the English monarch on behalf of the men in her family, speaking Latin in court, although it was said she also spoke English.

Pick through the records of rebellion and war – those manly pursuits that too often dominate history – and you'll find a rich seam that tells the story of the women who ran house-holds, acted as political advisers and intermediaries, and had a measure of power in their own right.

'Women often have significant behind-the-scenes political authority,' says Dr Tait:

> They often came from noble families themselves. They are a linking point between the nobleman and her family. When you marry, you make a marriage alliance. A woman might give advice, pass messages, putting forward the case for one side or the other. We tend to think of women in the past as being very politically powerless but they had a soft power.

Some were educated and others had their own means. Honora Fitzgerald of Ballymaloe, for instance, had the means to buy a silver reliquary for a relic of the true cross. She had it inscribed with the words 'Pray for the soul of Honoria'. The wills of noblewomen of the time give an insight into what they had and valued – clothes and jewellery, for instance.

Most clothes were manufactured in Ireland but there were many imports of more luxurious items. As the century progressed, tastes became more sophisticated and diverse.

Excavations from a sixteenth-century tailor's workshop in Upper Bridge Street in Dublin yielded pieces of continental velvet and silks and an array of ornamental trimmings such as silk braids, bands and laces.

We don't know what Katherine Fitzgerald wore but if she had money – and taste – she could have chosen from an increasingly luxurious range of goods that were being imported from Bristol, such as silks from Paris and Milan, and taffeta and damask. More and more accessories were also becoming available, including spectacles – although they are not, strictly speaking, an accessory. (Incidentally, the first pair of spectacles in Ireland was recorded in 1542.)

Hospitality was an important part of a noblewoman's role so the countess would have played hostess at Inchiquin Castle when the political climate allowed it. Luke Gernon, magistrate for Munster, opens a wonderfully evocative window on Irish hospitality in an account he wrote a little later in 1620.

Castles are built very strong and with narrow stairs for security, he wrote: 'The hall is the uppermost room, let us go up, you shall not come downe agayne till tomorrow …' The lady of the house greeted you in the hall and after salutations everyone was presented with 'all the drinkes in the house', starting with ordinary beer, then aquavitae, then 'olde-ale'. 'The lady tastes it, you must not refuse it.'

A big fire was blazing in the middle of the hall and guests could sit in front of it until supper time when the table was plentifully furnished with a variety of meats – 'but ill cooked, and with out sauce'. There might be red deer, or an Irish speciality, mutton roasted in its skin and served at the table. 'They say that it makes the flesh more firme, and preserves the fatt.'

While supper was being eaten, the harper played and sang ancient Irish tunes, often composing a song especially for the occasion. When guests had eaten and drunk their fill, they were invited to stay the night. If you chose that option, though, Gernon warned that the Irish bedroom did not have a canopy or curtains. In the morning, another cup of aquavitae was served. 'It helps [digest] the crudities of Irish feasting.' Breakfast was leftovers from the night before and when you were ready to go, the hosts called for 'Dogh a dores' – to drink, at the door, the same array of drinks you had the night before.

However, in contrast to Lord Bacon who said the Irish were long-lived, Gernon reported that they aged very quickly, particularly women. While he thought the women of Ireland 'very comely creatures, tall, slender and upright. Of complexion very fayre & cleare-skinnd (but frecled)', he said the old proverb applied: 'soone ripe, soone rotten'. They are women at 13 and old wives at 30; he never saw fairer young women nor fouler old ones, he added.

Which brings us back to the aged Old Countess who, it has to be said, is not done a service in any of her supposed portraits: they show a stern and sullen woman, peering out from a hooded cloak. Katherine probably was born later than is suggested and certainly died earlier than 1604. In the nineteenth century, antiquarian Mary Agnes Hickson suggested her advanced age was part of a clever plot by Sir John FitzEdmund Fitzgerald, a member of the House of Desmond, to hold on to the castle at Inchiquin. The widow had the use of the castle for her lifetime and then it was to revert to Sir Walter Raleigh. It made sense then to prolong Katherine's life.

In any case, as the *Cork Constitution* so eloquently put it in 1885, 'pens, paper, and time without measure have been spent in her service – hunting up her history, her residence, where she was born, who was her husband ...' It's a debate that continues, along with an enduring fascination about a woman who survived the many challenges of the sixteenth century.

If a theme emerges from all that is written about this venerable old lady, it is that she was immensely strong and hardy. For example, one account of her last days made a point of saying that she did not die from the fall from the cherry tree, aged 140-plus: she suffered an injury to her leg, which led to a fever. It was the fever that killed her, not her age, the writer insisted. Whatever her age and whatever the reason for her death, here at least is an account of a woman who emerges from the sixteenth century in her own right, rather than on the arm of her long-dead earl. For that reason alone, she is worth commemorating.

Katherine Jones, Lady Ranelagh

INTELLECTUAL, WOMAN OF SCIENCE,
PHYSICIAN – AND THE BRILLIANT OLDER
SISTER OF CHEMIST ROBERT BOYLE
(1615–1691)

[A] lady remarkable for her uncommon genius and knowledge.
Thomas Birch, Robert Boyle's biographer

Katherine Jones, Lady Ranelagh, would become one of the most influential women of science, politics and piety in seventeenth-century Ireland and England, but in late 1642 she was close to despair. For 22 weeks, she and her four young children were held under siege in the 'most miserable captivity' at Athlone Castle. The rooms of her lodgings, built to house the President of Connacht, had a sweeping view of the River Shannon with its corn mills and eel weirs, but that was obscured now by Irish Confederate Army troops amassed on the arched stone bridge, just south of the castle. Had she stolen a glimpse through the large windows of her living quarters, she would have seen the armed ranks, some uniformed and carrying muskets, pikes and pistols; others, ragged and barefoot, making do with scythes, clubs and stones.

Earlier that year, a plot to seize the castle and surprise the family as they made the short coach ride across that same bridge to St Mary's church failed. A musket went off accidentally, giving a premature signal to the troops to open fire on the castle. The Ranelaghs had not yet left for Sunday service, but they were left in no doubt that the Catholic rebellion, which broke out in Ulster the previous October, had spread to the gates of Athlone.

The months that followed were tense and uncertain, and in mid-June the rebels finally besieged Athlone, completely cutting it off. Nothing could get in – or out. One woman who tried to get a dispatch through the Irish blockade was stoned to death by women from the town.

Inside the castle, the situation was growing more desperate with each passing day. The walls were reputed to be impregnable, but the soldiers defending them had become so weakened from lack of food that they were no longer able to fight. They were said to be dying faster than the survivors could bury them. Disease was rife and smallpox had taken hold, yet there were very real dangers outside the walls too. Fleeing Protestant families, who took sanctuary in the castle, came with terrifying accounts of arson, dispossession and slaughter at the hands of what they called the barbarous Catholics bent on destroying them. Lady Ranelagh must have worried that she and her children would not get out of Athlone alive. Her youngest child, Richard, was only one year old. Frances was three; Elizabeth, six and Catherine, the eldest, eight.

Lady Ranelagh captured something of the desperation of that 'time of universal misery' in a letter to her father, Richard Boyle, the First Earl of Cork. She described feeling hopeless and friendless within a castle enclosure that would have been fetid, overcrowded and alive with rumour. For more than four months she held out hope of escape until, she said, her patience was quite tried. When it was clear there was no friend to deliver her from captivity, she turned to foe. 'The desperateness of [my] condition forced me to put my selfe into the hands of my enemys, without any other security for my safe getting out … [than] Sir James Dillon's word,' she wrote to her father, at pains to stress that she was in no way on the side of the rebels.

Sir James, however, was not exactly an enemy. The Confederate Army colonel was of Old English stock and had been on friendly terms with the Ranelaghs before rebellion shattered the country's fragile political equilibrium. The old English, descendants of the Norman settlers, now sided with the Gaelic Irish in a battle to force concessions for Catholics from the new English settlers.

Sir James Dillon was of the same social rank as the Ranelaghs and spoke about respecting the rules of God, even in the midst of a bloody uprising. He was also a man of his word which, Lady Ranelagh conceded, he kept 'most punctually and civilly' by safely delivering the family to Dublin. Once there, she set about rallying a relief force for the besieged town. About 900 men and 200 horses were dispatched to bring munitions and food to Athlone, but Lady Ranelagh would never live there again.

When she was escorted out of the town that October, passing near the bowling green, the great garden, meadow and orchard, she left behind not only her husband's demesne but her 10-year marriage to Arthur Jones, heir to Viscount Ranelagh. He was conspicuous by his absence during the siege and it fell to his father, Roger Jones, First Viscount Ranelagh and Lord President of Connacht, to negotiate his daughter-in-law's safe passage. That was not surprising as the young couple had lived apart since Katherine produced a long-awaited male heir in 1641.

The birth of a healthy boy must have come as an immense relief to Katherine and not just because it meant that she had fulfilled her marital duty by giving birth to a successor. She had been brought close 'to death's doore' when her first son was born prematurely two years earlier. There were considerable risks associated with pregnancy as Katherine's father, the Earl of Cork, knew only too well. He lost his first wife and child in childbirth and took a keen interest in his daughter's pregnancy. He had instructed her not to travel from England to Ireland as the journey might risk the 'loss of the blessing I know you desire soe much'.

The Earl later praised God when he heard that the 'boy-wench' and his mother were doing well, but the improvement was short-lived. The little boy died shortly after he was christened Frank and his mother, left 'weake and sickly', was confined to bed for six months. Unlike many others, she did recover and the arrival of a healthy baby boy in August 1641 marked the effective end of her marriage.

The difficulties in that union had been apparent for some time. Katherine referred to her husband's gambling – 'he is guilty of play' – in the letters she wrote to her father in Youghal, Co. Cork who, in turn, made a veiled reference to his infidelity.

Jones had few admirers. Sir John Leeke described him as 'the foulest Churle in the world; he hath only one vertu that he seldom cometh sober to bedd.' The Duke of Ormonde and the Earl of Clarendon were equally condemning. They said he was 'the worst man in the world' and failed to provide for his wife and children.

It might have been different as Katherine's father had promised her to another man when she was just eight years old. In fact, he was so pleased with the match that he paid £3522 (close to half a million euros today) of her £4000 dowry up front. But then he had the means. Richard Boyle was one of the most successful Elizabethan colonisers of the sixteenth century. He had come to Ireland in 1588 and acquired land, rank and considerable wealth in Munster. After he lost his first wife, he married Catherine Fenton and they had 15 children together. Their seventh child, Katherine Boyle, was born on 22 March 1615. Her youngest brother, Robert Boyle, was born 12 years later. He would go on to be recognised as the father of chemistry, thanks in no small part to his two-decade collaboration with his older, brilliant sister Katherine.

It is to her credit that Katherine managed to secure an education at all. Her father didn't believe girls needed to be educated and sent her, aged nine and a half, to live with the family of her betrothed, Sapcote Beaumont, in Leicestershire. Four years later the marriage was called off when the family increased the dowry by a further €2000, but her time in England had not been wasted. She had been introduced to the idea of education, an interest she vigorously pursued for the rest of her life. When she was 10, the household chaplain, Thomas Pestell, gave her a Bible and told her in the inscription that this was her first ABC. It was, he said, a path to literacy and salvation.

It's likely that Katherine was tutored too. Her father, it seems, was none too pleased with the results as he complained she had lost the foundations of her religion and civility when she returned home. Others, however, celebrated her exceptional intelligence – and her faith. Her memory was so sharp that she could hear a sermon, then go home and write it down verbatim after dinner. Sir John Leeke wrote of the 20-year-old Katherine in a letter to Sir Edmund Verney: 'A more brayve wench or a Braver spirit you have no often met wth ...'

He went on to describe her as a sweet, disposed lady who held her head down a little. There was nothing of that reserve evident in the woman who, seven years later, showed a steely resolve in negotiating her way through a rebellion that claimed the lives of thousands on both sides. For Lady Ranelagh, though, the balance of cruelty lay firmly with the Irish. Not only had she endured a four-month captivity at Athlone Castle, she was also in mourning for her brother, Lewis Boyle, First Viscount of Kinalmeaky, who died on the battlefield at Liscarroll, Co. Cork.

In a letter written at the end of 1642, the depth of her grief is evident but so too is a deep, consoling faith, underpinned by the belief that all burdens came from God. She went further, saying that her brother died in 'so noble a cause' she looked on it as 'a stroke of Gods hand & therefore dare doe nothing but submit to it'.

In early 1643 she left Ireland and the rebellion behind, only to arrive into the ferment of the English civil war in London. In effect, she was a single mother with four children and no income. If it was unusual for a seventeenth-century woman to separate from her husband, it was more unusual still for a woman to fight for a financial settlement. Over the next two decades Lady Ranelagh pursued her husband for money, which she planned to spend on her own daughters' dowries.

In the meantime, she moved to an address near St Paul's Cathedral and opened her new abode to family members left homeless by the Irish rebellion. Her elder sister Lady Joan Fitzgerald, Countess of Kildare, and her children were the first to join her. They fled a pillaged Maynooth Castle in Co. Kildare. They were joined by younger sister Lady Dorothy Loftus and her children, who took refuge in London after Irish forces 'dismantled' Rathfarnham Castle in Dublin.

Katherine was also joined by her sister-in-law Margaret Jones, whose husband, Sir John Clotworthy, was an influential Member of Parliament. He may well have helped her to establish herself in London, but Katherine Jones was already well connected in English society. When she was younger, she had dined at the royal table 'amongst all the great Lords and Ladies' when her brother Francis married royal maid of honour Lady Elizabeth Killigrew. In any case, she soon found her feet in London. Less than two years after her arrival, she was firmly established in intellectual and religious circles and was already integrated into parliamentary circles. When her youngest brother Robert visited her after returning from his Grand Tour of Europe, he remarked that he had been introduced to several 'persons of power & influence in ye Parliamt and their party'.

From 1644 Lady Ranelagh addressed those 'persons of power' in persuasive and authoritative letters aimed at promoting peace and reconciling king and Parliament. At first, she stood behind King Charles I, but as the civil war ground on, she thought him too full of pride and argued for more powers for Parliament. She said so forcefully in a letter to his sister, Elizabeth Stuart, Queen of Bohemia, who was exiled in The Hague. Lady Ranelagh hoped king and Parliament could work together to create a country that would act as a beacon for Christian virtue where people were treated with care and compassion.

She also expressed her opinion on a range of subjects including natural philosophy, religion, optics, chemistry, mathematics and horticulture. She was a member of the Grand Tew Circle, an intellectual network, and later became one of the most prominent members of the Hartlib Circle, an extensive association of friends who often met in her house to discuss the issues of the day.

Of the Circle's 766-strong membership, she was the seventh most important member, according to a mathematical analysis of its surviving letters completed by Dr Evan Bourke. That meant she was at the centre of a network that was pushing for political reform in Ireland, educational reform and the promotion of scientific investigation.

Katherine Jones was now Viscountess Ranelagh, but she continued to be most commonly known as Lady Ranelagh. Her opinion was sought by politicians, physicians, religious leaders, even royalty. There are multiple references to her eloquence and wit in the letters and diaries of her contemporaries. Her striking personality and her exceptional piety were commented upon – and celebrated. The poet John Milton described her as 'that most exemplary woman' and she later engaged him as a tutor for her son. Diarist John Evelyn said she was 'a person of extraordinary talent'. The word 'incomparable' began to be the adjective most commonly used before her name.

While her intellect was admired, she was motivated almost entirely by faith and a desire to unite Protestantism. She learned Hebrew to deepen her understanding of the scriptures. Her teacher William Robertson was so impressed by how quickly and expertly she mastered the language that he dedicated his guide to learning Hebrew to her. Her achievement made him see that 'the Female sexe is, fully, capable enough of this kind of learning'.

He even went so far as to say he hoped it would encourage other women to 'improve their abilities'. Lady Ranelagh and her Irish-born aunt, Dorothy Moore, also a prominent member of the Hartlib Circle, were avid supporters of education for girls.

Her life was now in England but there was still unfinished business in Ireland. In 1656 Lady Ranelagh returned to Cork with her daughters Catherine and Frances and spent the next two-and-a-half years trying to recover land and lost income from her late father's estates. She also pursued her husband, Arthur Jones, for a settlement but without success. Another decade would pass before a separation was finally agreed.

While in Ireland, she continued to correspond with the Hartlib Circle in England. She sent one member, John Beale, a discourse on dreams. It no longer survives, though Beale mentions that he spent much time meditating on it. Lady Ranelagh also contacted members of the Circle based in Ireland. Oliver Cromwell's land surveyor William Petty and Major Miles Symner, the first professor of mathematics at Trinity College Dublin, were among them.

She later expressed some reservations about Oliver Cromwell, but not because of the ruthlessness of his Irish campaign. Her personal experiences had turned her firmly against the Irish Confederate Army and their cause. Her main concern was that politics relied too much on one man – Cromwell – while failing to promote a godly society that might remedy all social ills.

—

Lady Ranelagh was woken in the small hours of 15 February 1659 by a furious thud that seemed to strike the ship just under the cabin she was sharing with her brother, Roger Boyle, Lord Broghill, and her daughters Catherine and Frances as they sailed for England. She had been asleep on a bench – 'I left [Lord Broghill] the bed' – when the ship ran into a sandbank during a storm so violent that she feared the hull would shatter into pieces.

Her brother cried out, saying they would all die, and Lady Ranelagh prepared her daughters for the worst: 'I expected … that [every] minute the [waves] should in and sweepe us away', she wrote. The crew members on deck were at their wits' end when Lord Broghill went up to see the damage while, in the cabin below, his sister was sure the loosened rudder would 'beate out his brains'. The ship, however, had not taken in any water and Lady Ranelagh later told another brother, Richard, First Earl of Burlington, that they had been 'plucked … out of the jawes of death' by the merciful saviour and that God 'who holds the winds in the hollow of his fists' then guided the ship safely ashore.

Her unwavering faith, so evident in the letter, shaped her world view. She saw the continuing turbulence of the world around her through a religious lens. Civil unrest, war and violence were all interpreted as signs of God's anger. When, in 1665, the plague turned London into 'a ruinous heap', as she put it, she considered it a punishment from God.

Yet she was not by any means unsympathetic to the victims of a disease that 'scattered death so plentifully about'. She wrote a treatise on the plague and spoke up for the non-conformists jailed for their religious beliefs (it was an offence to pray in groups of five or more without using the Anglican Prayer Book). With prisons being disease-ridden murder holes, a prison sentence amounted to a death sentence, she argued. She called for a society tolerant enough to allow its people to live according to their conscience.

When the monarchy was restored under Charles II in 1660, Katherine had moved to fashionable Pall Mall in central London. Despite the changing political landscape, she continued to be in favour. She had gained a reputation as a physician and her medical remedies were widely distributed. She was the one the royal court turned to when the young Duke of Cambridge was sick in the late spring of 1667. His younger brother, the Duke of Kendal, was also seriously ill. Lady Ranelagh disagreed with the physicians who had treated him and was not afraid to say so. She was later asked to give her opinion at the autopsy when the Duke of Kendal died before his first birthday. The Duke of Cambridge died one month later, aged three.

Two months later, she was called to attend Lady Clarendon who had lost her speech after suffering a convulsion. Again, Lady Ranelagh found herself in the company of other physicians and disagreed with them. She was critical of their methods and said they could not rouse the patient. She succeeded in bringing the woman around by holding her own remedy, spirit of hartshorn, under her nose. The relief, however, was short-lived – Lady Clarendon died the following day.

Nonetheless, Lady Ranelagh was convinced by her own preparation. Hartshorn, or smelling salts, was a solution of ammonia made from distilling shavings of deer (or hart's) horn. She later recommended it for her brother's wife when she became ill, asking him to send up the antlers of either stags or bucks from his parks so that she could make up the remedy for him. Her sister-in-law went on to recover fully.

Lady Ranelagh had medical remedies for all of life's ills: palsy, festers and inflammations, pains of the joints, sharp hot humours, lost appetite, lost memory, giddiness of the head and cold dispositions of the liver, to mention a few. She used plant-based ingredients, grinding them in a mortar, but she also experimented with new scientific techniques and had a laboratory built in her garden.

Her interest in science and chemistry developed alongside that of her brother's, Robert Boyle. He moved into her London home in 1668 and for 23 years they collaborated on a wide range of scientific and philosophical projects. Her influence on him was well known and, in some quarters, she was considered a little too influential. The Duke of Ormonde commented that she governed her family absolutely, although Robert Boyle treated her as an equal partner in professional and private matters.

She had persuaded him not to join the Royalist army when he was younger and encouraged him to work in the field of ethics.

While they lived together, she read and commented on drafts of his manuscripts. He held her in such high esteem that he offered to bequeath her his collection of medical recipes in the event of his death so that they would not fall into the wrong hands.

Lady Ranelagh's youngest daughter Frances was also part of the household at Pall Mall. She had never married and mother and daughter were extremely close. Her mother successfully nursed her through ill health as a baby but was not able to cure her when she fell ill as an adult. She died in 1672, aged 34. It was a terrible blow – but another was to come when her eldest daughter Catherine died just three years later.

The two daughters who had once accompanied their mother to Ireland were now dead but Lady Ranelagh continued to keep up with what was happening in the Williamite wars – a 'sad and mournful time' in Ireland. Or at least she tried to. She heard many stories, but very little truth, she said in a letter to Margaret Boyle, Countess of Orrery, in 1689. She said she was glad to hear the latest news – that the walls of Derry survived the siege by the deposed king, James II. Given her own experience in the rebellion of 1641, it is not surprising that she would side with the Williamites and want to maintain Protestant rule in Ireland.

She celebrated His Majesty's (William III) continued success after the Battle of the Boyne and was upset by 'the most unpleasant news' of a setback during the siege of Limerick.

She was 75 years old yet continued to follow political events in Ireland. In August 1690 she wrote in detail about the siege and the Williamite forces who tried, unsuccessfully, to reclaim Limerick city from the Jacobite army who had retreated there after the Boyne defeat.

In a letter to Anne Hamilton, Duchess of Hamilton, written on 28 August 1690, she referred to Patrick Sarsfield's famous raid on the Williamite siege train of munitions at Ballyneety. She wrote of the munitions lost, the soldiers who apparently slept on their watch and the 'cruel' Irish who killed not only the 'unready soldiers but many poore women and children' before they were eventually stopped. Yet, for all of that, Katherine Jones, Lady Ranelagh, was of Ireland and while she did not condone Irish-led rebellion, she maintained a fondness for the country throughout her life.

Four centuries later, it is Robert Boyle who is remembered as the first modern chemist and the man who first described Boyle's Law (when the volume of a gas is decreased, pressure increases by the same proportion). But in the seventeenth century his name was inseparable from that of his elder sister, Katherine Jones.

She was revered as something of a prophet within the Hartlib Circle. What she said in her letters and manuscripts carried considerable weight. While those letters were intended for private circulation, they had far-reaching influence. It would have been considered improper for a woman to commit her words to print, but Lady Ranelagh succeeded in crossing boundaries while remaining modest and pious. That decorum, though, partly explains why her influence was largely forgotten in the centuries that followed.

Her letters survive in part because of her connection to the powerful men in the Boyle family and because, in recent years, a number of academics have worked to bring her life and work to light again. To appreciate the reach of Lady Ranelagh's influence in the seventeenth century, let us turn to the funeral oration given at her brother's funeral, which took place just eight days after hers in December 1691. The Bishop of Salisbury, Gilbert Burnet, said Katherine Jones went about her charitable work 'with the greatest Zeal and most Success that [he had] ever known'. Of her influence, he said that she had 'lived the longest on the publickest Scene, she made the greatest Figure in all the Revolutions of these Kingdoms for above fifty Years, of any Woman of our Age'.

Ellen Hutchins

IRELAND'S FIRST FEMALE BOTANIST
(1785–1815)

Miss Hutchins amazed me by the extent and depth of her botanical knowledge … almost the best botanist, either Male or Female that we ever met with.

Lewis Dillwyn, botanist

Ellen Hutchins was dreading the journey home. The carriage ride from Dublin to West Cork was long and arduous and, in the early 1800s, the roads were so treacherous in places that men were sent ahead to fill the boggy potholes with furze bushes and stones to allow safe passage. But that was the least of Ellen's worries. She was returning to Ballylickey House in Bantry Bay to care for her frail mother, an elderly grand-aunt and her brother Thomas, who had been paralysed as a schoolboy after a bad fall on the ice. What she feared most was not so much her familial duty, but the isolation. The house received few visitors and there was nobody of her own age nearby.

She had also just recovered from her own health difficulties. She had taken ill as a teenager while at school in Dublin. Her niece Alicia Maria Hutchins later explained that her aunt had simply not been given enough to eat: 'She had been insufficiently fed, healthy appetites not being considered ladylike.' The Hutchinses enlisted the help of family friend Dr Whitley Stokes, a physician, polymath and keen botanist. He took Ellen into his home on Harcourt Street in Dublin and gradually nursed her back to health.

Ellen's niece described how he did it: 'Dr Stokes warned Mrs Stokes to take no notice of Ellen's nervous state, nor of her disinclination for food, and advised that some small thing should be left in her room, which might tempt her to eat, when alone. This plan was successful and after a time Ellen regained her appetite and health.'

Her return to health, however, also meant that it was time to return home. To ease the transition from the stimulation of the city to secluded country living, Dr Stokes suggested Ellen develop her interest in botany. She had already read widely on the subject, it seems, taking advantage of the doctor's well-stocked home library. He gave her some of his books and possibly a microscope, and advised her to pursue the subject as it would allow her to get out of doors and explore the countryside.

Ellen's French teacher – described only as 'an exiled French lady, a refugee' – gave her the same advice, telling her that botany had been a solace to her at times of difficulty.

That guidance set Ellen Hutchins on a course which shaped the rest of her short life. Despite ongoing health difficulties and family disputes, she made remarkably swift progress. Less than a decade later, her exceptional ability to find new species (she found more than 20) brought her to the attention of international botanists. Her achievements are all the more remarkable given that she looked after her elderly mother, a grand-aunt Bel who, Ellen said, hadn't left her room in three years, and her invalided brother Thomas. We get glimpses of the level of care needed in some of her letters: 'My poor brother requires to have me always near to write for him and attend him in all the little matters that make him comfortable and that no person who has not nursed the sick can imagine,' she wrote.

Yet, despite her duties, she still managed to find time to pursue her new-found passion. The house was beautifully situated. Ellen gave this vivid description: 'The view from our door is very soft & pleasing particularly at evening when the sun retiring behind a beautiful mountain sugarloaf just gilds the high ground & leaves the little cove before us in deep soft shade, or when the moon shines bright upon it.' She added rather caustically: 'I often think of the strong & melancholy contrast between the peaceful happy looking scene & the restless minds of its inhabitants.'

More than the beauty of the place, though, it was also an ideal place for plant hunting. Ellen set out to explore the rocky shores, the riverbanks beside the house and the woods, bogs and mountains nearby. She made many new 'dear friends' – plant specimens so precious that she spoke about them as if they were people. She talked about meeting and visiting her 'treasures' and 'exquisite little beauties' and she took immense pleasure in finding out their names and 'family'.

Her own family origins went back to the 1600s when the Hutchinses of Devonshire, England, moved to Ireland, her niece Alicia recorded. Ellen herself was born on 17 March 1785, one of 21 children born to Thomas and Elinor Hutchins. Just two daughters and four sons survived into adulthood. Even by the standards of the time, when between a quarter and a third of children died before their fifteenth birthday, that was an unusually cruel loss.

Thomas Hutchins was a Protestant magistrate who opposed the anti-Catholic Penal Laws. In one celebrated case, he took the side of a Catholic priest who sought his help. A Protestant had coveted the priest's horse and paid £5 for it. Hutchins said the sum was too low and ordered the horse be returned to the priest.

Ellen's father was a landowner and ran a profitable fishing trade in herring, cod and ling. He also rented from the Catholic landlord Lord Kenmare who once remarked that he had persuaded Thomas Hutchins not to follow his father into the smuggling trade, as it would end in ruin. Thomas's father had illegally imported French wine into Bantry Bay, a notorious haven for smugglers in the eighteenth century. His son may have done likewise for a time. He was certainly a frequent visitor to France. His grand-niece Alicia Hutchins even reported that he had once been detained in Paris on suspicion of being a spy. She wrote: 'He was said to be a remarkably good sword's-man and to speak French "like a native".'

Thomas Hutchins died when Ellen was just two years old, but her mother saw to it that her younger children were educated. Two sons went to Trinity College Dublin and Ellen got a good education. Money, however, was often tight and, in later years, there were bitter family disputes over who should occupy Ballylickey House.

For now, though, Ellen spent her free time tending her garden and collecting specimens, which she sent to her old friend Dr

Stokes. He introduced her to James Townsend Mackay, curator at the Botanic Garden of Trinity College, who suggested Ellen focus on a neglected branch of botany – seaweeds. Ellen did just that and began to explore the shoreline around her home.

In 1805 Mackay visited Ellen and spent a few days with her at Ballylickey. She was delighted to find someone who shared her 'pleasure in plants' and, says her great-great-grand-niece Madeline Hutchins, she realised for the first time that she had something significant to offer: 'Mackay could see how skilled she was at identifying tiny differences in the plants studied, how knowledgeable she was about local habitats, and how determined and careful she was in all that she did. Together they "botanised" on the shores of Bantry Bay, in the woods, bogs, heathland and went as far as the summit of Sugar Loaf mountain.'

Mackay wrote later: 'I am a little proud of having been instrumental in setting her a-going in a branch of botany in which she has made such a conspicuous figure – she had never examined nor dried a sea plant until I gave her the hint in the summer of 1805 when I had the pleasure of spending a few days with her at Ballylickey.'

The visit propelled Ellen into action and, a few months later, she wrote to tell Mackay that she would soon be able to widen her exploration: 'I am to have the boat and crew all the next summer to go where I please so that you may expect a good parcel at the end of it. I have high hopes of adding to our collections.'

She sent James Townsend Mackay that good parcel, as promised. He, in turn, sent some of her specimens to bota-nist Dawson Turner who included Ellen's discoveries in his book on seaweeds, *Historia Fucorum*. He wrote to thank her, establishing a long and mutually beneficial correspondence. Over the next seven years, Dawson Turner would become her mentor and friend. He even named his own daughter after Ellen and asked her to be godmother as he knew 'of no other female in the world that he would earnestly wish a child of his to emulate'. They never met but wrote to each other frequently, exchanging letters, specimens and opinions on everything from botany and Byron's poems to Sir Walter Scott's writings.

In 1808 Ellen sent him her first drawing. She had seen a particular species of seaweed in fruit and recorded it in a watercolour. 'I had great pleasure in finding *Fucus tomentosus* in fruit ... fearing that drying will alter its appearance, I have attempted to draw it as it appeared when recent.'

Her discovery was significant – and timely, as it came just as botanical experts were considering re-categorising the seaweed as a sponge, rather than a plant. Ellen was the first to record it in fruit, proving emphatically that it was a plant. Her discovery not only underlined her gift for botany, but also for art. She started to record her beloved seaweed specimens in minute and beautiful detail in watercolour drawings, many of which are now at the Royal Botanic Gardens in Kew.

Her reputation as a botanist was also growing, even though she was relatively new to the field. In three years, she discovered several new plants but was very modest about her achievements. In a letter to her brother Emanuel in 1807, she wrote:

For some time past, I have amused myself learning Botany. I am told by those that are good judges that I have made great progress for the time I have been learning, in a curious and difficult branch, that of marine plants.

I also sent a great many [plants] to Dr. Stokes and have made him a very fine collection. He says he is quite aston-ished at the progress I have made ...

Later, she explained to her brother Sam that she had done most in sea plants and had made a great many discoveries. Dawson Turner, 'a great botanist in England', was so impressed that he sent her some of the rarest plants to be found in England, as well as some foreign ones, she wrote.

But there were obstacles too. She said she didn't have as many reference books as she needed because those on botany were expensive and her mother couldn't afford to buy them. When she did try to buy books, she had difficulty getting her brother Sam to act on her requests. In May 1807 she wondered if he hadn't received her last letter because he hadn't replied: 'I begged you to make enquiry about a book for me that I wish very much to get. Will you acquire of Mr Sowerby No 2 Mead Place Lambeth whence "Dillwyn's British Confervae" is to be had, how many numbers of it are published and the price of each number. Let me hear from you as soon as you have made this enquiry for me.'

She was also careful not to impose high postal costs on others. Postage was paid by those who received rather than sent letters. With this in mind, Ellen often wrote over what she had written. When she had completed one page, she turned it at a right angle and 'crosshatched', or overwrote, what she had already written. A single sheet was half the price of a double sheet even if the result – to a modern eye, at least – was difficult to decipher.

Ellen Hutchins had another concern. Her fellow botanists wanted to publish her name as the woman who recorded several new plants, including a number of seaweeds and lichens, but she was slow to allow her name in print. It was considered unladylike for women to publish articles under their own names.

On 24 April 1807 James Mackay wrote to Dawson Turner: 'Miss Hutchins is as yet rather averse to her name being mentioned in any publication as the finder of any plant – so that in case you should describe any of the discoveries you can say they were found by a lady near Bantry – but I hope to be able to prevail with her to allow her name to be mentioned.'

In the meantime, Ellen wrote to her brother Emanuel seeking his advice. She explained that botanists publishing their work wanted to mention the place a new plant was found and also who discovered it. 'I desired that my name should not be published,' she wrote. 'I have since been asked to allow it to be mentioned. I am doubtful whether I ought to do so or not, I beg you to tell me what I should do … I hope you will excuse my troubling you on this subject & that you will tell me what is right for me to do.'

When he failed to reply, she tried her youngest brother Sam, who was still at school and living with his elder brother in London: 'I wrote to Manny [Emanuel] some time ago but as he has a habit of putting letters in his pocket without opening, I fear he has not read mine – will you ask him?'

A month later, she still hasn't heard from either brother and wrote to ask Sam again. The response – if one existed – is not recorded, but in December 1807 Ellen wrote to Dawson Turner giving permission for her name to be published.

Almost 200 of her letters survive, giving an exceptional insight into daily life at Ballylickey House and how her love of botany warded off loneliness. In 1807 she wrote to Sam: 'I am very well, quite strong. I walk, I botanise a good deal, to that I attribute my having health or strength, for living as I do without any person to take a walk with me, if I had not Botany to interest me, I should have no inducement to take exercise.'

On that day, though, the house was busy as her brother's children were visiting: 'Arthur's children are here. The little girl is a sweet tempered funny little thing. She is not at all petted but Tommy is the most troublesome obstinate ill-tempered child I ever saw. His Mother pets him so, that his temper is quite ruined ...'

She also reported that her mother was 'pretty well' and would write too if it wasn't so painful for her to stoop to the page. Thomas, meanwhile, had acquired a gig, or two-wheeled light carriage, which allowed him to get out every day. Aunt Bel died shortly after Ellen arrived home but had lived to be a ripe old age; she was reported to be 'about 100 years'.

If Ballylickey House had few visitors, Ellen didn't appear to seek them out either. She confessed that she was not at all inquisitive about her neighbours. Her passion was reserved for the seaweeds, lichens, mosses and liverworts she was discovering that were new to Ireland and new to science.

'Ellen's enthusiasm and energy for natural history are obvious from her letters,' says her great-great-grand-niece Madeline Hutchins, who has done so much to bring her life and work to public attention. 'Reading them, you get a strong sense of her writing quickly, and with feeling. She skips from one topic to another, covering a huge range in each letter.'

You can imagine her hurriedly dashing off this note to Dawson Turner, for instance: 'I now write in a great hurry as I am going to the mountains for a few days to a place where I shall do nothing but walk and gather beauties.' She was on her way to Hungry Hill, a 685m-high mountain where she found several botanical treasures – crowberry, an evergreen shrub that grows on rocks; harebell with its pale blue flowers; the herb roseroot and the perennial Arctic sage.

In 1809 Dawson Turner asked her to catalogue all the plants in her area. The request, she said, was the 'pleasantest prescription' she had ever received and she began a plant list that would ensure her place in botanical history.

She climbed Knockboy mountain and found several relatively rare plants growing on its summit, including dwarf willow and stag's-horn clubmoss. She wrote: 'The world felt light and full, ranging over the heath. Here I find advantage in such a remote country that one can ramble about as one wants. Where else could I be left alone to ramble among the rocks and mountains or take only a little boy or girl to bring my basket and box.'

At Whiddy Island, she found many previously unknown seaweeds and managed to navigate her way into inaccessible places to find plants on the rocks. At Snave beach, she gathered shells and identified a new type of wing shell. At Glengarriff woods, she discovered a plant that would eventually carry her name, Hutchins' hollywort.

When her health was good, she explored mountains, woods, beaches and islands all over West Cork. After one trip, she wrote: 'I am quite strong and out and about before 7 o'clock in the morning with the workmen. I sometimes think you would be amused to see me among a dozen mountaineers, some of them wild enough like goats. I envy their spirits and activity, poor and ragged as they are.'

Her reputation among her fellow botanists grew. Botanist Sir William Jackson Hooker enthused that her discoveries alone would form an appendix as long as the monograph (*British Jungermanniae*) he was writing on liverworts.

Once reluctant to be named in print, some of the plants she discovered were now named after her. When botanist Lewis Weston Dillwyn named an alga after her in his book *British Confervae*, he wrote that he knew 'few, if any botanists, whose zeal and success in the pursuit of natural history better deserve such a compliment'.

He was equally effusive after meeting Ellen on his tour of south-west Ireland in 1809: 'Miss Hutchins amazed me by the extent and depth of her botanical knowledge … almost the best botanist, either Male or Female that we ever met with.'

He was equally impressed by her character, saying she had very strong senses and pleasing unaffected manners. Of her appearance, he said: 'Miss Hutchins is a very sensible, pleasing, square-made and tolerably good-looking woman of about 30 years old.' Praise indeed, had Ellen not been 24 at the time.

There is no surviving portrait of Ellen (although she is imagined at the beginning of this chapter) but she described her own 'tall figure' and said she was 'stout' and 'fat'. Later, when ill, she spoke of being so thin that she scared others. When she could, she continued to 'botanise', as she put it, but her health was deteriorating. She suffered 'bilious complaints, coughs and headaches'. She was prescribed mercury for a liver complaint, a treatment that added significantly to her problems. (In the 1800s, mercury was still widely used as a treatment for a range of health complaints including syphilis, typhoid and nervous complaints including anxiety and depression.)

She was increasingly confined to the house. 'My time is now so entirely occupied with my new domestic concerns and I may add troubles that I have little leisure and less spirit to attend to anything amusing ... How my spirit flies to the mountains when my limbs will hardly bear me about on the plains,' she wrote.

Worse was to come. In the summer of 1813, it seems a family dispute forced Ellen, her mother and brother to leave Ballylickey House: around the same time, they were also travelling to Bandon to get medical help for Ellen's mother. In any case, the ongoing family quarrel took a terrible toll on Ellen. Madeline Hutchins explains:

From documents and letters it appears that Ellen's two eldest brothers, Emanuel and Arthur, were in a long-running series of disputes with each other over property. The members of the family at Ballylickey were often drawn into these disputes, or accused of taking sides, and they caused great anguish, heartache and anger. Ellen let her feelings show very strongly in some of her letters to Emanuel, but was extremely discreet about this in her letters to Dawson Turner and only alluded to 'troubles'.

It's clear, though, that she was deeply upset. In June of 1813 she wrote to Dawson Turner: 'My situation is one of uncommon misery. I look around me & see no person so surrounded with troubles. But why my dear sir should I trouble you with my sufferings when I cannot explain my story. I can only say that some disputes in my family have for years oppressed my spirits & broken my heart.'

When Ellen's mother died the following year, she moved in with her brother Arthur and his family in Ardnagashel near Bantry. Her health was failing but her physician was hopeful of a recovery. Her cousin Thomas Taylor, however, wrote to Dawson Turner telling him he felt her physical and mental suffering was caused by the ongoing family strife and he didn't think it likely she would improve.

Ellen's decline continued and, at the end of 1814, she wrote to her dear friend Dawson Turner:

> I am settled up in bed to write you a line. I have been many months in bed not able to turn or move myself. I am, thank God, greatly relieved but very ill still, reduced to a skeleton, I frighten everybody. I cannot write more. I cannot read at all now or amuse my mind in any way and this is worse than pain for a mind once active and though struggling with disadvantages seldom unemployed. Send me a moss; anything just to look at.

That was her last letter to a fellow botanist whose letters had sustained her over the previous decade. She died on 9 February 1815, a month before her thirtieth birthday, and was buried in an unmarked grave in Garryvurcha graveyard in Bantry. She left her herbarium to Dawson Turner but its shipment was threatened when another row erupted between Ellen's brothers. One of them stormed Ballylickey House with 40 armed men but failed to oust the brother living there. It's not clear which brother was living there at the time.

Ellen's botanical interests would not be forgotten after her death – at Ardnagashel at least. Several years later, her nephew

Samuel emigrated to Australia and served in the Australian Mounted Police shortly after that country's first gold rush in 1851. He returned to Ireland not with gold, but with 650 Australian seeds for the garden at Ardnagashel. He used Ellen's botanical connections to develop an extensive arboretum there – a fitting if unintended tribute to his late aunt.

Ellen Hutchins overcame many obstacles during her short life to gain a lasting place in the field of botany. Several plants and algae bear the description *hutchinsiae* in her honour. Even in her own lifetime she was acknowledged as a pioneer in cryptogamic botany (the study of non-flowering plants). Her contemporaries praised her 'zeal and knowledge' and 'her extraordinary talents and no less extraordinary industry'.

A century after her death, Ellen's niece Alicia recorded her aunt's considerable achievements which survive on nine type-written pages that were tied into a limp card folder. The family tried to have the memoir published – in the 1940s and again in the 1980s – but there no was interest. Ellen Hutchins had been forgotten.

Then, in 1999, the National Botanical Gardens in Dublin republished Ellen's list – the 1200 plants she catalogued for Dawson Turner over three years – along with some letters and biographical notes edited by Michael Mitchell, Professor of Botany at University College Galway. The notes mentioned that there was no memorial plaque on Ellen's grave, something that was corrected in 2002 by the Hutchins family.

Now an annual festival in Bantry during Heritage Week in August celebrates her work. Madeline Hutchins is one of its organisers and she continues to research Ellen's life and work.

She says of Ellen:

She was talented as a botanist and a botanical artist. She was determined and careful. When her health allowed, she was hard working and energetic. Bantry Bay has a wonderful range of habitats and a rich biodiversity. Its remoteness and the terrible state of the roads at the time meant that it had not been explored by botanists, and there were many new species waiting to be found.

In the first two decades of the nineteenth century, natural history, with botany as part of it, was predominantly studied by individuals outside of universities, making collections and working in their own homes. Later in the century, once botany was taken over by the universities, women had less chance of being involved as these were men-only establishments.

In many ways, Ellen Hutchins was the right person, in the right place, at the right time.

Lady Sligo

LANDLADY, STYLE ICON, HUMANITARIAN
AND MOTHER OF 14 (1800–1878)

*I fear there must be a great deal [of] distress & poverty about
Westport now that there is so little money spent in the Town, &
I do not … grudge the money you gave away in charity for me.*
Lady Sligo, Hester Catherine Browne, May 1845

Westport House in County Mayo was a place of
nicknames. Hester Catherine Browne's new husband called her 'Chatte' (pussycat) and she, in
turn, called him 'Poux' (louse). The new mistress of the house
also fondly referred to her mother-in-law, Lady Louisa Browne,
as 'Mink' and rather cheekily poked fun at her ample figure.
'[If] Poux was only to show you to his enemies they would
run away in a fright at the sight of your Minkship,' she wrote
in 1817.

Her Minkship, however, did not take offence. The Dowager
Marchioness of Sligo was happy to see her only child, Howe
Peter Browne, settle down at last. Lord Sligo had spent his early
days living it up in the salons of Paris and the coffee houses

of London and 'supping with whores and bawds', as his friend and accomplice Lord Byron put it. His adventures overseas had also landed him in jail. He spent four months in Newgate Prison in London after being found guilty of enticing Royal Navy seamen to desert so that he could sail home with artefacts from ancient Greece.

After his release from jail, he turned over a new leaf and, aged 28, was ready to marry. He set his sights on Hester Catherine de Burgh, an aristocrat from Galway, and seemed genuinely smitten with her: 'I am happy as a Prince ... I assure you I am more in love every day.' The feeling appeared to be mutual. Hester Catherine, or Catherine as she signed herself in letters, was barely 16 when she assumed her new role as the Second Marchioness of Sligo and mistress of a large estate at Westport. She seemed to take to it with admirable ease but then she would have seen her widowed mother run an enormous holding on her own: Lady Elizabeth Bourke successfully managed the family's 56,000-acre estate in Galway when her husband, the Earl of Clanricarde, John Thomas de Burgh, died.

It wasn't long before the couple's first baby arrived: Louisa, named after her grandmother – or 'Kitten' as her proud father called her – was born in December 1816. Soon afterwards, Catherine became pregnant again. Her husband was delighted but confided to his mother, Mink, that Catherine was dreading the thought of having two wet nurses in the house at the same time. And besides, the builders were in.

Catherine and Howe Peter had embarked on an extensive programme of renovation. Catherine embraced the project with enthusiasm. She kept an eye on building work and used her knowledge of gardening to direct the design of the new pleasure gardens. But in May 1817 she must have had moments of frustration. She was two months pregnant, had a five-month-old infant and there was dust and noise and upheaval everywhere. Library shelving was due to be delivered as well as two enormous mahogany sideboards from English cabinet-makers. Lord Sligo sent an SOS for help to his mother: 'For God's sake send over a housekeeper as soon as possible, as I do not know what to do without one.'

In December the stress of building was laid aside when Elizabeth arrived exactly 12 months after her sister. The first son – and heir – George came along two years after that and a year later, in 1821, Catherine gave birth to a second son, Howe. It was a busy household – and building work was still not complete. The weather that year had been particularly bad and Lord Sligo decided it would be a good idea to get away. Catherine, her four small children and a large travelling party of nursemaids, servants and staff left for Paris.

The couple had honeymooned in Paris and in the late spring of 1821 they revisited all the fashionable places – and people. They were accustomed to moving in the highest circles. The King of Naples, Joachim Murat, was a friend. Lord Sligo once even boasted that he had been mistaken for him at a ball in Naples. The Brownes also knew the King of England, George IV. They had named their son after him, and he was the boy's godfather.

In the summer and autumn of 1821, the travelling adventure continued. The family left Paris to go south and then over the mountains into Italy. Lord Sligo's diaries, quoted by historian Anne Chambers in her exhaustive account of his life, give a fascinating and hair-raising insight into the perils of travel in the nineteenth century. On one occasion, the mules pulling the carriages broke into a gallop on the narrow hairpin roads cut high into the mountains. On another, in heavy rain, the wheel of a carriage was inches from the edge. Lord Sligo wrote of the close shave and the horrifying thought of seeing his children plunge to their deaths.

Despite the dangers, the family continued on and wintered in Florence. Catherine was expecting again and all seemed well. However, when she was seven months pregnant the unthinkable happened: her youngest son, Howe, died suddenly in February 1822. Catherine barely had time to grieve when she was a mother again. Her third daughter and namesake Catherine arrived two months later.

Back in Westport, the family's absence was noted and Lord Sligo was under pressure to come home. When he returned to Mayo in 1823, he found a country in decline and many of his 10,000 tenants unable to pay rent. Unlike many nineteenth-century landlords, Howe Peter Browne helped them when he could, earning the title 'the poor's man's friend' in the press. He spoke out against absentee landlords and campaigned for Catholic Emancipation in the English Parliament.

Lady Sligo was also socially and politically aware. Both she and her husband were supporters of education, a point made strongly in a *Dublin Morning Register* article that reported their financial contribution to the Tuam Free School. 'Lady Sligo had the greatest pleasure in affording any assistance in her power to a school which promises the species of instruction she most approves of,' her husband was quoted as saying. Her approved 'species' of education was one that was open to everyone, regardless of their religion.

Daily life was busy and bustling and the Brownes often travelled around Ireland and abroad. In London, they stayed at their home in Mansfield Street which, like Westport House, was lavishly decorated. Their movements were followed closely in the social columns of the newspapers and the list of guests at their balls, dinners and parties read like a who's who of nineteenth-century society.

In the late 1820s, there were extended stays in London and Paris but Catherine and Howe Peter always travelled with their children whenever possible. By the end of the decade there were seven children, but there would be more children and many more far-flung adventures.

—

Catherine was expecting her tenth child in 1834 when she agreed to set sail for Jamaica, more than 4000 miles away. There was no question that she and her children wouldn't go. Her husband made that clear when he agreed to take on a new role as Governor of Jamaica where he would begin the process of abolishing slavery. He wasn't going to leave Westport House in County Mayo without his family. 'My children are numerous, I grant you,' he told the Colonial Office, 'but surely no person would … seek to deprive me of the happiness of my family accompanying me.'

His wife must have thought long and hard before agreeing to go halfway around the world with her children. The family were already seasoned travellers – some of the children had been born abroad, but one of them had died there too. There were several dangers at sea: storms, illness, or worse, pirates.

Then there was the Jamaican climate to consider and the risk of tropical diseases, not to mention the challenge facing her husband – to implement the recent Slavery Abolition Act of 1833 on the Caribbean island.

Ironically, the Brownes themselves owned two plantations in Jamaica, and by implication, slaves. The profits from the Kelly's estate and Cocoa Walk plantations – and the work of some 386 slaves – contributed to the running of Westport House. This was not unusual. The inconvenient truth is that the Irish, English and Scottish owned most of Jamaica's 600 sugar plantations, along with the estimated 200 slaves of African origin on each one.

At least Howe Peter Browne had shown a rare concern for his slaves in the years before his appointment. On one occasion, when he heard the slaves on his plantation were 'wretchedly dressed and worse fed', as he put it, he asked for the exact age and size of each slave so that he could have clothes specially made for them in England.

He knew something of the conditions that awaited the Brownes in Jamaica and wrote ahead to arrange for his family to be housed in the coolness of the mountains, but they had to get there first. The first challenge was fitting everyone on board the HMS *Blonde*. The captain had gallantly offered Lady Sligo his cabin, but that still left eight Browne children (the eldest boy, George, was to remain at Eton), her husband and ten servants, including two nursemaids, a governess, a cook, a butler and a private secretary. It was a tight squeeze on board a frigate not designed for passenger comfort.

They set sail from Portsmouth, England, in February 1834 and it wasn't long before two of their fears were realised: the ship was tossed about in a violent storm in the Bay of Biscay and, around the same time, Lady Sligo became very ill. The doctor on board was so concerned that the captain considered coming ashore at Lisbon.

Whether Lady Sligo regretted embarking on such a challenging journey is not recorded but she comes across as a woman with remarkable resilience. She was 34 years old, a mother to nine and on her way to a country where she was going to witness cruelties 'beyond all idea' inflicted on people working on the family's plantations. Now she was ill and quite literally at sea, yet she rallied and decided that she was strong and healthy enough to continue on to Jamaica.

In early April, after more than six weeks at sea, the Browne family set down at the Caribbean island. They were welcomed with the customary gun salute and the new governor wasted no time in explaining why he had come. He stood on the grand steps of the governor's residence in Spanish Town, the then capital, and told the assembled crowd that he intended to abolish slavery on the island for ever.

In August Lady Sligo gave birth to Richard Howe who was nicknamed 'the young Creole'. By September she was ready to receive guests at the governor's official residence, King's House, on Tuesday and Friday mornings. But that was more the exception than the rule as the Brownes uncharacteristically did little socialising. Instead, they kept their distance from the other plantation owners who, for the most part, vehemently opposed the abolition of slavery.

It wasn't long before Governor Howe Peter Browne came under attack – politically and personally – but he held firm. As did Lady Sligo. She and her daughters were said to be horrified by what they saw around them. They probably did not directly witness the whipping, burning, beating and branding of slaves, but they were aware of it. It is Howe Peter's condemnation of the barbarity that survives: he spoke of the inhumanity of whipping women, the cruelty of preventing mothers from suckling their own children and the affront to humanity of witnessing people treated as 'semi-human' by plantation owners.

Catherine and her daughters spent their days doing charity work with the black and mixed-race communities, setting them even further apart from planter society. They must also have begun to understand the multiple strands of Jamaican society. White slave owners had children with many of their slaves which, over generations, led to a population defined by distinctions in colour and status. There were so-called 'free coloureds' and 'free blacks' and many of them advocated for freedom and education rights. Catherine supported them by becoming patron of a local school and worked with missionaries to promote education. Their efforts were greatly appreciated and spoken about in glowing terms in the pro-abolition newspapers.

To get some relief from the stifling heat of Spanish Town, the family moved to the mountainous district of Highgate and into a large, airy Georgian house with open verandas on both floors and sweeping views of the sea. The new residence was comfortable and cooler yet the younger Browne children still found it difficult to adapt to the tropical climate. In early 1835 Catherine decided to return to Westport with the four youngest children while the older ones stayed on with their father.

Lord Sligo faced steady opposition to reform and the Jamaican Assembly blocked his attempts to introduce the abolition law in 1836. He resigned his position and the pro-planter press hailed his departure with mocking jubilation. One of them, quoted by historian Anne Chambers, wrote a patois headline worthy of any tabloid today: 'Oh! Lard Oh – Big Massa Da Go at Last Fo True' and went on to denounce him as a 'mischievous' governor with not a single redeeming quality. He mustn't have been too upset, though, because he pasted the article into a scrapbook of newspaper cuttings.

When Lord Sligo returned to England he continued, with the support of Catherine, to lobby the British government to end slavery. In August 1838 the government finally announced the total and immediate emancipation of all slaves in the British Empire. Jamaica named its first free town Sligoville after the man still remembered today as the 'champion of slaves'.

Lord and Lady Sligo did much to end the abhorrent system they saw first-hand yet, like all slave owners, they were handsomely compensated for their loss of earnings. The family were awarded £3221 13s 11d for the Cocoa Walk plantation and its 167 slaves, and a further £2304 15s 2d for Kelly's, which had 119 slaves. The total is equivalent to well over €500,000 today.

—

In April 1837, *the Leinster Express and General Advertiser* reported that the Marquess and Marchioness of Sligo and family had left Dublin for London but that 'the Noble Lord has been suffering severely from gout since his return from Jamaica'. This was not entirely unsurprising: Howe Peter had a taste for the finer things in life – and a waistline to reflect that. Before he set sail for Jamaica, he sent to Cadiz for sherry to be shipped ahead and had organised the delivery of a dizzying array of fine wines, confectionery, pâtés and other delicacies.

In stark contrast, Lady Sligo was svelte, fashionable and exquisitely dressed. She also happened to be a mother of eleven. She was considered so stylish that she had something of a public following. A portrait sold by Churton's Gallery in Dublin in 1836 shows her wearing a fur-trimmed, low-cut velvet dress with strings of pearls around her neck. In another portrait, she is elegance personified in a French Empire-inspired gown and a rather daring oriental-inspired turban.

Her wardrobe was stocked with silk and satin gowns, furs and a range of the most decorated fans, as her surviving letters reveal. In one of them, she rather forthrightly asked the estate manager, George Hildebrand, to identify the correct fur and send it to London:

I think you are mistaking the kind of fur I want. – I want white ermine fur with long black tails. – Some of it has the tails taken off, & they are tied up together in the bag ... I want all the white fur, but I do not want any dark fur. Hanly says she thinks she saw it in the bottom of the press in my bed room.

There were more pressing concerns too: Lady Sligo was expecting again. In July 1837, daughter Hester arrived. In August 1838, Augusta came into the world, and Lady Sligo's last child, Marianne, was born on Christmas Day in Naples in 1839.

The decade that followed was one of the darkest in Irish history but it was also an exceptionally difficult one for the Browne family. By 1841, Lord Sligo's health had deteriorated. He had increasing difficulty walking and his speech was affected. He had short periods of respite but, by 1844, he was no longer able to run Westport House and Lady Sligo ably stepped into his shoes.

Worse was to come. In June 1844, Catherine's daughter and namesake died. The *Dublin Evening Packet* noted the family's intense grief and attempted to explain what had happened: 'It is supposed that the death of her ladyship resulted from a cold, terminating in inflammation. The deceased was able to dine with the members of her family on Wednesday, and on the following morning was seized with severe illness, from which she never recovered.'

The family moved from London to a smaller house in Tunbridge Wells and from there Lady Sligo kept a close eye on affairs at Westport House. Several of her letters to Hildebrand survive, offering an unrivalled insight into a woman who showed compassion for her tenants at a time when she had her own troubles. She was grieving for her daughter and her husband was terminally ill.

Howe Peter Browne died at the beginning of 1845 and was buried with his daughter Catherine in London. His wife had been at his side since she was 16 years old yet she found the wherewithal to continue running an estate in a county that was one of the worst hit during the Great Famine. The population of Mayo fell by 29 per cent from 1845 to 1851, which was much higher than the national average.

Despite the challenges and difficulties, Lady Sligo was hard-headed and decisive when she felt the situation called for it. Just three days before her husband died, she sat down to write a strongly worded letter telling Hildebrand to deal very harshly with thieves who had been discovered at Westport House:

Hildebrand,

You must prosecute the Flynns for the Robbery, & the mother as a receiver of the stolen things. – I hope the Mother will be severely punished – She deserves it – & it will be a great advantage & a good lesson to her children if they see her punished – For the last ten years, Westport House has never been without some petty little stealing going on, & we never proved who committed these little robberies, the thieves found themselves safer, & were bold enough to keep continually turning away with one thing or another – it is quite necessary now to make an example of the Flynn family – if you let them off now, it will have such an effect on the people about the place, that we shall not be able to employ Westport people in the house.

Yet she was also deeply concerned about her tenants' welfare when the first signs of potato blight became evident. In May 1845 she wrote to Hildebrand: 'I fear there must be a great deal [of] distress & poverty about Westport now that there is so little money spent in the Town, & I do not … grudge the money you gave away in charity for me.' She asked regularly about the potato crop in Westport and, following stormy and wet weather, asked her manager to give good-quality warm blankets to the tenants.

After her husband's death, she moved to Clontarf in north Dublin and continued to manage Westport from there, often in a very hands-on way. She sent seeds and a particularly high-yielding strawberry plant in the hope that they might produce similar yields in Westport to those in Clontarf. She gave detailed advice, which she wanted relayed to the gardener because she had never seen such wonderful results: 'The quantity of strawberries here is greater than I ever saw anywhere on so small a space of ground,' she wrote.

She was also involved in hiring – and firing – staff. In January, she advised Hildebrand never to hire one particular woman: 'She is a very bad servant; & she is so very lazy & careless, that I do not think she will ever improve.' It was a bad year for servants. In August, she had to let a housemaid go:

The worst servants in Dublin are housemaids – I have got all my other servants pretty good, but I have been unfortunate in housemaids.

I almost think it would be a good way to get a housemaid from England, for English housemaids are all better than Irish … A housemaid from the Country in England is much better than a London housemaid.

As the Famine took hold, Lady Sligo continued to support her tenants. She ran fundraising bazaars, sent food and blankets and was concerned about what the newspapers said about landlords. Life, however, went on as normal for the privileged classes, at least for now. In one letter, she wrote about the blight on the potatoes while, at the same time, confirming that she had received a delivery of grapes and venison. The parties, balls and dinners continued too. In May 1846, *The Morning Post* reported:

The Marchioness of Sligo gave a very brilliant ball last evening at the family mansion in Mansfield-Street. His Royal Highness Prince George honoured her Ladyship with his presence on the occasion, arriving shortly after twelve o'clock …

Dancing was commenced shortly after eleven o'clock, to the music of Jullien's orchestra, and the festivities were prolonged until an advanced hour in the morning.

A year later, however, her own fortunes took a turn for the worse. By 1847 Lady Sligo was back in Westport but not in her beautifully appointed house. High taxes forced the family to close Westport House and grounds and move to a much smaller house in the town. The family, she wrote, could no longer afford a carriage either.

Even so, she continued to donate to those in need. In January 1847 Dudley Durkin, the medical attendant at Louisburgh dispensary in Co. Mayo, wrote to the editor of the *Mayo Constitution* to thank Lady Sligo for sending nine hundred-weight of rice to the poor in the district: 'Many and very many times has the noble family of Westport House been distinguished for their generous spirit of benevolence and practical charity in relieving the wants of the distressed. Sickness, I regret to state, is raging to an enormous extent in this parish.'

The Famine claimed an estimated one million lives and another one million people emigrated to America, yet Queen Victoria received an enthusiastic welcome on her 11-day visit to Ireland in 1849. In 1853 she returned and was again warmly welcomed by the Irish people. The Dowager Marchioness of Sligo, as she was by then, was among them. She was one of the titled and the high-ranking members of society who were invited to dine with the queen at the Viceregal Lodge (now Áras an Uachtaráin) in the Phoenix Park in Dublin.

In Dublin, *The Freeman's Journal* reported, the excitement among the ordinary people was intense despite the rain, which fell all day in torrents. Crowds lined the roads in an attempt to get a glimpse of the visiting monarch: 'At the hill above Dundrum, and all along the road, triumphal arches of laurel and other evergreens intertwined with flowers, spanned the road. One arch, in particular, was very tastefully got up, and was decorated with the letters V.A. and a crown wrought in various-coloured flowers.' At this remove, the welcome seems incongruous given the social catastrophe that had just taken place, but perhaps the spectacle provided some sort of distraction.

Lady Sligo inspired similar excitement, albeit on a much smaller scale. Whenever she returned to Westport, she enjoyed a rapturous welcome. She was greeted with blazing bonfires as the people of the town lined the streets. The event was written up in glowing terms in the local press. The reason was spelled out simply by the *Tuam Herald* in October 1857: 'Her ladyship's former acts of benevolence and Christian charity in this locality has endeared her name to a grateful people.'

That gratitude was still being expressed in 1865 when she donated a sum exceeding £50 (about €7000 today) to Westport residents affected by fever. The *Belfast Morning News* also noted that she had contributed £200 worth of blankets and clothing in the same locality 'some time since'. 'We are aware that her ladyship prefers doing good by stealth, but we think such examples of genuine feeling for the poor members of the community should be made public, in order to excite others to emulate such a noble example,' the writer noted.

There was time for entertainment too and Hester Catherine Browne was still dancing late into the night at her residence in

Mansfield Street in London when she was well into her sixties. In her later years, she lived between Ireland and England and continued her charity work. She died in February 1878, aged 78, and was buried with her husband and daughter at Kensal Green Cemetery in London.

She is one of many strong women to have lived in Westport House, which is on the site where Grace O'Malley (or Granuaile) built her castle in the sixteenth century. The famous pirate queen gained a reputation as an able leader who pushed the boundaries. Many others in Westport House would do the same. In more recent times, the visionary 11th Marquess of Sligo, Jeremy Ulick Browne Altamont, opened Westport House to the public in 1960 to ensure its survival. He was also a law-changer who in 1993, along with his wife Jennifer, took a private Bill through the Senate to challenge the male succession law. The couple had five daughters and no sons and wanted to ensure that their children would inherit the house. With the help of local solicitor Michael Egan and former president Mary Robinson, they successfully changed the law.

While Westport House is no longer owned by the family, without the work done by the Browne sisters (Sheelyn, Karen, Alannah, Lucinda and Clare), this singular place and the stories of the women – and men – who lived in it for over 400 years would be lost for ever.

Jo Hiffernan

PAINTER AND MUSE TO THE ARTISTS
WHISTLER AND COURBET
(CIRCA 1843–1903)

She was not only beautiful. She was intelligent, she was sympathetic. She gave Whistler the constant companionship he could not do without.

Joseph Pennell, artist and author

During that idyllic summer of 1865, Jo Hiffernan holidayed with two of the nineteenth century's greatest artists: her lover, the American James McNeill Whistler, and French realist painter Gustave Courbet. They took long swims in the freezing sea at Trouville on the Normandy coast in France, ate salad bowls of prawns slathered in butter and snuck out of the hotel casino when they were down on their luck. They painted the sea, the fish, the horizon and 'paid themselves in dreams', as Courbet later put it.

'Do you remember Jo?' Courbet asked Whistler in 1877. 'She played the clown to amuse us and, in the evenings, she sang those Irish songs so well. She had the spirit and the distinction of art … We were happy, and with no other worries than those of "art".

During those carefree days, Jo posed for a series of portraits that Courbet entitled *La Belle Irlandaise* (The Beautiful Irishwoman). He wrote about 'the beauty of a superb redhead whose portrait I have begun' and was so struck by her that he painted three more variations, each one slightly different. The portraits show Jo looking into a mirror, her auburn hair flowing in sensual waves. Critics have commented on the 'raw sexuality' of Courbet's portrayal, and perhaps that is the source of the rumour that Jo – Whistler's lover of six years – was not only Courbet's model but also his mistress.

Yet the fond reminiscences in Courbet's letter to Whistler, written 13 years after that happy summer interlude, are not those of a man writing to the supposed injured party in an illicit affair. You'll be hard-pressed to find proof that Jo and Courbet were lovers. If anything, the evidence suggests that they were not. Courbet's letters around this time refer to his love affairs – their beginnings, their complicated middles and sometimes awkward ends. Jo does not feature among them. The artist clearly admired his Irish muse and his portrait of her was a personal favourite. 'I still have the portrait of Jo which I will never sell … everyone admires it,' he wrote in the same letter to Whistler. Even on his deathbed, he refused to sell it. But there is nothing to suggest that Jo was ever his mistress.

If those portraits hinted at the relationship between Courbet and Jo, two other paintings supposedly confirmed it. Jo posed for Courbet's *Le Sommeil* (The Sleepers) in Paris around 1866, a portrait of two naked women on a bed, embracing erotically. She was also said to have posed for *L'Origine du monde* (The

Origin of the World), a graphic close-up that was shocking in its realist depiction of a woman's genitals.

Neither painting was intended to be shown in public. The more explicit *L'Origine du monde* was most likely commissioned by Turkish-Egyptian Khalil Bey, a larger-than-life figure in the Paris of the 1860s. He was said to have kept the canvas in his bathroom behind a green curtain, one of many in a collection 'devoted to the celebration of the female body', as one explanation put it.

When Khalil Bey was bankrupted by his gambling debts, the painting disappeared and later resurfaced in the collection of French psychoanalyst Jacques Lacan. In 1995 it was donated to the Musée d'Orsay in Paris where it is displayed among the art museum's vast collection of Impressionist and post-Impressionist masterpieces. The museum celebrates what it terms Courbet's 'daring and frankness' and says that due to the artist's 'great virtuosity and the refinement of his amber colour scheme, the painting escapes pornographic status' – an assessment open to debate.

Over the years, much ink has been spilt trying to give the torso in Courbet's painting a face. Jo Hiffernan emerged as a front runner – an assumption that no doubt added to an enduring image of her as the artist's muse and mistress. In many fictional accounts of Courbet's life, she is depicted as the auburn-haired temptress who had a torrid relationship with the great artist. It was often assumed that painters had affairs with their models.

Now, however, art experts are '99% certain' that the woman in *L'Origine du monde* was not Jo, but a Parisian ballet dancer called Constance Quéniaux. The revelation was unearthed in

2018 by French writer and Dumas biographer Claude Schopp who found a reference to the painting in a letter written by Alexandre Dumas, son of the author of *The Three Musketeers*. In it, Dumas described how Courbet painted 'the most delicate and the most sonorous interior' of Quéniaux. 'One of the greatest mysteries in the world of art has, without doubt, been solved,' wrote one French newspaper.

Surely, it's now time to extricate Jo Hiffernan from the shadowy and rather tawdry world of a decades-old art mystery and look at what it might really have been like for an Irishwoman frequenting the art worlds of London and Paris in the nineteenth century. Although remembered as a muse and model, Jo Hiffernan had an artistic ambition of her own. She painted and sketched and sold her work to art dealers under the name Mrs Abbott, although none of her work is known to have survived. Her letters reveal a woman who knew the art world from many angles – as an artist, as a model and as an artist's agent and manager. She sold Whistler's paintings and when he went to Chile in 1866, he gave her power of attorney to manage his affairs. She and Whistler parted ways after that – amicably it was said – but she remained a loyal friend. When he had a child with another woman, Jo and her sister Bridget Agnes raised it.

Jo met James McNeill Whistler in the summer of 1860. At the time, her family was lodging in Newman Street in London, just doors away from the artist. Jo was born in Ireland around 1843 but her parents, John Christopher and Katherine Hiffernan, moved to London to escape the catastrophic effects of the Great Famine of the 1840s. It's not clear when the family arrived in London but, by 1851, there were some 109,000

Irish-born people in the city – an all-time high, according to the census. The large Irish population meant that the city was a hotbed of Fenian political agitation and violence, as borne out by Old Bailey records.

Those records also paint a portrait of daily life for the thousands of ordinary Irish migrants who made their way to the city in the eighteenth and nineteenth centuries. Historians Clive Emsley, Tim Hitchcock and Robert Shoemaker provide this snapshot:

> Hawking, costermongering (selling fruit and other wares from a barrow), and street selling were occupations in which large numbers of Irish men and women could be found. In the early 1850s, Henry Mayhew [in his survey of London street life] estimated that there were 10,000 Irish men and women employed in these quasi-beggarly professions ... Similarly, in London, many building labourers, chairmen, and porters were Irish, as were the owners of lodging houses, alehouses, and chophouses frequented by Irish clientele.

Jo's father was either a clerk or a writing master, though Whistler's friend and flatmate, the caricaturist George du Maurier, described him as an 'impulsive & passionate' Irishman of uncertain occupation. He was 'a sort of Captain Costigan,' he said, a reference to a cheerful but slightly suspect character in William Thackeray's novel *The History of Pendennis*. Du Maurier, however, was impressed by his daughter: 'Joe, as everyone called her, had little formal education but was quick and intelligent, with something rather attaching in her character & manner.'

Joe, or Jo as her name was more commonly spelled, met Whistler when she was about 17 years old. Whistler was already something of a charmer as his friend, and it seems fellow charmer, George du Maurier revealed: '[Whistler] talks women over to him and I sing them back to me,' he wrote. Whistler, however, was very taken with Jo's deep blue eyes, pale skin and copper-coloured hair and she soon became his favourite model. Not long afterwards, she became his partner too. She joined him at his lodgings in The Angel Inn on the Thames at Wapping where he rowed up and down the river in an attempt to capture the spirit of the wharfs, jetties, warehouses and dockers.

Around 1861 he added a woman – Jo – to the portrait of two sailors smoking their pipes on the balcony of The Angel Inn. No matter what he did, however, he could not get her expression right. He described the difficulties to French painter Henri Fantin-Latour, but told him that he was 'jolly certain' the painting, his first of Jo, would become a masterpiece:

I will try to explain it – Firstly it is on a balcony right above the Thames. There are three people – an old man in a white shirt … then on the right in the corner, a sailor in a cap and a blue shirt … who is chatting to a girl who is jolly difficult to paint! And that is why I wish above all to have you here so that we could discuss it – Well I have painted her three times and I do not want to get tired – besides if I fiddle about with her too much I will have hardly any time to do the rest – Well you can imagine! I have managed to give her an expression! really my dear friend! a real expression – ah but if only I could describe her head – She has the most beautiful hair that you have ever seen! a red not golden but copper – as Venetian

as a dream! – skin golden white or yellow if you will – and
with the wonderful expression I described to you – an air of
saying to her sailor "That is all very well, my friend! I have
seen others!" you know she is winking and laughing at him!
… Hush! Not a word to Courbet!

He wrote that he did not think he would paint Jo again but
his most celebrated works feature the woman who would be
part of his life, in one way or another, for decades to come. We
don't know if he ever discussed his artistic difficulties with Jo
but she must have been aware of them because he repainted her
three times before temporarily abandoning the portrait and
moving back, with Jo, to the cramped quarters of a one-room
flat on Newman Street in London. It was, said previous tenant
George du Maurier, a 'blasted apartment'; 'draughty, disor-
dered, uncomfortable, wretchedly cold, illuminated by candle-
light, and darkened by clothes hanging all over the place'.

Little wonder that Whistler regularly retreated for some creature comforts to the Sloane Street home of his sister Deborah
(or Debo as he affectionately called her) and her husband, art
collector and surgeon Francis Seymour Haden. As Whistler's
biographer Hesketh Pearson wrote: 'The Sloane Street house
was a paradise of splendour to these poverty-stricken artists,
who drank champagne and ate roast beef and stood in awe of
the butler and slept in snow-white sheets and had their under-
wear sent to the laundry.'

It was not a place where Whistler felt he could bring Jo – she
was Irish, Catholic and an artist's model, a combination that
barred her from the drawing rooms of so-called 'respectable
society'. Whistler, however, did not think twice about bringing

her to France when he was advised to travel to a warmer climate for health reasons. In 1861 he got rheumatic fever and was told to take the sea air. Before he made it to the coast, he and Jo went to enjoy the delights of Paris, staying in lodgings on the boulevard des Batignolles. They visited friends, galleries and studios and dined, often on credit, in the bohemian Latin Quarter. Whistler also spent what money he had keeping Jo in the fashionable clothes she loved. George du Maurier wrote that she was 'got up like a duchess' when he met her and the 'mere making of her bonnet by Madame somebody or other in Paris had cost 50 Fr'.

They mixed with gallery owners, agents and fellow artists. They met Edgar Degas and artist Ernest Delannoy lodged with them for a while, at Whistler's expense – at Jo's too, it seems, as he was rather flippant with her and the two of them argued frequently. Some claimed Jo had a temper and superior airs, although others thought her exceptional. American artist and author Joseph Pennell, for instance, wrote of her: 'She was not only beautiful. She was intelligent, she was sympathetic. She gave Whistler the constant companionship he could not do without.'

In the winter of 1861–2, Jo sat for *Symphony in White, No. I: The White Girl*. It would take Whistler months to complete a full-length portrait of Jo on a canvas that was over 7ft tall. Whatever about the artist, it must have been exhausting for the model who posed from early morning until the light faded. Jo, standing on a bearskin rug, wore a full-length white dress and held a lily. Critics argue over the interpretation but the painting was, as Daniel E Sunderland noted, 'Whistler's first tentative step *away* from narrative painting, which was becoming one of the great artistic controversies of the century.'

In April 1862, Jo wrote to Paris art dealer George Aloysius Lucas to tell him how the painting had been received:

I note the W[h]ite Girl has made a great sensation – for and against. Some stupid painters dont understand it at all while Millais [the artist John Everett Millais] for instance thinks it spleandid, [sic] more like Titian and those old swells than anything he [h]as seen – but Jim [Whistler] says that for all that, p[e]r[h]aps the old duffers may refuse it altogether ...

With love from Jimmie and myself,

Joe

Remember me kindly to your little girl.

She and Whistler were not wrong about the 'old duffers' at the Royal Academy who rejected the painting in April 1862. However, the portrait caused great excitement in London. Later in Paris, at the Salon des Refusés (an exhibition set up for those rejected by the official salon), it also caused a sensation. Even Courbet, who called Whistler his 'student', thought it 'an apparition'.

For now, though, Whistler's attention was focused on Jo who had lost her mother Katherine a month earlier. He fondly referred to her as his mother-in-law and was said to be 'quite sentimental' when he came to London for the funeral. Whistler was also worried for his grieving partner and he leased a new home in Chelsea. As Sutherland observed: 'His status as a successful artist demanded a house, and Jo deserved it. Being Whistler's muse was no easy job, but Jo loved him, appreciated his genius, and intended to be the woman behind the man.'

Later that year, however, she almost lost him. In the autumn of 1862, the couple went to Guéthary, near Biarritz, where Whistler painted *Blue Wave*. While painting another canvas he went for a swim and almost drowned. According to one account, Jo raised the alarm and helped to rescue him. Whistler later recounted the trauma to his friend Henri Fantin-Latour:

A fifteen-foot wave swallowed me, I drank a ton of salt water, and went under it only to be swallowed by another twenty-foot wave in which I turned cartwheels and found myself engulfed by a third! I swam and swam and the more I swam the less I came closer to the shore! Oh, my dear Fantin to realize the futility of effort! and the specta-tors were saying, Oh but see how the monsieur is amusing himself, he must be awfully strong! I cried out, I howled in despair – I disappeared three or four times. Finally someone understood! A brave railroad contractor ran and rolled over twice on the beach! The 'bather' (my model) heard the call, came at a gallop, and jumped into the sea like a Newfoundland, managed to grab me by the 'paw' and the two pulled me out!

Once back in London, the couple moved to Lindsey Row in Chelsea. Their neighbour, poet and painter Dante Gabriel Rossetti, was interested in spiritualism. Whistler thought Jo something of a medium herself and the couple attended seances at his house and also held several at their own home.

Jo, however, would soon have to move out. If her family embraced Whistler, his did not welcome her. Whistler's brother-in-law Francis Seymour Haden had dined with Jo and been in her company several times but when he was invited to dine at her home, he refused, saying he did not approve of Jo being the mistress of the house. Whistler's biographer Hesketh Pearson takes up the story:

> Whistler, in a rage, went to 62 Sloane Street and spoke his mind. Haden, indignant, severely reprimanded him. Whistler marched out of the studio at the top of the house and descended the stairs; Haden pursued him, scolding all the way. At the front door Whistler found that he had left his hat upstairs, said wearily 'And now, have we to go through this all over again?' and went back for it.

If Whistler defended Jo against his brother-in-law, he sided with his mother a few months later. Anna Whistler did not approve of Jo either and when she moved to London in 1864, Whistler moved Jo to a cottage so that his mother could stay with him. All the same, when the artist later decided to go to Chile as part of a dubious scheme to provide the country with naval weaponry to help it in its war against Spain, it was his mother who spoke up for Jo. She asked her son to give Jo £100 to help promote 'a return to virtue in her'. She added: 'I never forget to pray for her.'

Whistler went much further and gave Jo power of attorney over his affairs, cited her in his will and gave her the authority to sell his paintings. If only his paintings would sell. In May 1866 Jo wrote to her solicitor, James Anderson Rose, asking for help:

> Being at the present Moment rather in want of Money, owing to the fact that none of Mr Whistler's pictures have

yet been Sold I take the liberty of asking you if you – would
be willing to lend me ten pounds for which I will give you as
security any one of Mr Whistlers, – Sea views that are now
at Mr Rosettis [sic]. would you kindly drop me a line to let
me know if you could – oblige me in this – and believe Me
yours very truly
Joanna Hiffernan

Before she received a reply, a letter from the bank arrived
to say that the Whistler–Hiffernan account was in the red.
It was around this time that Jo travelled to Paris, unknown
to Whistler, to pose for Gustave Courbet's famously contro-
versial painting *Le Sommeil*. She would have been paid
something for modelling, a much-needed income given her
financial straits. Her trip to Paris and her decision not to
tell Whistler was later interpreted as evidence of an affair. It
was also noted that she and Whistler separated shortly after
this; an understandable response to Jo's unfaithfulness, the
commentators said.

Yet in 1870, when Whistler had a son with a 21-year-old
parlour maid called Louise Fanny Hanson, he described it as an
infidelity to Jo. The boy, Charles James Whistler Hanson, went
on to live with Jo when he was two. She raised him, together
with her sister Bridget Agnes, although his father assumed
financial responsibility for him.

The following year Whistler had a new partner: Maud
Franklin, a woman who would be his model and mistress for
the next 15 years. He continued to stay in contact with Jo and
wrote to his son regularly. During a trip to Venice with Maud
in 1880, he wrote fondly to his son:

My dear little Charley –

I am very much pleased with your pretty letter which proves to me what an industrious nice little gentleman you have been during my long absence. – much longer has it turned out to be than ever I looked forward to – and very anxious am I to get back to you all and hear all the good accounts of you from Auntie Jo and see the tall fellow you have grown – It was very kind in you to send your first letter to me and very much I value it and shall put it away with my treasures …

I am so glad my dear boy to know that you are doing so well with your studies and are so obedient and attentive to your kind Auntie Jo – Tell her with my love that she must expect a letter from me at once – as I shall write tomorrow …

and now my dear boy with much love to you all
Goodbye – Your fond papa

In 1881 the census showed that Jo Hiffernan was living with her sister at 2 Thistle Grove Lane in London. A year later, Juliette Courbet, the painter's sister, was apparently told in a letter that 'the beautiful Irish girl' was selling paintings and antiques in Nice in the south of France. There were other reports that she now called herself Mrs Abbott along with speculation that she must have married. Abbott, though, was one of James McNeill Whistler's Christian names and Jo had used it when selling to art dealers when they were still a couple.

In any case, after that, Jo Hiffernan all but disappears – there are no documents to tell us what she did or where she lived. Whistler, by contrast, left a detailed record behind him; of his lovers, his paintings, drawings, etchings, his philosophy of 'art for art's sake', his legal case against the art critic John Ruskin and his many public spats. We know that Jo was still alive when he died in 1903, as she came forward to pay her last respects.

Art patron and feminist Louisine Havemeyer later described the scene in *Sixteen to Sixty: Memoirs of a Collector*. She wrote:

As she raised her veil and I saw the dark eyes … the thick wavy hair, although it was streaked with grey, I knew at once it was Johanna … 'la belle Irlandaise' that Courbet had painted with her wonderful hair and a mirror in her hand … She stood for a long time beside the coffin – nearly an hour I should think … I could not help being touched by the feeling she showed toward her old friend.

Jennie Hodgers

A WOMAN WHO FOUGHT AS A MALE
SOLDIER IN THE AMERICAN CIVIL WAR
(1843–1915)

*She wanted to be a man, and because Nature cheated her of
this privilege she did the next best thing, disguised as a man,
so she could do a man's work, lead a man's life and be a man
in everything, but sex.*

Rev Fr PD Curran, chaplain of the
Old Soldier's Home, Quincy, 1913

At five foot three, Albert DJ Cashier was one of the
smallest men in his company, but he was also one of
the bravest. He was hailed as a hero by his sergeant
when, during the Battle of Vicksburg, the company flag was
taken down by enemy fire and he scrambled up a tree to
reattach it to the highest branch. His sergeant later said he even
taunted the retreating Confederate soldiers from his vantage
point.

On another occasion, he was captured while out on recon-
naissance. But Albert Cashier, private first class of the 95th

Illinois Infantry, seized a gun from his captors, knocked down the guard and ran back to his camp. In three years of service during the American Civil War, he saw action in some 40 battles and skirmishes. When he died in 1915, he was buried with full military honours.

The story might have ended there, a fitting tribute to a soldier whose name was inscribed on the Illinois victory monument for his role in breaking the Confederacy at Vicksburg. After the war, like so many others, he lived a fairly unremarkable life. He might be all but forgotten had it not been discovered that Civil War veteran Albert Cashier was in fact a woman – and an Irishwoman at that.

He had kept his secret for decades and, after the war, continued to live as a man working in a series of jobs – janitor, handyman, herder – in the state of Illinois. In 1910, however, he fell ill and his neighbour, Mrs PH Lannon, sent her nurse to look in on him. The nurse did so and discovered the truth. She ran home and told her employer: 'My Lord, Mrs Lannon, he's a full-fledged woman!'

How did a woman – born in Clogherhead, Co. Louth on Christmas Day 1843 – keep her gender secret so effectively, and for so long that she had the distinction of being the only woman-soldier to complete a tour of duty and receive a Civil War pension? An estimated 400 women disguised themselves as soldiers in the American Civil War, but many of them were rumbled when they were injured or captured – or even when they gave birth. Other women died on the battlefield and were discovered only when they were buried.

Some didn't bother to disguise themselves at all, although women were forbidden in the military. One unnamed Irishwoman went into battle at White Oak Swamp Bridge in Virginia in 1862 armed with nothing more than a large umbrella. She fought alongside her husband in the Irish brigade and when she saw anyone trying to sneak to the back, she would 'seize him by the nape of his neck and place him in the ranks again, calling him a "dirty, cowardly spalpeen", and other choice epithets', according to William Davis, writing in 1886.

Some 200,000 Irishmen fought in the American Civil War and an estimated 25,000 died – little wonder that historian and archaeologist Damian Shiels has called it 'Ireland's Forgotten Great War'. While Irishwomen were involved in various ways – fighting beside their husbands, giving medical aid – there is, to date, just one known case of an Irishwoman who completed a tour of duty as a male soldier. And that is Jennie Hodgers.

It is not even surprising that the 19-year-old succeeded in enlisting in Company G, 95th Illinois Infantry in August 1862. Medical examinations were so cursory that it was said army policy was not to test eyes, but simply to count them. Years later Robert Hannah, who served with Albert in Company G, said the medical exam was very superficial. 'When I was examined for enlistment, I was not stripped and a woman would not have had any trouble in passing the examination,' he said.

The army was also desperate for new recruits and, as American local historian Frank Crawford puts it, all a soldier had to do was show he had teeth so he would be able to tear open the cartridge to load a gun.

Jennie Hodgers had probably already been living as a man when she went to enlist. She would not have been asked for proof of identity and when she gave her place of birth as New

York and occupation as farmer, it was accepted as fact. Official military records noted that the new recruit was five foot three with auburn hair and blue eyes.

Men – and, as we know, many women – joined up for a variety of reasons, not least financial ones. A soldier could count on a regular salary and an enlistment bonus. The day before Jennie Hodgers became a Union soldier, the Boone county board approved a sign-on bonus of $60 for new recruits. Some were motivated by patriotism, others by the notion that war was some kind of adventure. But what of Jennie Hodgers?

Towards the end of his life, Albert Cashier gave a possible explanation when he said: 'Lots of boys enlisted under the wrong name. So did I. The country needed men, and I wanted excitement.'

Albert Cashier made a reliable and fearless soldier. One of his superiors said he was selected 'whenever dependable men were absolutely necessary'. His unit fought in many of the war's bloodiest battles, engaging in combat on the western theatre of war – in Louisiana, Mississippi and Tennessee. They travelled nearly 10,000 miles, some 1800 miles on foot, often in blistering heat. Cashier was said to be good on the march and in battle and was singled out for bravery at least twice.

It's clear that Jennie Hodgers made a convincing male soldier but what is less clear is how, in the cramped reality of camp life, Albert Cashier was not exposed as a woman. In the initial days of the military campaign, soldiers were issued with a tent each so there was no need to share sleeping quarters. Ironically, the tents – dubbed dog or pup tents – were considered a nuisance as 'none but the very shortest men could sleep beneath them unexposed to the weather'. That suited Albert Cashier but not the other soldiers who were forced to sleep with their heads, or their feet, exposed to the elements.

The tent issue was soon remedied and, after that, it seems Albert Cashier insisted on 'bunking on his own', Company G comrades later said. In winter, when the soldiers felled trees to build substantial warm log huts, Albert must have slept in a dormitory-style arrangement. That wasn't necessarily a problem either as soldiers often wore their uniforms for weeks on end.

In any case, Albert Cashier was a person who kept to himself. Others in Company G recalled a man who was 'very quiet in manner'. He didn't take part in games or sports and kept his uniform buttoned to the chin – perhaps to hide the absence of an Adam's apple. It was noticed that he didn't shave, but that wasn't unusual as many of the recruits were just boys.

One of his closest comrades was Samuel Pepper and they both worked on the unit's laundry service. In a letter home to his wife, Samuel said Albert had a nickname, Chub, but also that he was a 'foul-speaking, foul-acting belligerent individual'. That's quite a contrast to the other soldiers' view of him but the two had fallen out in an argument. Maybe that was what coloured Albert's language or perhaps, as has been suggested, he was simply trying to appear 'soldierly'.

What was more remarkable was how he managed to stay healthy, unwounded and, indeed, alive. In three years, he missed only one day of duty but, when admitted to the army hospital, refused to be undressed or examined by a doctor. At least an ill-fitting uniform could obscure the female form when fully dressed, or Jennie may have bound her breasts to hide them. And, given the harsh conditions, it is quite possible that menstruation had stopped.

The company was often 'footsore and hungry' and, during one stretch, there was nothing but corn on offer at the mess table. Although the soldiers made jokes about it – wondering when they were going to be issued with rations of hay and a horse's draw halter – it was very bad for morale, as former adjutant of the regiment Wales W Wood noted in 1865: 'There is no thing about which a soldier is more sensitive than his appetite, and he very much dislikes to have it restrained or interfered with, unless under some great and pressing military necessity. He will go months without receiving a dime of pay, without a murmur, but place him upon short rations for a day even, and you will hear from him immediately.'

In a sense, that was the least of it. The Illinois 95th Infantry unit suffered heavy casualties during a tour of duty that included the Vicksburg Campaign in Mississippi, the Red River expedition in Louisiana and the Nashville Campaign in Tennessee. Of the 983 officers and enlisted men who went out to fight, fewer than half came home. Some 190 were wounded and discharged during service. 'Many of these returned to their friends, pale, haggard, and broken down by the sufferings and diseases incident to camp life,' Wales W Wood wrote in his history of the regiment. Another 83 men – including the unit's commander Colonel Humphrey – died in action, while 177 others became 'the pitiful victims of disease'.

Private Albert DJ Cashier did very well to survive the war – and to do so undiscovered. He was honourably discharged on 17 August 1865 and went back to Illinois. For the next year he took a job in Belvidere in the north of the state, working in a plant nursery. He continued to live as a man and, according to one account, decided to move to a small town some time later as it would be easier to keep a secret there.

Around 1869 he moved to Saunemin in central Illinois, a town with a population of about 400 people. He took a variety of manual jobs, working on a farm at first, then at a hardware shop and, after that, maintaining the local church. He was given a small house, which can still be visited today.

Mary Catherine Lannon, a descendant of the woman whose nurse first uncovered the truth, said he was remembered by many with affection and retrospective amazement. In 1969 Mary Catherine completed a master's thesis on this curious woman-soldier's life. She wrote: 'Albert – herder, lamplighter, janitor, handyman – was notably eccentric; but the people of the town called on her services, often paying her with meals and, at times, a place to sleep, never really suspecting that this peculiar man was in fact a woman.'

It is easy to see why Albert Cashier decided not to return to life as Jennie Hodgers. There were few opportunities for an illiterate woman in nineteenth-century America. If she was able to secure work, it would have been poorly paid and she would not have been able to vote. As a man, however, Cashier could vote, which he did with enthusiasm. He could also find work relatively easily and enjoy continued contact with his military friends. He was proud of his career and wore his Union uniform to town parades where he was nicknamed 'the little drummer boy'.

Nobody knew anything of his Irish background or true identity and it very nearly remained that way. Some learned the truth, but they kept it under wraps.

When his neighbour Mrs Lannon and her nurse found out in 1910, for instance, they said nothing. A year later Albert

Cashier's gender was revealed for a second time but, again, the doctor who discovered the truth was discreet. Albert had been working for the state senator Ira Lish who accidentally knocked him down with his car. Albert was now in his late sixties and the fracture did not heal well; he was also said to be in a weakened mental state. Senator Lish and the doctor arranged to have him transferred to a home for veteran soldiers in Illinois. The superintendent of the home was told of his identity but again agreed to keep Albert's gender confidential. He even agreed to give Albert more private quarters – 'out of respect for her desires' – and the veteran fitted in quite well, mingling with other soldiers around the grounds, joining them for meals and in their storytelling and games.

It was at this point that the broad outline of Jennie Hodger's background started to emerge. The Catholic chaplain at the Old Soldiers' Home was a man from Cavan called Rev Fr PD Curran. He took a particular interest in finding out more about his compatriot:

> Whenever I want to get some information from 'Albert', I had only to address 'him' in Irish and immediately Albert began to speak about Ireland. She (I suppose we must say 'she') spoke on one occasion of her father, whereupon I asked her what his name was. She answered 'Hodgers' and told me she came from Clogherhead, Co. Louth.

The chaplain supposed that Hodgers – they didn't yet have a first name – left Ireland as a stowaway, disguised in boys' clothes. He also imagined her departure was due to some failed love affair 'back in her mysterious past'. Another version had it that Jennie Hodgers quickly realised there were more job opportunities for boys and made the decision to become one before getting his first job in a shoe factory.

Whatever the exact course of events, the chaplain seemed to understand Jennie's decision very well, as he explained in a remarkable letter to the editor of the *Anglo-Celt* in 1913. He wrote: 'She wanted to be a man, and because Nature cheated her of this privilege she did the next best thing, disguised as a man, so she could do a man's work, lead a man's life and be a man in everything, but in sex.'

By then, her secret was widely known because the Civil War Pension Board opened an investigation as they suspected Jennie Hodgers of fraudulently claiming Albert Cashier's pension. Many of Albert's former comrades came to his aid and were gobsmacked to learn the truth. Without exception, they said they had no idea that their fellow soldier was a woman. Despite the highly unusual circumstances, the Pension Board acquitted Jennie/Albert and continued to pay the pension.

The press had also got wind of the story. It was front-page news in the United States – and in Ireland. On 4 May 1913, the *Quincy Whig* ran the story under the headline: 'Woman masked as man fought in civil war'. Two days later, the *Evening Herald* in Dublin trumpeted: 'EXTRAORDINARY CAREER'. The article read:

> The extraordinary career of a woman who for over fifty years masqueraded as a man was – says the New York correspondent of the 'Daily Mail' – disclosed on Sunday at the Soldiers' Home at Quincy, Illinois.

The man-woman has been an inmate of the Home for over two years, being enrolled on the books as Albert Cashier. She is a veteran soldier of the Civil War, and might have preserved her secret until her death, had not growing mental enfeeblement, and the resultant neglect of her physical well-being caused the authorities to give her a bath. Unable to escape the ordeal, the veteran appealed to a female nurse to whom she confessed her identity. According to her narrative, she is a native of Ireland, and went to America as a stowaway, disguised as a boy.

The article went on to say that the authorities did not know what to do with this 'war-scarred woman'. Albert's chaplain friend, however, did what he could to help. He wrote to the *Anglo-Celt* to try to locate the Hodgers family. The letter was sympathetically printed under a large headline that read: 'BRAVE WOMAN'S SECRET'.

A few days later, the paper published a letter to say the brave woman's relatives had been found. Patrick Hodgers claimed Albert Cashier as his sister Jennie and said she had left for America 'between 50 and 60 years ago'. He went on: 'My father and aunt left her to the boat in Drogheda, as my mother died when we were very young. I am in communication with the Rev P. D. Curran who has so kindly written to you.' Her parents were later revealed as Denis and Catherine Hodgers from Clogherhead, Co. Louth.

While some of the newspaper reports were dismissive – 'Find Old Soldier is Just a Woman', said the *Chicago Tribune* in 1913 – many of them were full of admiration for what Albert Cashier had achieved. *The Hartford Republican*, for instance, wrote about Albert Cashier/Jennie Hodgers' remarkable heroism in a front-page article under the headline 'REMARKABLE WAR VETERAN'. The unnamed reporter visited Albert in hospital, and was surprised by what he found:

> I had expected to meet an Amazon. A woman who had fought in the death grapple of a nation and had lived and toiled as a man through half a century should be big, strong and masculine.
>
> And when I entered her hospital ward there rose and came to meet me, in her faded soldier's uniform, just a little frail, sweet-faced, old lady, who might be anybody's grandmother. She was so little and so gentle ... And her face was a face for a painter to dwell on. Half a century of sun and wind had bronzed that face, sowed it with freckles and seamed it with a thousand wrinkles.

The reporter went on to outline, in a rather patronising way, the achievements of this frail old lady who had shared the soldier's lot in camp, on sentry duty, in bivouac and in the line of battle. The account is interesting, however, as it gives a concise summary of Albert's experiences during three years of war:

> She had built and guarded a railroad in the advance on Memphis. She had been through the battle of Guntown when her company was nearly annihilated. She had helped pursue Hodd's defeated army to Tennessee. She had toiled in the swamps against Gen. Johnston's Confederates, and triumphed with Grant amid the thunders of Vicksburg.

She had taken part in the siege of Natchez, the battles of Kennesaw Mountain, Chattahoochee River, Jonesboro and Lovejoy Station. She had been in the battering campaigns against Price in Arkansas and Mississippi, and Hood in Alabama, and with Sherman in his Atlanta campaign, where one soldier out of three was killed and had followed him in his devasting march to the sea.

The article also noted that Jennie/Albert was unaware of all the media attention. Life went on as normal for him and the veterans in the Home continued to address him as Albert.

But that was not to last.

In 1914, Albert Cashier developed dementia and was committed to the Watertown State Hospital for the insane. He was then admitted to a woman's ward and forced to wear a dress. It was said Albert was deeply distressed and pinned the skirt of the dress in an attempt to fashion makeshift trousers, but that made him trip up.

Charles W Ives, of Company G, was deeply saddened by what he found on a visit to the hospital: 'I left Cashier, the fearless boy of 22, at the end of the Vicksburg campaign. When I went to Watertown [hospital], I found … a frail woman of 70, broken, because, on discovery, she was compelled to put on skirts. They told me she was as awkward as could be in them. One day she tripped and fell, hurting her hip. She never recovered.'

Albert Cashier/Jennie Hodgers died, aged 71, in mid-October 1915. Even though he had been forced to live as a woman in his final years, he was never aware of the publicity that his story had generated. He was buried, in his uniform, by the Grand Army of the Republic Veterans' Society and given a military funeral.

A few years after his death, the *Chicago Tribune* singled out Jennie Hodgers for another distinction. She was one of only two female soldiers, who fought as men, to receive a military pension. The report, published on 30 April 1923, said the unique records of two women serving as private soldiers, one in the American Revolutionary War and another through the Civil War, had been discovered in the files of the Department of the Interior Pension Bureau at Washington. Both had hidden their identities, which were revealed only after they were awarded pensions by the government.

The other woman was Deborah Gannett who fought under the name Robert Shurtleff and served in a Massachusetts regiment from 1781 to 1783. She was wounded and honourably discharged but her identify was not revealed until after the war. In 1838 Congress passed a special Bill, awarding her heirs a pension. In it, she was described as 'Deborah Gannett, a soldier of the Revolution'.

Meanwhile, in Sunnyslope Cemetery, Albert Cashier's headstone was marked with his name, rank and company. Six decades later, the community in Saunemin thought it apt to add his second identity – Jennie Hodgers, the girl who emigrated to the United States.

Whatever Jennie Hodgers' reasons for reinventing herself as Albert Cashier and embarking on a long and successful military career, the Civil War veteran very definitely pushed the boundaries of what was believed to be possible in his (and her) lifetime.

In recent years the story is more widely known thanks in no small part to Fiona Ní Eidhin whose documentary, *Jennie*

Hodgers – Saighdiúr Lincoln [Jennie Hodgers – Lincoln's Soldier], was aired on Irish television in 2017. She believes Albert/Jennie realised very early on that the odds were stacked against her as an illiterate female in the US all on her own:

'Jennie Hodgers hadn't travelled all the way across the Atlantic to fail. Thus, Albert Cashier was born, and with it came a whole host of exciting opportunities. Albert was a man on a mission, and his gender would not get in the way of that.'

Fiona Ní Eidhin says it's important to tell these stories of remarkable courage:

Aside from the fact that Albert Cashier was a biological female, and so gave us this fascinating story, Albert was also a soldier of the Union Army that ultimately went on to win the American Civil War, preserving the United States as a republic, and strengthening the movement to abolish slavery. Jennie Hodgers, the unassuming girl from Clogherhead, Co. Louth, played a part in that vital piece of history, however unorthodox a way she went about it.

Also, stories like Albert's make us realise just how far we have evolved as a society. The fact that Jennie felt she had to become Albert in order to succeed in life should make us appreciate the completely different world we live in today.

Lizzie Le Blond

ALPINE MOUNTAINEER AND PHOTOGRAPHER (1860–1934)

My grand-aunt, Lady Bentinck, sent out a frantic S.O.S. 'Stop her climbing mountains! She is scandalising all London and looks like a Red Indian!' for I was usually copper-coloured when I returned to England after a series of ascents.

Lizzie Le Blond

Dressed in high-heeled buttoned boots and shady hat, Lizzie Le Blond set out one beautiful winter morning in 1881 and zigzagged along a mountain path at the base of Mont Blanc. At the edge of a glacier she saw four men emerge from the ice, equipped with axes and ropes and, as Lizzie put it, 'all the other thrilling accessories of an expedition to the summit'. They greeted the all-female group and said they supposed they were on their way to Grand Mulets, about two-thirds of the way up the highest mountain in the Alps.

'We hadn't supposed anything of the kind,' Lizzie wrote later, 'but at the same moment at least two of us began to suppose very hard indeed.'

Their guides casually said they *happened* to have a rope in their knapsacks and urged the women to think about it. Two turned back, but a third woman joined Lizzie to face the heights. Soon they were roped up, 'dodging in and out of crevasses' on their way to Grand Mulets hut at 3051 metres. When they arrived, they were exhilarated if a little worse for wear. As Lizzie recounted:

> Our boots were pulp, our stockings wet sponges, our skirts sodden, but somehow we were rigged out in dry clothing, which included enormous felt slippers that dropped off at every step as we clambered to the top of the rocky pinnacles behind the hut to watch the sunset. By that time we were altogether reckless, and did not hesitate to ask: "Why not go to the top of Mont Blanc tomorrow?"

The guides were not against the idea but told them to put it off for a week as they would need proper boots and clothing. Excited, the two women made a 'delightful descent', even if Lizzie's climbing companion was greeted by a furious uncle who reduced her to tears. As far as Lizzie Le Blond was concerned, though, she had made her start.

Lizzie's first climb was all the more remarkable as she had gone to the mountains not to climb, but for health reasons. As she herself explained: 'My mother's family had a long record of lung trouble and in those days "consumption" as it was called was considered incurable.' Initially, she was sent to the warmth of Algiers, but on one trip she was caught in a snowstorm on the journey home and got severe 'congestion of the lungs'. When she recovered, her doctor advised she move to Switzerland. Before her first ascent of Mont Blanc, she sought her doctor's permission to climb. When he gave the go-ahead, she never looked back. Her health didn't seem to bother her after that.

Two successful ascents of Mont Blanc followed and then she felt entitled to call herself a climber – not that she thought anybody would be interested:

> The long story of my twenty years' mountaineering is of no interest to the general reader. My longest climb lasted for two nights and two days going all the time. The slowness of the pace, for usually I was pretty quick on the mountains, was due to the extremely bad state of the rocks, which were glazed in ice.

She corrected people when they claimed she was the first woman up Mont Blanc, giving credit to her predecessors – 18-year-old local maid Marie Paradis who summitted in 1808 and the 44-year-old French aristocrat Henriette d'Angeville, who made it to the top in 1838. She was equally bemused when her books on mountaineering were well reviewed: 'I climbed like a child, ardently, engrossingly, thinking not at all of onlookers, and indeed unaware that such even existed, and when one day I came across an allusion to myself in a paper as "an Alpinist of world-renowned fame" I wondered what idiot could have written it.'

By the time she wrote her autobiography in 1928, she had several accomplishments to recount, even if she downplayed them. She was the first president of the Ladies' Alpine Club, an early pioneer of nature photography, an accomplished writer and a World War I volunteer. In that time, she had also been married three times and widowed twice. She had one son, from her first marriage, and Harry Arthur, like his mother, had been advised to live outside England for health reasons. He eventually settled in California.

His mother, however, found the Alps most beneficial for her lung complaint, although she never imagined the mountains would come to mean so much to her. Her mother used to read extracts from Edward Whymper's *Scrambles Among the Alps in the Years 1860–69* to her as a child, and while she loved the vigour of the stories, the idea of climbing never gripped her.

Elizabeth Hawkins-Whitshed, or Lizzie as she was later known, was born on 26 June 1860 to Captain Vincent Hawkins-Whitshed and his wife Anne Alicia. She spent a happy – and privileged – childhood at Killincarrick House in Greystones, Co. Wicklow, going to lessons only when she felt like it. She had her own governess from the age of eight but confessed that she had been a terrible student: 'It has been an ever-present regret to me that I learnt absolutely nothing. I was a somewhat delicate child and had only to imagine a headache in order to be sent out into the garden to play for the rest of the day.'

At the age of 17 she deeply regretted her failure to learn but the merest smattering of French as she faced her first dinner party in London in 'secret terror'. What would happen if she found herself surrounded by ambassadors who spoke nothing but French? she fretted. As it turned out, her linguistic shortcomings were never exposed but Elizabeth Hawkins-Whitshed did admit to feeling overwhelmed to be cast from her 'simple outdoor girlhood' into a life among 'the Prince of Wales set'.

There was a social whirl of balls, dinners and encounters with a host of high-profile family friends that included the Misses Shelley (the elderly sisters of the late poet), George Bernard Shaw and George Eliot. On one occasion, she was even introduced to Queen Victoria: 'When I bent low to kiss Her Majesty's hand, I was struck by her small stature and great dignity and, though her hand was plump and pink, she was every inch an Empress.'

Before the end of the season, she was engaged to Captain Fred Burnaby, a writer and swashbuckling adventurer who was said to be the strongest man in the British army; his party trick was to bend a poker around his own neck. Years later, she said she was still filled with surprise 'that a man whose adventurous travels filled edition after edition took a fancy to an inexperienced child of 18', although he said at the time that he was utterly charmed by Lizzie. Of course, she was also a young lady of means, having inherited the house and estate at Greystones after her father died in 1871.

Their wedding in South Kensington in June 1879 was a high-society affair that filled column inches in the following day's newspaper. The bride, *The Morning Post* reported, wore a dress of duchesse satin, a tulle veil, diamond tiara (a present from the bridegroom) and a diamond bracelet and pendant (gifts from her mother). The newspaper also said there were numerous presents, among them a three-foot dining-table centrepiece from her Irish tenantry.

The couple's only son, Harry Arthur, was born in 1880, but shortly afterwards Lizzie and her husband began to lead separate lives. Captain Burnaby went on to become the first man to cross the English Channel in a hot-air balloon but later died in Sudan in 1885.

Lizzie, meanwhile, moved to Switzerland initially for health reasons. When she first started to visit St Moritz in the 1880s and 1890s, it had no railway, no electric light and no heating and she recalled luging down the village street on tiny sleds. It soon became popular with the elite as tobogganing, skiing and skating gained popularity. Lizzie mixed with duchesses, countesses and even princesses, but she had no time for vanity. She was scathing about those who, when unrecognised, indignantly asked the question: 'Don't you know who I am?' In her autobiography she recounts cheekily answering: 'Yes, of course I know who you are. You are a man with more money than manners.'

Lizzie was grateful to the mountains for knocking any illusions of grandeur out of her. When she first got there in 1881, she had never actually put on her own boots and confessed that she wasn't entirely sure which boot went on which foot: 'It did not occur to me that I could do without a maid, and it was not till one of the species had incessant hysteria whenever I returned late from an expedition, and another had eloped with a courier, that I gained my independence.'

It came at a cost, however, as her mother faced the music on her behalf when her grand-aunt, Lady Bentinck, sent out a frantic SOS: '"Stop her climbing mountains! She is scandalising all London and looks like a red Indian!" for I was usually copper-coloured when I returned to England after a series of ascents.'

She didn't stop, of course, and was soon guiding others up the mountains on early morning expeditions behind smelly lanterns to light the way. She started to take photographs too and got her first camera in the early 1880s – 'a cumbersome concern' – when few people were taking photographs. She photographed the stunning views and also the people who were now coming in increasing numbers to the Alpine resorts. After one fancy dress party at the five-star Kulm Hotel in St Moritz, Sir Arthur Conan Doyle terrified a newcomer in his Viking costume as he made his way to Lizzie's improvised studio to be photographed.

Her favourite subjects, however, were the mountains, which up to then had not been photographed at close quarters. She wrote:

It was trying work setting up a camera with half-frozen hands, hiding one's head under a focusing cloth which kept blowing away and adjusting innumerable screws in a temperature well below freezing-point. But one learnt one's job very thoroughly and I confess that even now I never felt satisfied unless I have done all the developing, printing, etc., of an exposure.

She later made a series of short films, capturing tobogganing, skating and bobsleigh racing on the Cresta Run, the famous toboggan track which ironically banned women in 1929 on the grounds that it was 'medically unsafe'. The ban was lifted in 2018, although it might have happened sooner had Lizzie Le Blond been on the case. During her lifetime she success-fully challenged the organisers of a men's skating competition to open it to women. She was never particularly interested in skating, she admitted, but when a man told her she would never be any good at it, she set out to prove him wrong. And she did, by becoming the first woman to pass the highest test set up by the St Moritz Ice Skating Club.

In the meantime, she found time to marry again. In 1886 she married John Frederic Main but that marriage didn't last very long either; he went to live in America a year later and died there in 1892. Lizzie now spent most of her time in Switzerland and had taken up cycling. She cycled to and from climbs but also went on long cycling tours, sometimes with friends and sometimes alone. 'Once I rode from St Moritz most of the way to Rome, with my luggage on my machine, carrying my bicycle over portions of the narrow up-and-down path (for there was then no complete road) along the Lake of Como,' she wrote of one trip that continued on to several places in Italy.

She had also started to write – newspaper articles, books on mountaineering, travel books and even a book on Italian garden design. But, as she said, life was not all fun and pastimes. She helped to set up the St Moritz Aid Fund so that those who did not have the money could avail of the health-promoting climate of the Alpine resort.

She wrote often of accidents on the mountains but said her own trips were free of all disasters thanks to her excellent guides, Joseph Imboden and his son Roman. The only part of her that ever got caught up in an avalanche was her skirt, which was in a bundle under a rock with other climbers' belongings. Her guide Roman watched as a wind lifted up the bundle and brought it out of the way of the avalanche in the same way that an old woman sitting outside her chalet door had once been transported by the wind of an avalanche to the top of a pine tree, where, quite uninjured, she calmly waited for help to come.

Tragedy did strike, however, as shortly afterwards Roman was killed in an accident. When that happened, Lizzie couldn't face the Alps and instead travelled to Norway to venture into territory that was not only unexplored but unmapped, 'a climber's playground well worth exploring', as she put it. She made 19 new ascents with her two guides and was captivated by the remoteness and perpetual daylight in a region so little known. They camped and fished for food or bought salmon from the local people, who thought they were prospecting for gold when they saw their ice axes.

It was also a haven for photographers:

Our only visitors were occasional Laps and now and then a reindeer would wander close to our camp and nose around till he discovered us, when he would disappear like a flash to join the herd. One day a great eagle settled on our rubbish heap, but departed the moment he spied strangers, his widely-spread wings appearing for a moment to darken the sky.

Lizzie managed to set up an improvised dark room in a tent covered with a mackintosh sheet and developed and printed as she went along.

She kept an eye on her family property in Ireland too and came up with the progressive idea of turning it into the country's first planned housing estate. In 1889 part of the estate was opened up for a golf course and a few years later, roads were laid and houses built in the fashionable 'domestic revival style', with high-pitched roofs, tall chimneys and dormer windows. Gardens were also considered a crucial part of the design.

While Lizzie referred to it as 'my building estate', the development bore the name of her late husband Burnaby. Her name is memorialised in the nearby Hawkins Lane and Whitshed Road in Greystones today.

In 1900 Lizzie was ready to marry again. This time, though, she did so in a low-key ceremony and married Aubrey Le Blond, a man ten years her junior, in what the *Morning Post* described as a very quiet ceremony with 'only the nearest relatives of the bride and bridegroom being present'. The couple remained together until Lizzie died more than 30 years later.

By the early 1900s Lizzie had all but stopped climbing but she remained very involved in the sport. When the Ladies' Alpine Club – the world's first climbing association for women – was established, she was elected its first president. The Journal of the all-male Alpine Club praised her physical courage and sure judgement which, it said, was 'never surpassed in any mountaineer, professional or amateur, of the so-called stronger sex'.

She began to develop new interests too and over the next three decades travelled all over the world. In 1912 she toured China and Japan with her husband and was deeply affected by the aftermath of the 1911 revolution, which had overthrown the country's last emperor to establish the Republic of China. Their boat was fired upon while it travelled up the Yangtze River and she was horrified when a guide leaned in to tell her that they had cut the throats of 25,000 people – men, women and children – the previous year. The whole of China, she said, was like one vast graveyard. Yet the couple stayed a month in Beijing visiting the sites and her husband added to his already large collection of porcelain.

The following year the couple went to Moscow and St Petersburg and Lizzie stayed on for two weeks' sightseeing when her husband returned home. At the Winter Palace in St Petersburg, she was less than impressed with the emperor's plain bedroom. 'On his writing-table was a common ash-tray and writing accessories that would have been dear at half a crown,' she commented. Yet, in the Gallery of the Romanovs, she was delighted to spot the resemblance between her distant relative, Catherine the Great, and her own great-great-great-grandmother, Charlotte Sophie, Countess Bentinck.

She continued to make frequent trips to Switzerland and on one of those visits, in the late summer of 1914, World War I broke out as she was returning home. Herr Stilling, a German man, helped her to find her way through the 'seething mass of humanity' at all the railway stations and she noted the irony that she had been helped by 'an enemy subject'. Herr Stilling, meanwhile, commented with chilling prescience: 'It [is] hard to believe that millions and millions of people are getting ready to kill each other.'

When Lizzie arrived home, she wanted to volunteer for the war effort but found that the Red Cross in England were looking for younger women, so she went to Dieppe in France to see what she might do. The very first hospital she approached – a large, improvised military hospital – welcomed her with open arms. There were just two doctors and one partially trained nurse to care for the hundreds of wounded German prisoners held there after the Battle of the Marne. A few months later, she was moved to a French ward in a hospital in the Hôtel Métropole. 'My job was to make myself generally useful: that is to say, I made beds, washed patients, helped them with their meals, gave medicines, took temperatures, sterilized instruments and did so many other trifling jobs in our ward of fifty beds.'

Though the 'very starchy English nurses' would have been scandalised by her methods, she said. There was no early-morning bedmaking, no polishing of brasses at night and no set time for washing. 'Sometimes,' she wrote, 'a patient would remark, as I prepared to dump a basin of warm water beside him, "Not now, Mees. I want to finish this letter."' She let him do so and she saved books for those who were depressed after operations. *The Scarlet Pimpernel* was an extraordinary success, she said.

She also called on her old network of mountaineers to help, and they sent money, equipment and boots to an ambulance corps in the Vosges mountains in France. She went back to England in the winter of 1916 and was put in charge of the Appeal Department of the British Ambulance Committee. She raised thousands of pounds during a series of fundraising activities while the war lasted.

When she wrote about the war afterwards, she said there was one story so characteristic of our Tommies that she had to recount it:

It was usual for English nurses to meet trains as they passed through the station and give our men cigarettes. One day they handed a packet to a Tommy who was escorting two German prisoners. Immediately, as was the wont of Tommies, the cigarettes were shared with his charges. The giver protested.

"Take care, lidy," said Tommy hastily, "Fritz 'ere, 'e understands English. Yer might 'urt 'is feelin's!"

When the war was over, the War Office sent her to lecture to the troops in France while they awaited demobilisation. Before she went to amuse the troops with tales of her adventures in the Alps, she went to Ypres on a solemn pilgrimage to see what she described as 'the sacred battlefields' of war:

It was indeed an overwhelming experience which awaited me. Not a single human being was visible at Ypres … On the stricken field, honeycombed with shell-holes full of stagnant, yellowish water, fourteen tanks were dotted about … mere empty shells, pierced through and through. Fragments of cloth, scraps of metal, ghastly remains, the nature of which one hardly dared to guess at, were pressed and rolled into what seemed a solid mass of congealed mud.

She visited Lens in northern France, which had been reduced to a 'rubbish heap'; the cathedral just a slightly higher mound than the rest. She visited Bailleul, a town 'reduced almost to powder' while the city of Reims, in the northeast, reminded her of the ruins of Pompeii. She was deeply saddened to see the damaged cathedral and later managed The British Empire Fund, which raised money for its restoration. In May 1927 she would return to see the great nave open again for worship but now her attention was on raising the spirits of the troops waiting to be sent home.

Lectures were at 10 am, and when Lizzie faced the first wall of khaki-clad youth her heart went pit-a-pat: 'I wondered very much indeed whether I could expect to hold their attention.' She invited them to smoke and to shuffle their feet loudly if they were bored but later reported that they were a wonderful audience and were fascinated by her experiences in the Alps, which she illustrated with some of the thousands of photographs she had taken.

She delivered hundreds of lectures – and in all conditions. On one occasion, the lantern slide projector caught fire and flames shot to the roof but they were dampened down and

Lizzie was soon back in front of a solid block of khaki telling them about her exploits.

The experience of seeing the damage done by war stayed with her for life. On her return to England she became honorary secretary of the Anglo-French Luncheon Club and worked to improve relations between England and France. She also made frequent trips to see her son in California – the climate suited him best there – and said she'd happily settle in Hollywood if she had to move to the United States.

All the same, she spent her final years in England and remained involved in her many activities until shortly before she died on 27 July 1934. Unlike other women of her generation, she wasn't forgotten. Her contemporaries spoke highly of her and the memory of her mountaineering achievements was kept alive. Claire-Elaine Engel mentioned her in *They Came to the Hills*, a history of mountaineering in the Alps. In 1953 *Tatler* reviewed the book and wrote of the amazing career of Elizabeth Hawkins-Whitshed, the 'utterly tireless' woman who was first to make 'manless ascents' of the mountains.

But it appears this utterly tireless woman had another story to tell. At the end of her autobiography, Lizzie Le Blond admitted she had told only those stories that were 'discreet to mention. I have plenty of the other kind, though Heaven grant I may never be tempted to relate them.'

What a pity she never did give in to that temptation, because what she left behind is an autobiography full of her own adventures, but one that gives us little insight into her private life as a mother and three-time wife.

Clotilde Graves

ACCLAIMED JOURNALIST, PLAYWRIGHT AND BESTSELLING NOVELIST
(1863–1932)

Miss Clo Graves … was an unusual figure in London literary life. She wore short hair and affected a masculine manner and cut of costume and smoked cigarettes in public some thirty-five years ago, when such characteristics were considered eccentric.
Obituary, New Zealand Evening Post, *1933*

Clotilde Graves put out her lamp at 3 am and tried to get some sleep. The cocks of Coram Street in Bloomsbury were already crowing in their backyard coops but she hoped, at least, that the students in the adjoining rooms would be quiet as she had to be down on Fleet Street by 10.30 am to pick up any job that might be going. That was how she got work on the *St. James's Gazette*, a London evening newspaper, and she was making a name for herself on Grub Street, as the famous centre of journalism was known at the turn of the century.

It was a mixed experience for women in newspapers, but some had succeeded in breaking into what had been described as 'the Bastille of journalism'. Women, explained nineteenth-century journalist Marion Leslie, had made 'a hop, skip, and a jump' into the profession and 'by their ready wit, light, facile pen, and indomitable pluck [had] made themselves necessary adjuncts to every editorial staff'. Not everyone agreed with that view, but Clotilde Graves was already considered one of the boys.

It helped that she wore her hair short, dressed liked a man, smoked cigarettes and liked cycling and fly-fishing. She fitted in admirably, one unnamed editor wrote in a London periodical in April 1890:

Clotilde Graves is an exceedingly clever young lady, an enthusiastic journalist, and 'quite one of us' in the matter of cigarettes, cut of the hair and of the coat, and in the adjustment and shape of the collar. I remember once correcting proofs in the same office at the top of a big building off Fleet Street. She struck me then as being one of the type who will presently invade the realm of journalism in driving us out of our editorial rooms into the cold and bitter outside world.

Women had certainly not driven men out of newsrooms but some of them had succeeded in getting a toehold in a male-dominated profession. To make things a little easier for herself, Clotilde had shortened her first name to the more androgynous 'Clo' to distract readers and editors from her gender. She was, according to Dr Jenny Bloodworth, who is an authority on Clotilde Graves, the very epitome of the vigorous 'New Woman' of the *fin de siècle*, and she was doing all right. She had moved to London when she was just 17 and since then had earned considerable respect. Indeed, English artist and cartoonist Leonard Raven-Hill even considered her to be the first female journalist. He said: 'She had to do a man's job in a man's way, and in those days there were no "sob sisters", lingerie chatterers, and the shrieking sisterhood hadn't started then.'

Respect, however, did not necessarily translate into financial reward. It was difficult enough to earn a single living, but Clo Graves was struggling to support her family. There were many other challenges. 'Where a man finds one obstacle we find a dozen,' fellow Irish journalist Charlotte O'Conor Eccles wrote in the late nineteenth century. Her father Alexander O'Conor Eccles founded the Home Rule newspaper the *Roscommon Weekly Messenger* and she followed him into journalism. Like her contemporary Clo Graves, she moved to London to get work and was trying to negotiate the unsocial hours, the challenge of assignments that might take you into 'unsuitable' places and the daily grind of meeting deadlines.

In 1890 the relentless demand for copy took its toll on Clo's health. She had her first bout of severe exhaustion after a prolonged stretch of overwork. She later wrote:

I had brain fever, all alone in a room on the top floor of a grimmish apartment home in Bedford Street, Russell Square, and when the percussion had stopped rolling by my bed, and the drumming and the trumpeting that had accompanied them were silent, I came back, a feeble wreck, to ordinary life again. That might be said to be a de-facto movement repeated many times in my life. A quite roaring success achieved and then a great breakdown in health.

Her letter went on to refer to other breakdowns, yet in a career that lasted nearly 50 years, she wrote 15 novels – including a bestseller – some 20 plays, nine short-story compilations and several thousand articles. She was invalided in her fifties and spent the last 16 years of her life confined to a bath chair – a rickshaw-like wheelchair – but she continued to write.

When she died in 1932, she was remembered as a brilliant writer who was Irish not only by her birth in Buttevant, Co. Cork but, to quote the *Cork Examiner*, because of 'her gift of humour and sense of the "tears of things"'. 'This writer for *Punch* and pantomime could feel the serious things of life,' the paper said. Her death was reported as far away as New Zealand. That country's *Evening Post* noted that she had much of the talent of her relatives, the Irish Graves family of Charles Larcom Graves, journalist and travel writer, and Alfred Perceval Graves who was a poet and the father of Robert Graves. She was also related to the Anglican Bishop of Limerick, Charles Graves.

Yet Clotilde Graves died impoverished and was almost forgotten although, as recently as 1971, she was still well known enough to be a clue in the *Irish Press* crossword, which asked for her male pen name (Richard Dehan). A few decades on, few remember this woman who could turn her hand to anything – illustration, art, acting, literary fiction, journalism and drama.

But then it was hardly expected that a girl born in 1863 in the barracks at Buttevant in Co. Cork would make such an impression on the literary world, even if the town had associations with Elizabethan poet Edmund Spenser, whose Irish estate at Kilcolman was once nearby. There are many references to the locality in his poem *The Faerie Queene*.

Clotilde Inez Mary Graves was the third daughter born to Major William Henry Graves, of the 18th Royal Irish Regiment, and his wife Antoinette Deane. There was also a son. She lived inside the barracks with its parading ground, stables, hospital, administration, dining and sleeping blocks, although she probably knew the town outside the military precinct too. The barracks had provided the town with an economic lifeline since it opened some 50 years before and by the 1860s there was much more interaction between the soldiers and the local townspeople.

'On Sundays, hundreds of soldiers in scarlet and black would provide a colourful spectacle as they marched to Mass in the local churches,' recounts local historian Frank Trimm. 'The echo of horses' hooves could be heard on the streets as cavalry units came and went for training and exercise while bugles would blast regularly from behind the high walls to bring the men to order.'

Garrison life was not very family-friendly, though. Some married soldiers were given houses outside the barracks but that was a few decades after Clotilde was born. She might have got some early tuition at the church, which doubled as a school for soldiers' children, but it is unlikely she got much more than a basic education there.

When the family moved to Southsea in England almost a decade later, a nine-year-old Clotilde said she awoke to the 'ugly fact that she was absolutely ignorant'. There was no money for even 'the barest pretence of education', as she put it, and she began to beg and borrow books to educate herself. A friend of her father's had a well-stocked study and she spent her happiest hours in it, sitting quietly under a table and feasting on Shakespeare, Spenser, Ben Jonson, Plutarch, Dryden and many others.

That love of books stayed with her all of her life and she amassed a personal collection of over 4000 volumes, which she considered the indispensable tools of her writing trade. By the age of 16, she was already plying that trade, writing for a number of weekly magazines to support herself and her family. She gave up on a career as an artist as it was impossible to earn a living as a freelance illustrator but she persevered as an actress throughout the 1880s.

In 1885 she came back to Ireland to perform at the Gaiety Theatre in Harry Paulton's *The Babes*. The burlesque 'evoked an immense amount of laughter and applause' and 'Miss Clotilde Graves made a sprightly Ben Bosun,' the critic from *The Era*, a British weekly paper, said. There were many other performances in provincial theatres around England where she acted with her sister Maud, but her main source of income was her writing. Her output was extraordinary. Throughout the 1880s, she wrote an incalculable number of articles for several publications, including *The Gentlewoman*, *The Illustrated London News*, *Lady's Pictorial*, *The London Magazine*, *The Pall Mall Gazette* and *Punch*.

One of her editors, Sidney Low, recognised a literary quality in her articles, something rare among writers for the press: 'I always felt that if Miss Graves had been able to release herself from the stress of constant journalism, she would have produced imaginative work of exceptional merit. This impression has been confirmed by many of her short stories and essays, which I have read in magazines and weekly journals.'

Even with the demands of tight deadlines, Clotilde Graves was incredibly prolific, moving easily between genres to write poems, stories, essays, plays and countless articles. Her first play *Nitocris*, an Egyptian drama in poetic verse – and playing over five acts – ran in Drury Lane in November 1887 to mostly positive reviews. The critic at *The Era*, however, sarcastically noted that it was hard to gauge the play's quality as he could barely hear it: 'It is quite possible that amidst the descriptive passages of Miss Graves's piece may lurk gems of the richest poetry, treasures of melodious imagery. We cannot say, for the simple reason that only the more striking portions of the dialogue reached our ears.'

That year and into the next, she also collaborated on a four-act farce (*The Skeleton*) and two stage adaptations (*She* and *Puss in Boots* for the famous impresario and so-called 'father of modern pantomime', Sir Augustus Harris) as well as writing articles and short stories and also acting on the stage herself.

Little wonder that the *Sheffield Evening Telegraph* gave the impression that Clotilde Graves was a resounding financial as well as critical success when it ran a flattering profile of her in 1888 under the title 'A Lady Journalist': 'Clo Graves is very versatile in her genius. She is a dramatist, a novel writer, a burlesque poet, an artist, and has even worked at stereotyping her own sketches. Introductions to her charming chambers in Henrietta Street, Covent Garden, are much sought for by the literary Bohemians of Fleet Street. Not to know Clo Graves is to argue oneself unknown in literary and Press circles.'

By 1893 she had already written three books and five plays. In one of them, *Hey for Honesty!*, she firmly established her credentials as a 'New Woman', questioning Victorian hypocrisy,

which overlooked promiscuity in men but condemned it forcefully in women. Throughout her career, she created female
characters who were strong and independent in their dealings
with the messy complications of real life. Clotilde Graves was
not afraid to tackle contentious issues and she wrote about
domestic violence, sexual abuse, adultery and abortion even if
society preferred to sweep those uncomfortable subjects under
the carpet.

In 1896 she was celebrated as the first woman ever to have
two plays (*A Mother of Three* and *A Matchmaker*) running
in London at the same time. The weekly journal *The Sketch*
marked the achievement: 'It has never before occurred in the
theatrical annals of London that two plays by the same woman
have been running at the same time.'

But the relentless pace of work took its toll. The 'brain fever'
she had once described to a friend struck again and, soon after,
she 'went a tremendous purler [suffered a spectacular fall]', as
she put it. Around this time she converted to Catholicism,
which tempered her views on certain issues such as abortion,
but she continued to be firmly feminist.

Her health failed again in 1902. She continued to write but in
the years that followed found it increasingly difficult to get any
new commissions or to sell existing manuscripts. She applied
to the Royal Literary Fund – a benevolent fund set up in 1790
to help struggling writers. The Fund's archive reveals the difficulties faced by writers of both genders and across all genres.

The well-respected Kerry-born antiquarian and writer
Mary Agnes Hickson, for instance, applied for assistance a
few decades before Clotilde Graves. So had fellow writer and
journalist Elizabeth Owens Blackburne, who moved from Co.

Meath to London in the 1870s. She lost her sight at the age of 11 but had it restored by Sir William Wilde, the eminent eye and ear surgeon and father of the more famous Oscar. The two Irish women may have known each other. It's possible they met at The Society of Women Journalists; Clotilde was a member. Or they may have crossed paths while using the Reading Room of the British Museum, which intellectual women of the late nineteenth century turned into a kind of knowledge factory.

It was clear that Clotilde Graves had talent, contacts and an exceptional ability to write in any style, yet it was never enough to generate an adequate living. In 1903 she also faced significant health difficulties. She was very ill with pleurisy in March and later that year she had surgery to remove a uterine tumour, which might have killed her.

We know that because Clotilde's financial woes and serious health risks are spelled out in poignant detail in a further appeal to the Royal Literary Fund. Her friend Lady Colin Campbell (*née* Blood), an Irish-born journalist, author and playwright, made the following case on her behalf:

I have known Miss Graves intimately for six or seven years during which time I have hardly ever known her to stop work, even when seriously ill. She has had a life of great work and privation having supported herself and helped her family since she was fourteen. Last year Dr. Bland Sutton told her she had just two months to live if she did not consent to an operation for a tumour. Not being able to afford long convalescence, she went back to her writing. A month ago she collapsed with heart failure and was partially paralysed on the left side. She needs nourishment and is

distressed by her debts for rent, taxes and to those who have
supplied her with food.

Clotilde's application for aid was successful but the payment,
and the others that followed, were never enough to cover her
living expenses. She was also severely restricted by ongoing ill
health and it is a measure of her remarkable tenacity that she
continued to write and to garner widespread respect. In the
early 1900s she was celebrated as one of the most successful
women playwrights of the age, though that success was measured in recognition rather than in pounds, shillings and pence.
There was the occasional bad review: in 1906 one critic colour-
fully remarked that the first act of *The Bond of Ninon* fell upon
the audience with 'the heaviness of a cold suet dumpling', but
that was the exception rather than the rule.

She hit another low in 1909 when her mother died, but there
was more to the bereavement than emotional loss. She had
been staying with her mother as a paying guest and now had to
try to scrape together enough money to rent somewhere else.
Once more she was obliged to apply to the Royal Literary Fund
and, tellingly, she referred to her mother's passing 'as the death
of a near relative'. Perhaps she didn't want to admit that she was
paying her mother rent. She doesn't seem to have been close to
her two remaining siblings, even though she had supported the
entire family earlier in her career. Her father died in 1882 and
her only brother died, aged just 37, in 1902. Her elder sisters,
Maud and Dora, were in touch with each other but apparently
not with her.

—

In 1910 Clotilde Graves decided that she was 'more than a little bored' with Clotilde Graves and would 'like to drop her for a while'. She adopted a male pen name, Richard Dehan, and went on to write her most successful work, *The Dop Doctor*. It became an international bestseller that sold more than a quarter of a million copies. In other circumstances, this publishing triumph might have brought an end to Clotilde's financial worries but, unfortunately, that was not to be.

Richard Dehan was an unknown writer so, ironically, the manuscript did not command the fee that Clotilde might have secured were she writing under her own name. Also, because she was in dire financial straits, she sold it for a one-off payment with no claim on the considerable royalties to come.

When it came out, the book was praised for its plot, characters and convincing portrayal of a South Africa on the brink of the Second Boer War. Clotilde had never set foot in the Transvaal but wrote about it as if she had, gleaning details from her enormous library, which she had managed to keep intact.

She also impressed critics with her knowledge of military life and strategy, early Christian history, the customs of Western Australia and the politics of the German state, to mention but a few of the impressively long list of themes. The book's expansive canvas was a testament to the breadth of her imagination and her skill as a writer, but *The Dop Doctor* also did something else; it revealed the real Clotilde Graves. That was why she adopted a *nom de plume*, or *nom de guerre*, as she more evocatively put it:

[It] was to serve as my mask when the thoughts, reflections, experiences and griefs of a life-time, contained between the battered leaves of eighty-seven notebooks and wrought into the chapters of a novel, should be sent out into the world. I had written articles and stories and verses and plays, but the book I had entitled *The Dop Doctor* was another matter. I had filled my fountain-pen from the veins of my heart!

In its 671 pages the book deals with any number of difficult issues, from alcoholism (the doctor of the title suffers from it) to abortion, prostitution and sexual abuse. It is impossible to say how, or if, any of those issues directly affected Clotilde Graves but her study of sexual violence was so insightful that it led Dr Bloodworth to suggest she may have been writing from personal experience.

Some of the incidents in the novel may or may not represent real events in Clotilde's life or in the lives of those close to her, but her descriptions of child cruelty and sexual abuse are remarkable. Even more than a century after they were written, they remain insightful, thought-provoking and deeply moving. She describes, in beautifully measured prose, how publican Hans Bough's mistreatment of a young orphaned girl moves gradually from physical to sexual violence.

The girl, who doesn't even have a name at this point in the book, used to fear the blow of his heavy hand but as she started to outgrow one dress and then another and another, she became aware of something much more sinister – the publican's knowing smile as he licked his lips and followed her around with 'light, cautious, padding footsteps': 'Beating she comprehended, but this mysterious change in the man Bough filled her with sick, secret loathing and dread. She did not know why she bolted the door of the outhouse now when she crept to her miserable bed.'

Much later, the girl escapes and is adopted by a kindly Irish Mother Superior who gives her a name (Lynette) and acts as a mother figure. She spoke 'with the velvet Southern Irish inflection … and the soft melodious cadence that made her pure, cultivated utterance so exquisite'. She is also incredibly strong, like many of the female characters who drive the narrative of Clotilde Graves' books.

However, the terror of those early abusive years never leave Lynette and are described with an awareness and understanding that you might not expect to find in an early twentieth-century novel. For instance, when a well-intentioned young army officer, Lord Beauvayse, attempts to kiss Lynette, she is filled with panic:

> She swayed to him, as a young palm sways before a breeze, and he caught her in his strenuous, young embrace, and held her firmly against him. Her old terrors wakened, and dreadful, unforgettable things stirred in the darkness, where they had lain hidden, and lifted hydra-heads. She cried out wildly, and strove to thrust him from her, but he held her close.

The horror of child cruelty and sexual abuse is partially offset by Clotilde's brighter portrayal of motherhood. The abused Lynette is taken in and protected by a substitute mother – the Irish Mother Superior – who fights to the death, quite literally, to protect her charge. Clotilde Graves never became a mother herself – indeed none of her siblings became parents – but she wrote often about the subject and even thought women could be single mothers.

After the unexpected success of *The Dop Doctor*, she continued to write under her own name and also as Richard Dehan. Her circumstances, however, did not improve and at the age of 66 she (and her entire book collection) moved into a Catholic convent in Hertfordshire where she lived as a paying lodger.

Around that time she was yet again forced to appeal for financial assistance. This time she wrote directly to the Prime Minister, Ramsay MacDonald, asking to be included on the Civil List Pension Fund:

> My health had long been precarious and in 1912 it completely broke down. For nearly 16 yrs I have been an invalid, suffering frequently from severe pain, and so crippled that I cannot move from my wheeled chair. I require constant assistance, and have nurses with me day and night.
>
> Most of my savings have passed to doctors, surgeons and nurses, and the sales of my books are now so limited that I derive very little from them. At the age of 66, I am faced with poverty and something like destitution: and without extraneous aid I do not see how I can obtain the skilled attention without which I can not live.

She was eventually awarded a pension of £100 a year but it came too late, just months before her death in 1932. A friend paid for her burial plot and later her sisters paid for a headstone. The obituaries, which appeared in newspapers all around the English-speaking world, did not hide the many hardships she faced in her life.

As Dr Bloodworth noted, Clotilde Graves put it very succinctly herself: 'Authorship is a terrible profession when all is said and done.'

In the decades following her death, her work went out of fashion and she was largely forgotten, though that is starting to change. Her life and work feature in a few online articles and, at the time of writing, Cork library – in her native county – had plans to feature her in an exhibition celebrating five local female writers. There was renewed interest in her hometown of Buttevant too and even if authorship proved a terrible profession, there is reason to hope that new-found recognition will now come.

Sr Concepta Lynch

BUSINESSWOMAN, DOMINICAN SISTER AND PAINTER OF A UNIQUE CELTIC SHRINE (1874–1939)

Hoisting herself on planks, lying supine (another Michelangelo), she painted ceiling and high walls – often her right arm, powerless, had to be held aloft for her, often she had to stop work when her fingers could no longer guide her brushes.

Dr George A Little

By day Sr Concepta Lynch taught art and music to the pupils at the Dominican Convent school in Dun Laoghaire, Co. Dublin, meticulously preparing her lesson plans on the back of Bird's jelly boxes. When the school bell rang, she pinned her habit under an apron with safety pins and lay on a scaffold – Michelangelo-like, as Dr Little suggested – to paint the walls and ceiling of an oratory built on the convent's grounds in thanksgiving for peace at the end of World War I.

For 16 years she spent all of her spare time in the cold, lamp-lit chapel breathing life into her exquisite Celtic designs with nothing more than ordinary household paint mixed according to her detailed instructions. She developed a special pigment to mimic gold leaf and applied it to enchanted birds, mythical animals and intricate interlace reminiscent of the earliest illuminated holy books. Her playful monks pulled each other's beards as they had done in the Book of Kells, but Sr Concepta incorporated many of her own designs. She cut stencils from the blackout curtains so recently used in wartime and mapped out motifs of such striking originality that they are without parallel a century later.

For inspiration she turned to the monks of the early Irish Church and set herself a very clear challenge – to follow in their footsteps. Indeed, it would have been shameful not to do so. She made that point emphatically in verse:

It will be no small disgrace
If we do not keep the pace
With those men whose meditating
Brought us first illuminating

She made time to paint, even in a day that began at 5.30 am with breakfast and prayers and continued with a full day of teaching. When her health failed, she continued to perch on her makeshift scaffold while a favourite pupil held her arm and brush aloft. Her work in the oratory was her prayerful homage to God. Just like the monks she was so fond of quoting, her illustrated sermons were an expression of a deep faith. To her, prayer and art were two sides of the same coin.

Again, in verse, she explained how the lines drawn by the monks should be seen as 'roads to God'. Likewise, the dots they drew for stones and the curves that represented hills were all to be seen as prayers.

Her interpretation of the earliest manuscripts was prayerful and personal, yet she was not alone in looking to the past in an attempt to shape a more 'Irish' version of the present. The Celtic Revival, which began in the 1880s, had already given rise to a cultural renaissance that embraced the Irish language, Irish literature, music and art. Irish artists were painting in their own style. Irish work was being produced at the new Abbey Theatre in Dublin and Irish literature was flourishing.

Although Sr Concepta led a cloistered life, she was aware of the ongoing revival outside the convent and had a deep appreciation of Ireland's rich national heritage. That was evident in the vivid stories she told her pupils about the beginnings of Celtic art. For her, the monk-artists who illuminated the earliest manuscripts were true pioneers. In her introductory lesson to First Years, she explained that monks got the idea of making the first quill when they saw a feather fall from a bird flying overhead. They made thin quills to draw fine lines and larger quills for wide lines, she told them:

No work seemed wrong. Old men with shakey [sic] hands made use of their shakey hands and put them into wonderful ornaments. Later they made colours from the barks of trees and when they wanted material to paint on they used the skins of animals which they prepared in some wonderful manner … All creation is represented in this Art, Birds, Animals, Serpents, fish, the Sky, the Sea, men, women, etc.

She was doing the same now, portraying all of creation in brilliant reds and oranges, blues and browns, on the walls of the little house of prayer built to remember the local men who died on the battlefields in France and Belgium in World War I.

Many of them joined the 1st Battalion Irish Guards, a regiment that played a major role in stopping the Germans breaking through to the Channel ports in November 1914. Private Thomas Kelly, from Dun Laoghaire, was among those who defended the Belgian village of Zillebeke in what became known as the first battle of Ypres. Rudyard Kipling, whose son John fought and was killed with the Irish Guards, described the action:

There were many casualties in the front trenches, specially among No. 3 Company, men being blown to pieces with no trace left … The line was near breaking point – they were shelled and machine-gunned at every point. Here the officers, every cook, orderly and man who could stand, took rifle and fought, for they were all that stood there between the enemy and the Channel Ports.

The soldiers held the line but at a huge cost. Thousands died and many thousands more were injured or missing. Private Kelly was badly wounded and later died behind the battle lines. His effects were sent home to his widow Marie Kelly in a little brass box. He was buried in Poperinge, near the French border, where Irish troops once prayed in front of a statue of the Sacred Heart in the town's church. The statue, it was said, had even accompanied them into the trenches to offer protection, or solace, though many soldiers never returned home.

It's possible that very statue made its way to Dun Laoghaire to form the centrepiece of the little hidden church, or another may have been brought from France. In any case, what marked out the nuns' plan to build a memorial chapel was that they were almost alone in honouring the Irish war dead.

Outside the convent gates the political tide had turned against the 200,000-plus Irish men who served in the British army during the Great War. They returned to find a country changed utterly by the Easter Rising and the ongoing War of Independence. The new heroes were those who fought for the nationalist cause, not the veterans of the world war who were forgotten or ostracised. The nuns at the Dominican Convent, however, were not swayed by the prevailing mood. Prioress Mother Mary Laurence was determined to honour the local dead and she fundraised with persistence to build an oratory that was modelled on the style of an early Irish church. It was simple and unadorned and measured just 5.8 by 3.6 metres.

When the statue – a plain plaster model – was in situ and the chapel complete, Sr Concepta invited her cousin Shaun Glenville and his wife Dorothy Ward to visit the newly named Oratory of the Sacred Heart. Glenville was a music hall and pantomime star and when he saw the undecorated church, he bluntly exclaimed: 'It looks like a stable in Connemara.'

He suggested that his gifted cousin paint the walls and promised he and his wife would run a series of concerts to fund it. Acting as well as art was in the Lynch family. Shaun's mother and Sr Concepta's aunt, Mary Browne (*née* Lynch), had managed the Mechanics' Theatre, a theatre and music hall that had been on the site of the newly openly Abbey Theatre in Dublin. Her son Shaun followed her into the theatre and now he and his wife were a roaring success, appearing in pantomimes and comedies as far afield as New York and Birmingham.

Sr Concepta said she would think about her cousin's suggestion. That night she had an elaborate dream in which she saw the oratory alight with colours. It was a 'harmony of wonder' according to Dr Little's vivid account, which describes how she woke up the following day convinced of her vocation to illuminate the chapel. She didn't have to canvass support because the Mother Superior had always intended to ask her to paint the alcove behind the statue. She was so pleased with the results that she asked for the entire church to be decorated.

Sr Concepta's exceptional gift as an artist had been carefully nurtured since early childhood. She was born Lily Lynch in 1874 to Mary and Thomas Joseph Lynch and was their only child. Her father was a craftsman and illustrator whose original work earned him the title 'the King of Celtic Revival art'. Lily's mother died when she was ten and her father took her under his wing, teaching her the 'Lynch method', the artistic code he developed at the end of the nineteenth century. At just 15, Lily Lynch was as skilful a calligraphist and illuminator as the old master himself.

There are tantalising glimpses into life in those early days in the mementos Lily kept in a little leather-covered trinket box she made herself. She had lantern slides made of family photographs and the newspaper clippings that lavished praise on her father's work, most notably the detailed illuminated addresses – or speeches – that were presented to church leaders and public dignitaries.

In 1880 the illustrated vellum address Thomas J Lynch completed for Cardinal Newman was praised as 'a work of great interest, beauty and merit' in the prestigious *Art Journal*. His daughter kept a copy of the article that could, a few decades later, describe her own work:

> There are borders of interlacing riband-work and scrolls, quaint serpents and birds, fantastic groups of most conventional animals and scroll-work, all studies after the fashion of the Book of Kells, the Gospel of Mac-Regol, that of St Chad, the Book of Durham, etc. The ornamentation has been executed in rich colouring, picked out with gold and silver.

It went on to say that Thomas J Lynch's work had put him among the long list of Irish artists who took 'high place among foremost men of the age'.

Another article in her box of memories recalls what must have been a cause for great celebration in the family. On 5 February 1881, 'The Irishman' column in *The Irish Times* reported that 30 of Thomas J Lynch's friends gave a banquet in his honour at the Gresham Hotel. His daughter even kept a copy of the menu, which offered mock turtle soup, turbot with lobster sauce, Limerick ham and Swiss pudding or wine jelly.

Given the lavish menu, there was a certain irony: the artistic work they were celebrating was done for the Duchess of Marlborough in recognition of her charity work after the Famine of 1879. The Duchess had established a fund to give food, fuel and clothing to the worst affected. To thank her, Thomas Lynch was commissioned to illustrate the borders of a 60-page address, which he presented to her in London. The 'intricate devices and unrivalled colours produced on every page' were singled out for mention. The Duchess herself said the work reflected the art treasures that Ireland had inherited from her ancient masters.

That rich ancient tradition was inherent in all of Thomas J Lynch's work. He passed on his famed Lynch method technique to his daughter but, more than that, instilled in her an appreciation of the earliest Celtic art that stayed with her all her life.

Lily was just 16 years old when her father died. She left school at the Dominican Convent in Dun Laoghaire and took over the running of the family art business at 31 Grafton Street in Dublin city centre. She proved to be a very able business-woman and, according to one account, 'soon became the inspiration of even her father's experienced employees'. She had established herself as an artist in the creative sense, but she also showed a flair for the art of business.

In the six years that she ran the family business, she also earned a reputation as a musician. Her friends said she played the piano and sang with the sweetest voice. She composed her own music and wrote lyrics, often religious in nature. It was not entirely surprising then that she decided to return to her old school in Dun Laoghaire, but this time as a Dominican nun. It has been suggested that a fire in the family business was what finally prompted her to act on her vocation – and that may well be so – but Lily Lynch was a deeply spiritual woman and the decision to enter an enclosed convent was not completely unanticipated.

On 3 July 1896 Lily Lynch entered the Dominican Order at St Mary's Convent at her old alma mater in Dun Laoghaire and took the name Sr Concepta. Her talents were soon recognised and she was appointed art mistress. She is remembered as an innovative and precise teacher who taught art and music. At primary level she taught boys and they gathered around her as she played the piano. She taught her pupils the words of songs, which they played on the kazoo – all 90 of them. Two of those pupils recalled, as elderly men, her lively lessons and said her bright eyes made them forget their bare feet.

She played the cello and gave piano and violin lessons. She also produced plays and concerts, involving her pupils in each part of the process. She kept the programme of one of those productions, a one-act play performed on St Patrick's Day depicting the school in Iona on the day before St Colmcille died. 'The costumes, all hand-painted in Celtic design were very pretty and striking, and the scenery was very effective,' it noted.

The 12-pupil cast, all girls, was led by Molly Daly who played Colmcille. Maureen Kelly played Brendan, a student monk – she would later pass paint to Sr Concepta when she was lying on a plank, placed across two ladders, painting the oratory ceiling. Her teacher fondly nicknamed Maureen 'Little Flower', a reference to her own great devotion to St Thérèse of Lisieux. Sr Concepta was one of the first in Ireland to venerate the saint.

It was as an art teacher, however, that she is best remembered. She carefully smoothed out her detailed teaching notes into large sheets and covered them in plastic. Materials were scarce and she made use of everything. Classes began with a series of finger exercises to help keep hands and arms supple. Sr Concepta also asked her students to pay particular attention to the mind, keeping it busy at all times so that they could build up the pattern they were drawing, before applying colour.

Some of her instructions sound stern, made more so by her categoric underlining. In one lesson, for instance, she wrote:

'They get <u>no help</u> no matter what mistakes are made. They are taught to <u>correct</u> with <u>brush</u> in <u>black</u> paint, leaving the wrong pencil line to be seen so that they <u>see</u> how they <u>are progressing</u> later on when they look back ...'

Pupils, however, remember her as a kind and patient woman who compared painting to stroking a cat. She told her charges to make strong, slow brushstrokes as if caressing a pet. 'Poor pussy,' she would repeat, mimicking how it was to be done.

Mary O'Rourke, who was in her art class from 1919 to 1921, remembers her as a shy, sensitive woman who liked fun and jokes:

> She gave us singing lessons and told me to whistle as it would be good for my voice but, for goodness sake, don't let the older nuns hear you. ... She was very approachable and she would play the piano for us boarders if it was raining and we were not able to go out, and she would sing for us with that wonderful voice she had. She was a real contemplative and we would often see her walking in the grounds praying.

Other sisters recall seeing her in ecstasy in front of the statue of the Virgin Mary.

On free days, she played and sang opera arias with her close friend Sr Imelda Connery. 'We will play every note for the love of Jesus,' Connie, as Sr Imelda called her, used to say. She was also highly strung and hasty – but when she lost her temper she would always go to the door of whomever she thought she had offended and beg their pardon before bedtime.

In 1902 members of the wider local community got to see Sr Concepta's work when they were invited to sing Christmas carols around the convent crib. The nativity scene was conceived and made by Sr Concepta, who had fashioned an impressive set of life-sized figures from wood and papier mâché and dressed them in Eastern costumes.

Nearly two decades later, she was still bringing her creativity to her full-time teaching role but had started to spend all of her spare time painting the oratory. She started behind the altar where she painted golden arcades to frame the showpiece statue of the Sacred Heart. Her ingenious use of gold leaf gave the impression that it was backlit. Every square inch of the altar was illuminated in a design that owed more to Byzantine influences than Celtic, though it was clear that she had conceived the design of the oratory as a whole.

Moving away from the altar, her work became so gradually Celtic that the design stands as a perfect whole – 'an outstanding achievement', according to early Irish art scholar Etienne Rynne.

She achieved the effect of a perfect whole through her ingenious use of the stencils she made from whatever material was at hand – blackout curtains or spare rolls of paper. She used them as templates to lightly map her designs on the walls, working freehand to complete them. She used each stencil several times, but in different ways so that features on one wall found a mirror image on the opposite wall.

One pupil remembers her sitting in the hall at breaktime, cutting stencils from a roll of paper with a small scissors while the convent cat Bobbins sat at her feet. She asked fellow teacher Mrs Glynn to buy ordinary house paint in nearby Glasthule. The shop owner was delighted with the regular orders because Sr Concepta wanted bright, vivid colours rather than the buff and green that were the big sellers in 1920s Ireland.

She used those vivid colours to paint magnificent designs on the walls, frieze and entrance – interlacing serpents, fantastical creatures, peacocks with open mouths and a dragon that looks like one on the Cross of Cong, the exquisite relic made to house the remains of the true cross said to have come to Ireland in the twelfth century. She painted two magnificent red pelicans over the oratory's entrance, reminiscent of her father's business logo.

'Her work,' wrote Etienne Rynne, 'is ever *mouvementé* [dynamic], vibrant with life: her birds squawk, bite and even dance, her serpents wriggle and knot themselves as do her quadrupeds'. As she inched her way up the plastered walls, she became bolder, brighter and more innovative, remarks artist and oratory guide Jo Callanan: 'It's almost as if she got colours later on that she did not have in the beginning. As you go higher, her style is more flowy, almost Art Nouveau. Her birds are happier – singing rather than biting.' She painted blues and yellows next to one another – seen from a distance, it looks almost impressionistic. She also used an astonishing array of designs: a Chinese-looking dragon, a Maltese cross to mark the Eucharistic Congress of 1932, a fleur-de-lys, which was a nod to the war in France, and even, at a certain angle, something that resembles a hippopotamus with flared nostrils.

The breadth of her imagination is remarkable, but it was the painstaking attention to detail that particularly impressed members of her community. Sr Concepta once asked a visitor, Sr Julianna Tutty: 'Do you see this little square? It took me the last two hours to put in the dots.' Sr Julianna later remarked, 'For such a great artist, there was a great simplicity about her.'

Once she took up her brush, time stood still. She worked on into the early evening, totally engaged until it was time for supper. As she made her way to the refectory, the pungent smell of paint would herald her arrival to her fellow sisters.

That lead-based paint would eventually take a toll on her health: she spent hours every day inhaling its poisonous fumes. She was already 42 when she began to paint the oratory and the years perched on scaffolding weighed heavily as she became older. Her students helped, passing up paint to her when she was lying on her back painting a high wall or a section of ceiling. She allowed some of them to assist her in a more practical way, showing them how to paint the dots that are a recurring feature in several motifs. One pupil, Bunty Phibbs, later told how she had completed a section of dots just inside the door.

Meanwhile, Sr Concepta's cousins, Shaun Glenville and Dorothy Ward, continued to raise money, which helped pay for the seven stained-glass windows commissioned from the Harry Clarke studio. Her parents are represented in one window and her cousins in another. It might have struck her as incongruous that the money for this quiet place of reflection came from a flamboyant theatrical duo who made their name in panto. Her cousin Shaun played the leading dame in more than 40 pantomimes while Dorothy performed into her sixties, although she never revealed her age. When asked about it while playing Dick Whittington, she said: 'I want audiences to enjoy the pantomime, not to wonder if I've got my own teeth!'

Their artistic expression might have been public and boisterous yet Sr Concepta's cousins had deep admiration for her solitary, spiritual work. The exceptional character of that work was also valued by Sr Concepta's own community even if the chapel was sometimes used to provide shelter when the girls playing hockey nearby got rained off the pitch. Work continued throughout the late 1930s in spite of Sr Concepta's failing health. There are several accounts of her determination to keep going and how, at times, her brushstrokes were guided by her pupils and fellow sisters. For 11 of the 16 years she painted in the oratory, she suffered from breast cancer. She continued on until she became too ill and was confined to bed.

Just before she died, her beloved student Maureen Kelly had her first child. Sr Imelda snuck the baby into the convent under her scapular so that Sr Concepta could see him. She prayed the little boy would become a priest – and many years later he did. Fr Myles Healy, at Blackrock College in Dublin, recalls the story with great fondness and says his mother spoke often of her former teacher. He says Sr Concepta was remarkable to do what she did, given the convent's strict routine and the air of suspicion that still surrounded artists at the time. The nuns later said that Sr Concepta held on to see the little boy come into the world before she died, aged 62, with the community gathered around her bed.

The chapel was nearly complete; the ceiling had been mapped out and was partially painted. The community considered finishing it but decided against it. The door closed on the little chapel and it was all but forgotten until a new generation of pupils 'rediscovered' Sr Concepta's quiet genius when they were looking for a subject to photograph for the camera club set up by Sr Theodore in 1960.

She had suggested the oratory and the girls, who thought it was a mortuary chapel for the nuns, were awestruck by what they found. They photographed every detail, tape-recorded Sr Concepta's life story and presented the findings as their annual lecture to the club. Mass was celebrated in the chapel in 1960 for the first time in 25 years and, thanks to the camera club, Sr Concepta's work was once again in the public eye.

Three decades later, her work again came into the public consciousness. The Dominican nuns sold the convent and when plans were unveiled to build a £20m retail development, the fate of this unique vestige of Celtic Revival art was uncertain. A group of artists moved into the vacated convent and acted as caretakers. They could see the exceptional value of the oratory and one of the local artists, Veronica Heywood, launched a campaign to preserve it. She succeeded in rallying widespread support, enlisting the then Minister for Arts, Culture and the Gaeltacht, future President Michael D Higgins and even the supermarket developers.

In 1995, with Sr Frances Lally and photographer Edward Sweeney, Veronica prepared an application – complete with stunning images and beautiful calligraphy – and sent it to the EU to try to secure heritage funding. She argued: 'There is lots of Irish literature and poetry from the years of the Celtic Revival. But this is the only standing monument to the visual arts from that period. It's unique.'

The following year, the EU granted a restoration fund of £100,000 and the owners of the site, Monarch Properties, donated the oratory to the Office of Public Works (OPW). The little chapel is now encased in an OPW-built protective shell so that the visitor has to pass through two buildings to get to the gem inside. The experience, one observer wrote, is akin to unwrapping the prize in a game of pass the parcel.

Sr Concepta's singular achievement will be 100 years old in 2020, yet the woman and her work are still not widely known. Had she continued to work in her father's studio, it's likely that the lay woman, Lily Lynch, would have made as much of an impression as other women artists working at the time, such as stained-glass artist Evie Hone and enameller Mia Cranwill. Of course, Sr Concepta worked within the confines of an enclosed convent so she was cut off from a larger audience. The oratory is not her only work, but it is her best known. She illustrated chant books and poems as well as a series of linen rolls that are almost Moorish in design.

Her artistic style was considered traditional at a time when artists were embracing modernist ideas, although art historian and writer Síghle Bhreathnach-Lynch argues that the decoration of the oratory was radical in its own way: 'Sr Concepta imaginatively adapted the art of manuscript illumination, most unusually, to wall painting using an entirely new medium, ordinary household paint. The results are astonishingly beautiful and clearly point to an impressive creative talent.'

Thanks to the work of the Dominican sisters and other artists such as Veronica Heywood proof of her impressive creative talent survives. In 1992 the sisters donated a large body of Sr Concepta's work to the National Gallery of Ireland. 'Since our motto is "to give to others the fruit of our contemplation" we feel happy that this valuable work will now be in safe keeping and readily available to the public,' Prioress Sr Breeda Hourigan and Janitor of the Oratory Sr Frances Lally wrote in a letter to the gallery.

One hundred years on, the fruits of Sr Concepta's 16-year contemplation at the oratory have also been given to others. The chapel is open to the public yet it is still referred to as a hidden gem. Perhaps in its centenary year, this 'late flower of the Celtic Revival', as Jeanne Sheehy called it, will finally be allowed to come out of hiding.

The Overend sisters

FARMERS, CHARITY WORKERS AND
MOTORING ENTHUSIASTS
(LETITIA OVEREND 1880–1977)
(NAOMI OVEREND 1900–1993)

*I have got two parking fines and one parking summons from
Dundrum and my sister arrived just in time to prevent her
Rolls being towed away the other day by Corporation men.*

Naomi Overend, 1973

In March 1938 Naomi Overend watched as German troops poured into the Austrian skiing village of Kitzbühel, vaguely aware that she was witnessing the annexation of Austria into Nazi Germany in what became known as the *Anschluss*. She took several pictures and wrote home to tell her mother and sister not to fret; she had been assured there was no risk of any disturbances even though there were soldiers everywhere and the streets were full of leaflets and Nazi flags. When it became clearer what was happening, she said it was amazing to see people quietly going about their business when the country had just 'changed hands'.

'Don't be uneasy,' she wrote to 'dear Mogs' [her nickname for her mother]. 'It is quite alright and everything just as usual. They even held a slalom race this morning [in] the middle of it all! So if we are not wanted back in a hurry we will stay on here while the snow lasts. Very fondly written on a too high table.' Yet despite the jaunty tone, her sister Letitia noted in her diary that she was relieved when Naomi finally arrived home.

Both sisters had already experienced war – if at a relatively safe distance. When World War I broke out, Letitia Overend signed up to volunteer at the War Hospital Supply depot on Merrion Square in Dublin city. She had joined the St John Ambulance Brigade the year before and now worked daily helping to send supplies to hospitals in Ireland, Britain, France and Belgium. Sometimes she brought Naomi, 20 years her junior, into the depot where she made tea for the workers.

Meanwhile, their mother, Lily Overend, set up a work guild at home in Airfield House in Dundrum, making bandages and clothing to send to the front. In turn, the soldiers who received the welcome 'parcels of comfort' sent moving thank-you letters and postcards back to her. In one, JA MacMunn wrote that an Irish soldier 'went into raptures over a shirt when he saw "Irish Manufacture" printed on the collar'.

Another soldier, Arthur Verschoyle, who described his whereabouts as 'in the field', gave a more chilling insight into the reality of combat. He told Mrs Overend her package arrived just as they left an awful trench where they had been up to their thighs in mud and water. He said he had been hit by a piece of shell – 'just a scratch' – from a German artillery, which was more active than normal and 'as usual, unfortunately accurate'. Lily later wrote on the back of his letter: 'From Arthur Verschoyle written in France 1915 shortly before he was killed.'

Lily also sent parcels to her cousin Humphrey Butler who served in France with the 1st Royal Irish Rifles. In November 1915 he wrote to thank her for her parcel and said he was living about 400 yards behind the front line and he had to 'toil up to the fire trench several times a day'. 'The Boshes', he continued, shelled them every day and 'fired an odd round now and then just to let us know they are thinking of us'. The Germans also shouted at them in English and German, asking: 'Will you have a Woodbine?'

If the Overends did what they could to help soldiers fighting along the Western Front, they also did much to help people in need nearer to home. Charity and charitable causes were an intrinsic part of everyday life at the family home in Airfield. The Victorian cottage with its eight acres of prime farmland was initially intended to be a summer retreat but when Lily and the couple's two daughters, Letitia (14) and baby Constance, moved there in March 1894, they loved it so much they eventually gave up their city-centre home at 12 Ely Place. Lily and Letitia immediately embraced the outdoors and before long they were farming on a small scale, producing milk and eggs.

Lily's mother captured a sense of the bucolic charm when she wrote that it must have been a sight to watch Tot [Letitia's nickname] and the cow walking together. She wished the family and its 'two dear chicks' many happy years there, but added she was sorry to hear the baby was unwell and hoped the fresh air would help. The fresh air, however, did not help. Constance Overend died of meningitis in September 1895, just days before her first birthday.

The loss was incalculable. Lily Overend was already campaigning to improve healthcare for women and children but the death of her own baby can only have sharpened her resolve. The arrival of a third daughter five years later, when Lily was 46, came as an unexpected surprise. Naomi's birth in 1900 was celebrated by a large extended family who were regular visitors to Airfield. It was a happy, bustling place, to judge from surviving correspondence. Trevor and Lily were devoted to each other – though he seems to have been the romantic one, as his letters show. In one, he wrote: 'I don't care a pinch or snuff for any girl in the world but yourself … They say my lovely Lily that out of sight means out of my mind – but my beloved I am always thinking of you.'

The couple later sent sweet illustrated letters to their daughters from various holiday destinations. When Letitia was eight, her mother's letter included a sketch of Trevor battling a mosquito on a lake in Switzerland. When they reached Paris, she sent another of the couple at breakfast in the Grand Hôtel eating French bread which, she said, was 'long like poles'. The first letter Trevor wrote to Naomi ('My dearest Sweetest Peepsie'), when she was two, gives an insight into how Airfield House was developing as a farm. He asked about 'Bugley and Jersey and Suckey and Bon', with each name drawn inside an animal.

Lily Overend had started to develop the farm. She invested in the award-winning Dromartin Jersey herd, and famously named them after characters in Gilbert and Sullivan operas. She also went about expanding the acreage of rich farmland, wisely buying any neighbouring properties that came on the market. She sold produce to local creameries and traders but also donated milk and eggs to local children suffering from rickets, the bone condition caused by lack of vitamin D.

She set up a local branch of the Children's League of Pity and involved her younger daughter in fundraising efforts. When she was nine, Naomi raised money at her first garden fête at Airfield House; for her efforts she was presented with a certificate in remembrance of the 'sad and suffering children' she had helped. Lily instilled a sense of duty in both her children and taught them to help those less fortunate than themselves, something they did with vigour for the rest of their lives.

They might be remembered as the well-to-do sisters who drove a Rolls-Royce to the local butcher in the south Dublin suburb of Dundrum, but Letitia and Naomi Overend's wealth was recent. Their father Trevor was a solicitor. His grandfather had been a grain merchant and his father moved to Dublin to find a position. Lily Butler, meanwhile, was descended from the earls of Ormond, but the family estate at Broomville in Co. Carlow was no longer a going concern. Lily lived with her sister and mother in a rented house in Dublin before she married Trevor Overend.

Lily and Trevor Overend were well-off, no doubt, but in 1913 their eldest daughter Letitia Overend became financially independent in her own right. Her Uncle Tommy died and left the largest part of his considerable estate to her. Like his elder brother, Tommy had made his own fortune. He borrowed money to travel to India but went on to become a successful stockbroker, co-founding the Calcutta Stock Exchange. He kept close ties with Ireland and wrote regularly to his nieces Tot [Letitia] and Mick [Naomi], sending them unusual gifts. One New Year, he sent Letitia a present of a silver Burmese buckle. When his health failed, he went to live in London and Letitia visited him there just before he died in March. Two months later she noted in her diary: 'Spent the rest of the day unpacking & sorting Uncle Tommy's things. Very painful.'

1913 would prove a very significant year in Letitia's life as it also marked the beginning of her lifelong involvement with the St John Ambulance Brigade. During World War I she worked full-time – and voluntarily – for the war effort. When it was over, she would devote the rest of her life to the Brigade's service. In recognition, she received its highest honour – Dame of Justice – and when she was also conferred with an honorary degree from Trinity College Dublin decades later, she joked: 'I must have got [both awards] for eating and drinking.' Naomi was not in the Brigade but she sometimes acted as a patient for training purposes – 'and she was a very mischievous one' her sister once quipped to an *Irish Times* reporter.

Had she been in Dublin during the Easter Rising in 1916, Letitia would certainly have been with the members of the Brigade who tended the wounded on both sides of the conflict – soldiers and rebels – and helped civilians caught in the fighting. As it turned out, she was away on holiday with her family in Co. Down but she followed what was happening closely. On 25 April she noted in her diary: 'News of very serious trouble with Sinn Feinners in Dublin. The bank of Ireland reported taken. Stephen's green [trenched] & held by rebels. Grafton St [barricaded] & barbed wire up street-fighting in Dame & Sackville St. Said to be the G.P.O taken & set on fire – Sackville St. taken.'

—

Meanwhile, in Dublin, Letitia's Aunt Fanny tried to leave her home in Sandymount Avenue to check on the Overends in Airfield but couldn't get through. In any case, they weren't there. She noted in her diary: 'Everyone more or less in terror ... 7 soldiers camped in our front garden – we gave them tea etc & coffee & eggs – at night C. gave them cigars and cigarettes.'

When Letitia returned to Dublin, she continued to work at the war depot in the city. 'Records show that she contributed more hours to the cause than any of her co-volunteers often walking back to Dundrum after a long-day's work,' according to Bernadette Larkin, former head of education at Airfield. 'She was offered an OBE from the King in recognition of her work. She refused, on the grounds that "it would be impossible that everyone who did good work during the War can be recognised".'

Naomi was also involved in charity and helped her mother establish the Women's National Health Association, which set up the city's first pasteurised milk depot. She was also involved in the Blind Asylum and supported the jubilee nurses – the early district nurses who delivered care to people in their own homes in an attempt to eradicate some of the epidemics of the time, such as tuberculosis (TB), typhus, typhoid, diphtheria and polio. Naomi organised countless fundraising events and later became president of the Dundrum and Ballinteer District Nursing Association.

Both sisters knew Dr Ella Webb, a pioneering paediatrician awarded an MBE for her work during the 1916 Rising when she cycled through the city tending to the wounded from all sides of the conflict. In the early 1920s they collaborated to establish the Children's Sunshine Home to tackle high infant mortality rates and help children in the city slums disabled by rickets.

The new centre opened in Stillorgan in Dublin in 1924. *The Irish Times* reported it would help its patients by giving them fresh air and sunshine as well as a 'sufficiency of ordinary nutritive food'. The article continued: 'About the middle of August the first party of little patients will be in residence, the forerunners of many thousands who, it is hoped, will return straight and sound to their homes. It has been proved that rickets never recur in children when cured by this method.'

The paper also said the opening of the home was made possible by a gift of £5000 from 'a lady who will not permit her name to made public'. That lady was Letitia Overend. Dr Webb later wrote to Letitia saying the success of the project was entirely down to her. '[It is] one of the very few things of permanent value that I have accomplished in a life that has lasted perilously nearly half a century!' The home operated for several decades and, in 2011, the LauraLynn Children's Hospice opened on the same site.

—

Daily life for Letitia and Naomi Overend was filled with a variety of activities: fundraising and charity events, golfing, gardening, family gatherings, travel, services at their local Church of Ireland, Taney parish – and, of course, driving.

The sisters' interest in motoring is legendary and they received numerous awards for their vintage cars and attended countless vintage car rallies. Their mother had been interested in cars too but Letitia's fascination was first awakened in 1903 when 1500 cars arrived for the Irish Gordon Bennett Cup Race, the first international motor race to be held in Ireland.

In a country that had only about 300 cars on its roads at the time, it was quite an event. In the decades that followed Letitia and Naomi became motoring enthusiasts of such note that, on the 70th anniversary of that historic race, they were made honorary life members of the Irish Veteran and Vintage Car Club – the highest honour the organisation could bestow.

In 1927 Letitia bought a blue Rolls-Royce for £1700 and the car never gave her a day's bother in 50 years. She famously serviced the car herself, a skill she acquired at the Rolls-Royce school in London. 'I'm not a mechanic,' she told Averill Douglas in an *Irish Times* interview in 1973, 'just a good house maid.'

She wasn't keen on the model when she saw it first, though. 'My mother was there at the time and she said, "I don't approve of any other car but a Rolls; you must take that." "Oh but," I said, "I think that would be a very big undertaking and I don't think I will at present." She said: "It's that or nothing."'

Letitia certainly came around and, years later, said she wouldn't have a modern car for anything: 'They're always getting crocked up. As I am so lucky to have a car of this vintage, I wouldn't change it. I don't like the designs of modern cars. I don't like anything about them.'

Naomi drove a 1936 Austin Tickford and was an equally keen motoring enthusiast. The cars gave both women a freedom that was unusual at the time and they used it, travelling to attend vintage rallies but also to visit family and to explore the country. Letitia was particularly impressed by a visit to Skellig Michael, the early Christian monastic settlement off the coast of Co. Kerry. She said it was her 'most exciting excursion ever taken' and sketched the lighthouse and the beehive huts that were once home to monks in the eighth century.

They went much further afield too. Naomi was a keen skier and while she had to abandon the sport during World War II, she returned when it was over and skied in Austria into her early sixties. They both made trips lasting weeks, even months, to Europe, India, America and Australia. In 1935 Letitia went on a world tour with the British Medical Association and sent a series of letters home describing each stage. She was charmed by the military band that greeted them on the pier at Honolulu in Hawaii, the spectacular Jenolan Caves in Australia, and the police escort through the streets of New York: 'We drove on against all traffic lights, and without one halt! It was the most marvellous drive I ever had.'

When the sisters were at home, they kept equally busy. In 1932, for example, Letitia was working with the St John Ambulance Brigade at the International Eucharistic Congress. She said she enjoyed every minute, working from 9 am to 2 am for six days straight. The Congress, a demonstration of global Catholicism, generated huge public interest and took place over five days in June. Historian Rory O'Dwyer noted:

Visiting journalists and commentators, including the well-known Catholic intellectual G. K. Chesterton, were struck by the efforts of Dublin people, most especially the impoverished tenement-dwellers, to embellish their streets and laneways with bunting, festoons, banners, garlands, floral arrangements, grottos, shrines and various other forms of religious decoration.

Airfield House continued to be a working farm and the centre of the sisters' ongoing charity work. It also hosted many visitors including the Yeats sisters, Lily and Elizabeth, known as the 'Cuala girls' after the printing press they established to support the Celtic Revival movement.

The Overend sisters saw a new Ireland emerge and embraced many of the changes that came with it. Letitia, for instance, was in awe when she witnessed Dr Bethel Solomons perform a Caesarean section in 1943. 'Marvellously interesting such skill & such an atmosphere of quietness,' she wrote in her diary. However, they also held firm to what they valued as the world around them changed beyond recognition.

As the twentieth century progressed, their farm was literally engulfed by burgeoning suburbs and property developers were putting increasing pressure on them to sell their farmland oasis. The Overend sisters were not for turning, as was made gloriously clear in a wonderful interview they gave to Jim Farrelly in the *Evening Press* in March 1973. The article began: 'The magic crinkle of one million crisp pound notes cannot spellbind the Overend sisters of Dundrum into changing their life-style ... And today the pair, Laetitia and Naomi, have issued a stern warning to speculators and developers that their cherished Jersey cow[s] and nineteenth-century home are not for sale at any price.'

Developers wanted to turn the farm into a luxury housing development as demand for housing increased and the building of apartments gathered pace in the 1970s. The Overends, however, stood firm, saying they wouldn't even sell as much as half an acre.

'Where would one go with one million pounds?' Naomi mused. 'It would be difficult to find a happier haunt than this if one searched the world. Selling our farm would cause too much trouble. It would be awkward and inconvenient.' She went on to criticise the pace and the character of development: 'Houses of character were pulled down to make way for shopping centres. A fight should have been made that at least the village itself remained intact ... More [houses] are to be demolished to make way for a new office block. The place has changed so much that friends, when driving to our home, cannot find where we live.'

Letitia said a lot of their old friends had gone – she hardly recognised a face at Sunday service and it was difficult to get her old Rolls out of the front gate with the constant stream of traffic. The days when they used to pull up to the kerb outside the local shops, get what they wanted and engage in a little small talk were long gone, as Naomi opined: 'I have got two parking fines and one parking summons from Dundrum and my sister arrived just in time to prevent her Rolls being towed away the other day by Corporation men.'

Yet they were still farming, tending a herd of 33 Jersey cattle and earning a modest income by selling milk locally. They did most of the work themselves even though they employed a farm manager. They also kept the gardens and opened the estate to children who visited for school projects. They said the children of the new Dundrumites were 'dreadfully polite and courteous' even if they did ask a lot of questions. 'They submit us to police-like interrogation: how old are we [their ages were a sealed book], how many staff have we, how much do we earn, they ask without batting an eyelid. They are so enthusiastic that it is difficult to turn them away, but we get too many of them,' Naomi said.

Letitia was still heavily involved in the church and the St John Ambulance Brigade while Naomi was interested in theatrical productions in the Church of Ireland parochial hall: 'Our house has always been a source for props for the local plays. We are always called upon to supply churns, or farmyard equipment or period dresses. I like to help out behind the stage.'

Neither sister married and when Letitia Overend died in 1977, she left the estate in trust. Naomi remained on and held out against the developers who continued to try to convince her to sell. But, as her former tenant Barbara Carney recalls, she had a will of iron and was adamant that the farm and land were not for sale. Barbara and her husband rented the lodge in Airfield from 1985 to the mid-nineties. Naomi Overend asked for a reference before they moved in – 'she was very particular about who lived there' – but the rent was just £50 a month, in comparison to the £180 they had been asked to pay for a flat on the open market. The house had no mod cons, but it was an idyllic life. The sisters had been far ahead of their time in many ways, but by the time the Carneys moved into Airfield, it was like stepping back in time. It was an absolute oasis of calm, Barbara says.

She remembers Naomi Overend as a very frugal, disciplined woman who ate her meals at the end of a large table in the kitchen with her housekeeper/live-in companion, Mrs O'Brien. One Christmas Barbara gave her a box of chocolates after they had been invited for a sherry in the drawing room by a big open fire. 'She would eat just one every night after dinner until the box was gone. We are still very nostalgic about our time there.'

Naomi died in 1993, leaving Airfield in trust to the people of Ireland so that they might enjoy a little piece of the countryside in the middle of Dublin. In 1995 the house's period furniture was all sold at auction, fetching £1.3m, twice the pre-sale estimate. The house and the estate, however, remained intact. Or almost. Two fields were sold during the boom for €19m but the trust was able to buy them back for half the price in 2012, and the profit helped to part fund a €11m redevelopment in 2014.

While Letitia and Naomi Overend would be shocked at the pace of development in the area, Genevieve Whitfield, heritage and events manager at Airfield, thinks they would be pleased to see how the estate has adapted to a new millennium: 'They were really practical women who did not stand on ceremony and were not afraid to get their own hands dirty. Their foresight was amazing – they did not stand still. I think they would be pleased to see how Airfield is now.'

Today Airfield Trust welcomes over 200,000 visitors a year to its urban farm in the centre of Dublin. Its guiding principles of education and innovation go a long way to keeping the spirit of two remarkable sisters alive.

Mabel Colhoun

PIONEERING ARCHAEOLOGIST, ARTIST, PHOTOGRAPHER AND TEACHER
(1905–1992)

One evening [during World War II] *she was stopped by an army patrol on the quay and the soldier said to her, 'Do you realise, madam, that you don't have a rear red tail light?' And Mabel looked at him as only Mabel could and said, 'Do I look like the kind of lady to be associated with a red light?'*

Roy Hamilton, broadcaster and friend

On Saturday mornings Mabel Colhoun packed a leather satchel with measuring tape, magnifying glass, field books, T-square, sketch sheets, camera and travelling picnic basket and set off from her home in Derry city to explore the archaeology and heritage of the Inishowen peninsula. She cycled in all weathers – and in wartime – often covering distances of more than 60 miles a day as she bumped down dirt tracks and lanes to meticulously chart a range of archaeological monuments and record what local people had to say about them.

From the late 1930s to 1970 she systematically recorded thousands of archaeological monuments, some of them previously unknown. That in itself was a first: her findings would later be compiled into the region's first comprehensive archaeological survey. But Mabel Colhoun was a pioneer in another respect: she was also one of the first archaeologists to put people into the landscape. She sought out the stories associated with the monuments and wrote them down, preserving traditions and folklore that would be otherwise lost to us.

One of those stories offered a possible clue when four silver Viking arm rings were discovered at a ringfort in Roosky, Donegal, in 1966. Two decades earlier, Mabel had recorded the local belief that 'a Dane' had been buried there. Was her story, captured in local lore like an insect in amber, just a coincidence or, as archaeologist Brian Lacey wonders: 'Had Mabel recorded a genuine folk memory that had survived a thousand years?'

'She was passionate about finding the past, bringing it into the present and preserving it for the future,' says Denise Henry, an archaeologist also steeped in the heritage of the Inishowen peninsula and one who has done much to bring Mabel's contribution to the attention of a new generation. 'What Mabel did was remarkable,' she says, continuing:

> She was uncompromising and driven and left a path where there had been none, so that people might follow. On a local scale, her research prompted people to learn more about their own heritage and, on a national scale, she contributed to the development of archaeology as a discipline and showed that women could be a vital part of it.

Yet Mabel was not a professional archaeologist, although it is not accurate to say that she was an amateur either – she was painstaking and methodical in her research. She was, however, a part-time practitioner. After spending her spare time criss-crossing the Inishowen peninsula, she was back in school on Monday morning teaching her beloved children.

She made a significant and lasting contribution in the field of education too. Mabel was an early advocate of nursery education and thanks to her Froebel training believed children should be at the centre of activity-based learning. In 1935 she set up a preparatory school in her own home. The following year she got a job at the Londonderry High School and went on to become its first principal.

Her former pupils – her only niece Kyleen Clarke among them – recall a brilliant and imaginative teacher who was a gifted artist and keen naturalist. Kyleen remembers her aunt with exceptional fondness and recalls how she got her out of trouble when she once chalked the names of birds on the inside of her parents' newly painted garage. 'My aunt urged my parents not to scold but to encourage a developing interest in bird life,' Kyleen recalls.

Mabel had a lifelong interest in nature and her letters reveal her continual sense of wonder at the natural world. They show her sense of humour too. In one letter, she described chancing across two 'courting hedgehogs' at her home in Deanfield, Derry city, and capturing the moment in two coloured slides. She wrote: 'I found out what the grunting was about, rushed back into the house for my camera, took 2 quite close-up flash-light photos & they took no notice!' She was 83 years old when she wrote that and she remained active and involved until shortly before her death in 1992.

She led an extraordinarily full and eventful life not least because she lived through every decade of the twentieth century, witnessing much of its political turbulence. She saw soldiers going off to fight in World War I, experienced partition in Ireland in the 1920s, the outbreak of World War II in 1939 and, three decades later, the Troubles in Northern Ireland. None of it, however, stopped her pursuing not just one career, but several. She was a reforming educationalist, a gifted artist, a photographer, a naturalist and a pioneering archaeologist.

Mabel Remington Colhoun had talent – and endless dedication – but she was also lucky enough to have been given the educational opportunities to capitalise on her potential. She was born on 2 November 1905 into a wealthy Protestant and Methodist family, the second child of John Colhoun and Elizabeth Gordon. Her only sibling, brother John (Jack), was born two years earlier. Her grandfather Robert Colhoun was from Malin Head and had moved to Derry/Londonderry in the late 1800s where he and his son John worked as successful building contractors. They restored many significant buildings in the city, including the nineteenth-century Guildhall.

From an early age, Mabel was influenced by her mother's interest in heritage and took an interest in the environment around her. When her family built a house in Deanfield on the Waterside, she designed a remarkable bay-style window for her bedroom to make the most of the view of the River Foyle and its bridges. She fostered many interests – in sport, heritage and art, to name a few – during her years at school and had the opportunity to go to third level when she finished at St Lurach's College in 1922. From there she attended the independent Queenswood School just outside London and, from

1924 to 1927, studied at the Froebel College in Roehampton, where she learned the progressive teaching methods she would later introduce at home.

Most of her surviving letters from that time are full of cheery news and generous good wishes to family members but one, written in February 1927 and addressed to 'My dear Elsie', shows that Mabel was struggling with her health and a bout of depression. She confided to her friend that she was under strain and was finding it hard to sleep but dismisses her woes – 'that's enough!' – and entreats her friend not to say anything to her family: 'Still on no account must the family know the real state of affairs & neither father nor mother (especially latter) to think of coming over. Now dear, I've said enough. I'm getting tired & I've still to write a cheery letter home.'

It was not a side that Mabel showed often; she was reserved but also generally assured and upbeat. Her family and friends speak of a woman with boundless energy who was interested and involved in everything. One of those lifelong interests was travel and after she graduated later that year, she went on a long trip to Egypt and Palestine with her maternal uncle, Charles Wesley Gordon, a man with a keen interest in archaeology. He had a specimen cabinet full of prehistoric artefacts, which he later bequeathed to her.

On that trip, she too began to assemble the beginnings of her own extensive collection. She brought home a first-century oil lamp from Jerusalem and a glass bangle from the Valley of the Kings in Egypt, which she kept along with photographs, sketches and paintings of her travels.

On her return, she got her first teaching job at Bournemouth but came home to Derry/Londonderry to be with her mother after her father died in 1932. She established a preparatory school in her own home on the Waterside, filling a room with tiny chairs and tables for her little charges. She was deeply interested in education for young children and believed that nursery education was vital, particularly in a city with a large proportion of mothers working outside the home. 'As if [all mothers] don't work,' she quipped when making that point while campaigning for increased facilities for children of nursery-school age. She continued to champion the cause of nursery schools when she got a job at Londonderry High School preparatory department.

Mabel Colhoun was the kind of woman who established associations – or, at the very least, joined them – so it is not surprising that she chaired the Londonderry Nursery School Association when it was founded in 1943 by the Londonderry High School Old Girls' Association. Three years later, the association opened a voluntary nursery school in an old church hall on Hawkins Street to help, among others, the children who found themselves locked out while waiting for their mothers to come home from working in the factories.

In the decade that followed, Mabel and her association fought against what she described as apathy and prejudice to try to convince the local authorities and general public of the need for nursery schools. They had considerable success. By 1957 there were 25 nursery schools and the local education authority had agreed to set up nursery classes in primary schools.

Mabel told the personal stories behind those statistics in her annual reports, which described, in a very tangible way, how nursery education supported parents and helped to produce 'happy useful children'. In 1958 she described the progress of some of those pupils – thoughtfully using pseudonyms to hide their identities:

> Margaret: One of a large family, whose mother was working part time, was an aggressive child, but soon learned to cooperate with other children.
>
> Jack was shy, lazy and cried very easily but soon learnt to stand on his own feet, and before long became a 'tom boy'.
>
> Rhoda lived in a room with her mother, her father was in prison. She was very "difficult" but became more content.
>
> Florence lived with her parents in one fourth floor room. Her mother had TB and the father was unemployed.
>
> Grace and Harry, whose parents were separated, were recommended to the Nursery School by the Welfare Authority.

Even when there were setbacks – the nursery school was stuck in an old, unsuitable building for more than a decade – the association celebrated its achievements. In the late 1950s, Mabel wrote: 'We have succeeded gloriously all these years in helping so many children, and we know it is the **spirit** in the community that counts, not the **building,** and the life and happy atmosphere in the Nursery School far outshines the old unsuitable building.'

Meanwhile, she worked full-time at the Londonderry High School where she encouraged her students to take an interest in the world around them. Her niece – and student – Kyleen Clarke remembers art classes and being praised when she added a touch of black to give perspective to her painting of lavender.

Teaching was in her blood, explains Kyleen. Mabel's great-aunts, Eliza and Sarah Remington, and her grand-mother Harriet Remington had opened a ladies' seminary in Cookstown, Co. Tyrone, around 1834. Mabel was carrying on a tradition, yet she was far from traditional. She encouraged her students to be imaginative and was very impressed when a young Kyleen wrote an essay describing how two policemen had abandoned their bicycles in a hedge and commandeered her family car, instructing her father to follow the driver ahead who was drunkenly weaving all over the road. When the car failed to stop, the policemen shot at the tyre to bring it to a halt. 'Mabel reported to my parents that my essay-writing was much improved and showed good imagination except every-thing that happened was true!'

She also instilled in her students a love of their local heritage and got out into the open air whenever possible. As friend and fellow historian Roy Hamilton recalls: 'She wasn't one for sitting in a classroom on a sunny day. There are people who'd say that she wasn't one for sitting in a classroom on a wet day either!'

She told her students of the importance of heritage and passing on knowledge. As she used to put it, in a family of three generations, the grandfather knows 103 townland names; the father knows 50 and the son knows just 10. She spent a lifetime protecting, preserving and recording the heritage of Inishowen so that her pupils and their children might reverse that stark statistic.

She would take people out and show them around, says Roy:

Nothing pleased her better than to go out into Donegal on her field trips on her bicycle. She was even doing that in

1940, during World War II. One evening, she was stopped by an army patrol on the quay [in Derry/Londonderry] and the soldiers said to her: 'Do you realise, madam, that you don't have a rear red tail light?' And Mabel looked at him as only Mabel could and said, 'Do I look like the kind of lady to be associated with a red light?' I can always remember her with a twinkle in her eye. She always had a wee bit of devilment about her.

Yet she had a Victorian formality about her too. Several years passed before she would call 'Mr Hamilton' by his first name Roy.

—

Mabel Colhoun bought her first pair of trousers when she was invited to join an archaeological dig at Dungiven Priory in Derry/Londonderry in 1939. She was one of several experienced amateurs who helped prominent archaeologists Oliver Davies and Estyn Evans carry out the first comprehensive excavations in Ulster in the late 1930s and '40s. She probably knew them from the Belfast Naturalists' Field Club – all three were members – and under their guidance she learned how to conduct meticulous field research.

Evans encouraged her to put her new-found expertise to use on the Inishowen peninsula and over the next four decades she recorded countless features in the country's northernmost landscape. In the classroom, she was nicknamed 'the ferret' because she had a gift for getting to the bottom of things but the moniker – meant fondly – applied more than ever now as she cycled over tough terrain in all weathers to meticulously chart a peninsula.

'There are great stories of her going about on her bicycle, navigating down the worst back roads. Nothing deterred her,' says archaeologist Denise Henry of a woman who was able to talk to anyone. She goes on:

> This ability to interact with people of various backgrounds combined with the fact her family were well known in the area meant Mabel got much more than basic information on sites. She was fascinated by the pagan origins of sites and their association with myth and legend. This is reflected in her analysis of standing stones which had been altered when Christianity arrived.

She was also very scientific and methodical, noting the condition of each monument and any possible risks to its preservation. Mabel not only recorded monuments, says Denise, she protected them: 'If she went to a site and saw that there had been some kind of deterioration, she was in foul humour for the rest of the day.'

But she took action. Her letters recount how she informed the National Museum in Dublin of any risks posed by theft, development or weathering. In 1965, for instance, she wrote to tell Dr Joseph Raftery, the Keeper of Antiquities at Dublin Museum, of some disturbance to some of the stones, crosses, etc. in '*my* area', as she called her much-loved Inishowen peninsula. On another occasion, she noted that a carved stone at a church in Malin Head was in an 'unprotected position' and it was later sent to the National Museum of Ireland for safekeeping. She made several trips to Dublin to receive further tuition in archaeological techniques from Dr Raftery and museum director Dr Anthony Lucas.

In the mid-1970s archaeologist Brian Lacey moved to Derry/Londonderry tasked with doing an archaeological survey of Donegal with funds and equipment that Mabel could only dream about. Mabel was one of the first people he met as she was a widely respected figure in the field and every new archaeological discovery went to her first. He explains:

> She was the head of everything to do with heritage. She knew every blade of grass and every stone on the Inishowen Peninsula. Despite the fact that I was a Young Turk, and might have been seen as stealing her thunder, she was extremely generous with her time and knowledge. She was fundamentally an educationalist. Spreading knowledge was her main interest.

Brian Lacey was deeply impressed by the quality of her archaeological research – 'her 6-inch [Ordnance Survey] maps were works of art' – and over the following decades they collaborated on 'millions of things'. Like so many others who knew her, he recalls a woman who always made sure that she got to the root of the matter, a trait that endured right into her eighties as she illustrated with characteristic determination on a field trip to Mayo with the Londonderry Naturalists' Field Club. Brian was standing on Rathmulcagh ringfort, telling the assembled group that there was an extensive network of souterrains beneath their feet.

He had no intention of bringing them to see the under-
ground passages as they are notoriously muddy and inaccessible. When he looked around, however, Mabel was gone. 'She
wasn't going to stand around and listen to me talking about
it when she could go down and investigate it for herself. She
might miss something.'

Mabel Colhoun was the very epitome of active old age and
when she retired from her teaching post in 1969, she threw
herself more fervently into all her other activities. She was
also a keen sportswoman and honorary secretary of the Derry
Ladies' Hockey Club. She played badminton and tennis into
her seventies and remained fit and active all her life. That
must have stood to her when, in 1974, she was dealt a serious
blow: she was ordered to move out of her family house, which
was being demolished to make way for a proposed new dual-
carriageway link from Waterside to Caw.

Although deeply upset at having to move from the house
her family had built, she went about it methodically and rather
cheerfully. In October 1974 she wrote to her niece Kyleen:
'Thank goodness for my garden incinerator – it hardly has
time to get cold! I should hope to be ready (up to a point) in
time, but over 50 years in this house, all my accumulations &
those of generations before me!'

Among those accumulations was a large tea chest given
to Mabel by her Uncle Charles Gordon. It contained the
contents of the pre-war museum at Brooke Park, which had
been carefully packed and stowed when World War II broke
out. Mabel kept the chest in her attic and, many years later,
Kyleen and her husband Richard found it and donated it to
the Tower Museum in Derry/Londonderry. The artefacts,

which include a large range of fossils and flints, are now in the museum's collection.

Mabel, however, couldn't take everything with her as she was moving to a much smaller house. She offered her friend Brian Lacey a large button-back settee: 'I remember distinctly as she gave it to me, she sort of wagged her finger at me and said you know that couch belonged to a former bishop of Derry. She paused for a minute – and said something to the effect that there was to be no hanky panky on it. That was Mabel.'

It turned out that the bishop in question, the Church of Ireland Bishop George Chadwick, moved to Dublin after his retirement and lived on Brookvale Road in Donnybrook, the very same road where Brian Lacey grew up. 'Mabel was delighted with this coincidence.'

She was a committed church-goer herself and regularly attended the Great James Street Presbyterian Church, but wasn't in any way sectarian or political. She saw much political change in her lifetime: two world wars, partition in Northern Ireland and later the Troubles. She didn't allow any of it to stop her crossing the border on her bicycle and getting on with her work in Inishowen. She spoke to everyone, regardless of their politics or religion, and was proud of the fact that the nursery schools she did so much to help establish were non-denominational.

If she had a regret, it was that she didn't make more progress with the Irish language. She studied it – along with the ogham alphabet – so that she might better understand the place names and local lore she so diligently recorded. On a personal level, she might have regretted not having children, although she never articulated it. Her niece says she absolutely adored children, so it was a pity she never had any of her own. She was always so kind and gentle and would have been a great mother, Kyleen says.

Mabel Colhoun was very modest too, so her family were not fully aware of all she had achieved. Yet, in the field of heritage, there was little she didn't achieve. She was president of the Londonderry Naturalists' Field Club; vice president and fellow of the Royal Society of Antiquaries of Ireland; and she was also instrumental in founding the Federation for Ulster Local Studies so that all societies might work together.

She was also one of the founding members of the North West Archaeological and Historical Society and that society honours her annually with a memorial lecture in her name. It's a fitting tribute because, as the society's current president Roy Hamilton says:

> She was a natural teacher. That was her living but when you were in her company you felt you were going to learn something. She had a great ability to put a message across in a very friendly way. You never felt that you were being lectured to; you always felt as if you were being treated as an equal. Any question was never too stupid for Mabel, she would go into the great detail of it.

The society's president also went about publishing her work in a single volume. If Mabel were alive, she would never have been satisfied with the final proofs, Roy says. 'She kept adjusting and amending and she'd say, "I wonder if it has changed. I'll just take a run down to see."'

The Heritage of Inishowen: Its Archaeology, History and Folklore was published, posthumously, in 1995. Mabel Colhoun's cousin David Trimble, then leader of the Ulster Unionist Party, was invited to the launch. Brian Lacey, who was launching the book, recalls seeing him on the evening news in Downing Street and thought he'd never make the event in Derry/Londonderry. But he arrived that evening to commemorate his cousin.

Since Mabel's death, archaeologist Denise Henry has joined other volunteers from the West Inishowen History and Heritage Society to catalogue her vast collection at the Tower Museum in Derry city. It's an ongoing project, but those involved are glad to say that her recognition is growing. In 2017 the Ulster History Circle unveiled a Blue Plaque to Mabel Colhoun at the Tower Museum.

Says Denise: 'She devoted her life to helping others. She wanted to capture the importance of our past in the present and to keep that for future generations. For that reason alone, it's extremely important that we remember Mabel. Her work is unparalleled.'

Brian Lacey agrees. He says that Mabel was like a nine-teenth-century woman in some respects but was way ahead of her time in others:

She grew up in a very restricted environment but she broke through barriers and she was off at weekends with her equipment on her bicycle, travelling miles down back roads and bumpy bohereens to chart the heritage of the peninsula. Her life is indicative of a certain kind of Irish woman who was forced into narrow norms although they were bursting with interest and education and wanting to get away from their backgrounds. She succeeded. She was a marvellous person for young girls growing up. A great influence, showing them that there was a lot more to life than just the domestic sphere.

She didn't live to see her work in print, but she knew the society had agreed to support the publication before she died in 1992. When it came out three years later, Mabel Colhoun's singular work and lasting contribution to local heritage was widely acknowledged.

One reviewer, John Dooher, referred to her as an extraordinarily talented woman whose linking of folklore, with its stories of fairies, giants and local heroes, and archaeological research pointed the way for later professionals. She also showed how Seanchas (a detailed knowledge of the locality) could help pinpoint sites for further investigation.

'Mabel's sharp eye and ability to get local people to talk about their locality made her survey compulsive reading,' her friend and fellow archaeological society member Kathleen Gormley later wrote in a tribute. She continued: 'Mabel, during her long life which has spanned every decade of this century, has done a great service to local history. She once referred in an article to one of the Federation's past presidents as "an outstanding person full of knowledge and interest". I am sure he, and all of us, would say the same of Mabel.'

Rosemary Gibb

ATHLETE, SOCIAL WORKER, CLOWN AND ACCOMPLISHED MAGICIAN (1942–1997)

While she was performing at an autistic home in Philadelphia, a shout of laughter erupted from a child whom the staff had that morning decided was unreachable and would have to leave the home: they called Gibb's work that day 'a miracle'.

Pat Williams, 1997

In her student days at Trinity College Dublin, Rosemary Gibb (*née* Gibson) worked as a waitress for 10 shillings a night at the Soup Bowl, a restaurant off Molesworth Street in Dublin city centre famous for its celebrity clientele. One night in the early 1960s, Ray Charles – the American singer/songwriter also known as 'The Genius' – and his entourage dropped in during her shift. When they finished their meal, Rosemary issued a spur-of-the-moment invite to take them to see the lights of the city. They all piled into her clapped-out Renault Dauphine and she drove them up into the Dublin mountains to enjoy the view from the vantage point of the infamous Hell Fire Club.

Rosemary may well have been introduced to Ray Charles, but she had no idea who he was, much less that he was blind. That was typical of her. In those early waitressing days, she ran into all kinds of celebrities but didn't know, or care, who they were. She met famous musicians, artists and actors and, more often than not, would ask them who they were and what they did.

'She was never overawed or even interested in fame,' her husband Andrew Gibb recalls. Although he adds, with a delicious sense of irony, that Rosemary was also a rather good self-publicist who had an uncanny knack of finding herself at the centre of things. In January 1963, for instance, she made national headlines when she rushed off the upper deck of a passing bus to rescue a dog from drowning in the River Liffey. She also gave the dog – a fox terrier – a home and was later presented with a silver medal for bravery by the Kildare branch of the Irish Society for the Prevention of Cruelty to Animals.

A few unkind cynics claimed she had pulled the stunt for publicity and felt vindicated when, two years later, she again jumped into the Liffey fully clothed to rescue a crippled pigeon. As Andrew remembers it: 'They suggested uncharitably that she had chucked the bird overboard herself.'

The *Irish Independent*, however, was much more benevolent. It reported the event with great fanfare, describing how Rosemary gallantly jumped 20ft from the Ha'penny Bridge, watched by hundreds, to save the bird on the very same day that she received her BA degree (in Philosophy, Fine Arts and English) from Trinity College. 'I just had to do it. I love animals and I could not let it die,' she told them.

There would be lots more publicity in the years ahead, not because she sought it but because there was a 'madcap, storybook richness' to Rosemary Gibb's life, as her friend and admirer Pat Williams so beautifully put it. As a child in Ethiopia, she taught Emperor Haile Selassie's grandchildren to ride horses. As a teenager, she set an Irish swimming record in the 100m backstroke and turned down an offer to train for the Olympic Games. She studied Arts in Trinity College and later became a social worker, setting up the UK's first literacy programme for Travellers. She became a mother in 1970, a professional clown in 1980 and the first Irish female member of the male-dominated Magic Circle in 1995.

'She had this absolute ability to drop everything and go for any opportunity that presented itself,' Andrew Gibb says now, more than two decades after her death from cancer in 1997. 'If you told her something was impossible, she would set out to prove that it was possible.'

That determination is evident in the stories her father, eminent surgeon and hypnotist Dr Jack Gibson, tells about her in his own memoirs. He recounts how he once challenged a very young Rosemary to see which one of them could best withstand the pain of a bee sting. Rosemary lost the toss of a coin and was first to put a bee on her arm and allow it to sting her. Her father then did the same. 'The pain must have been enormous,' Dr Gibson wrote, but his daughter remained stoic. 'It seemed like a cruel competition, but Rosemary was glad she had withstood it and the same determination which she had that day, she used all her life.'

If she had a steely resolve, she also had a precocious taste for practical jokes. When she was just two years old, she went to her dad in the garden and told him that she had broken a window with a big stone. She then took him by the hand and led him to the window she had supposedly broken and told him that she was only having him on. Or, as she very sweetly put it: 'Mime [her word for 'I'] only pulling owns [her word for 'your'] leg.'

Rosemary was Dr Jack Gibson and his wife Elizabeth James's only child. She was born in Dublin, in Hatch Street, in 1942, and spent much of her childhood abroad. The family moved with each of Dr Gibson's medical postings, from Rhodesia (now Zimbabwe) to Guernsey and then Ethiopia.

When Rosemary contracted TB as a child, her father warned her mother not to expect her to be able to run around like other children. However, with that determination Dr Gibson had so proudly observed, she not only overcame the disease, but recovered so completely that she became an accomplished athlete in several disciplines – swimming, showjumping, netball and tennis.

—

In 1959 the family returned to Dublin from Ethiopia and Rosemary went to Alexandra College, where she proceeded to fail all her exams. As she admitted in an interview years later: 'I rejected all learning. I wanted to write and play games so I didn't get on with the teachers. Quite honestly, I was a disgrace to my family and country – [a] philistine.'

Nonetheless, she eventually passed her Leaving Cert and in 1961 secured a place at Trinity College Dublin where, to quote her fellow graduates, you couldn't be unaware of her. She was an ever-present personality in Front Square.

She was already a legend when Senator David Norris first came across her in the 1960s. He recalls her as 'golden-haired and effervescent with contralto laughter' – and always unconventional. She enjoyed a good cigar and loved to challenge stuffy bourgeois etiquette wherever she found it. She made quite a stir when she went to the Provost's garden party one year dressed in a black bin bag, with holes cut out for the arms and head. 'The Provost was fascinated and he could not be distracted from her,' Senator Norris recalls.

Trinity College was still a rather fusty male establishment where women students had to be off campus by 6 pm. Lunch in the Dining Hall was a segregated affair and full membership of some of the major societies, the Phil (the University Philosophical Society) and the Hist (the College Historical Society), was still a few years off, much to Rosemary's annoyance. To make a point, she once dressed as a man and briefly made it into a Hist gathering before being discovered and unceremoniously thrown out.

A different stunt brought her to the attention of Katherine Cohen, who would become a lifelong friend:

I met Rosemary in the Buttery of Trinity College. She was crazily chasing a very large African man, Solomon, around with some sort of liquid. They were both laughing hysterically, while the other denizens of the Buttery looked on in horror. Definitely not the kind of student I, a 20-year-old American girl from Minnesota, had seen there before, but the kind of person I was immediately attracted to. So, we made contact that day, and thus began a friendship that lasted until she died.

They went on to swim together on the TCD team, study together and later holiday together, with husbands and children in tow. Katherine recalls Rosemary's love of people, her devotion to dogs, her work with Travellers and her initial disdain for cooking – her main diet for years was coffee, roll-up cigarettes and Polo mints, she says.

Rosemary wasn't very fond of politics either, but she was a lifelong advocate of gender equality and social justice. Her one foray into political activism ended badly when she took part in a demonstration at the American Embassy to protest at the Kennedys' brinksmanship during the Cuban Missile Crisis in 1962. She and other protesters were mauled and bitten by police dogs. The case made national news when one of the protesters sued Gardaí. Rosemary gave evidence in court, saying that she had been bitten by a police dog, but Garda witnesses said they never saw their dogs biting anyone.

—

Rosemary first spotted Andrew Gibb under the arch at Trinity and invited the Modern Languages student, who was one year her junior, to hop on the back of her Vespa scooter. He did so, marking the beginning of a relationship that led to a happy 30-year marriage:

This madcap trajectory was laid down and off we went. I am not normally attracted to exhibitionists but she was kind of irresistible with her Pekinese nose and trademark haystack blonde hair. I envied Rosemary's spontaneity and challenging irreverence. She had everything I sensed I did not have myself: a free spirit, gutsiness galore, curiosity and a healthy disrespect for authority. She was whimsical and always mischief-making; breaking the rules if they deserved to be broken.

The Irish word 'craic' and the Latin phrase 'carpe diem' informed her student days and, for that matter, the rest of her life, Andrew adds.

Her final years in Trinity were filled with parties, pubs (she loved chatting to Brendan Behan's parents in McDaid's) and yet more photo opportunities. She and Bob Horlin won a National Twist Competition at the Eamonn Andrews Studios on Harcourt Street in the early days of television. But it was not all entertainment and merriment either. At Trinity College, Rosemary founded a literacy society for Travellers and would later do pioneering work in that field.

After sitting her finals in 1965, she and her 55-year-old mother went off on a hitchhiking trip to the Berlin Wall. She returned to Dublin fully expecting to fail her exams but when she passed, she was left at a loose end, not sure what to do. She went to Maine in the United States and got her first teaching job – helping children with dyslexia. Meanwhile, Andrew was still in his final year: once he finished his exams he worked 'all the hours in God's calendar' – eight straight days and nights – at a pea-canning factory in East Anglia to earn enough money to travel to see her.

When Rosemary returned to Dublin, she decided to do an MPhil on the poetry of Patrick Kavanagh, with David Norris and Professor Brendan Kennelly as tutors. Her husband recalls their dilemma during her studies – her ideas were good but her spelling was atrocious. All the same, she managed to write a 'distinguished thesis' and impress her supervisors. She was also rather a good poet herself.

As David Norris recalls: 'She was a great original, stylish rather than elegant, delighting in puncturing pomposity, but with no streak of cruelty in her own special brand of wit. In her company we got a glimpse of life as it could be, seen through her uniquely "Rosy-tinted spectacles".

After graduating, Andrew went to Paris to do a postgrad and Rosemary joined him. It was there that he asked her to marry him. 'She made me wait 24 hours!' he says. But she did say yes and, although she wanted to wear black leather on her wedding day, she opted for traditional white (complete with veil and gloves) to please her mother. She was 24 and he was 23.

When the young couple moved to London in 1967, Rosemary studied for a diploma in social administration at the London School of Economics and, once again, tried to improve education opportunities for the Travelling community. She became London's first officially designated Travellers' teacher. The Inner London Gypsy Education Group bought a caravan for £100, which was to act as a school on a halting site in Shepherd's Bush, and the Inner London Education Authority agreed to pay her a part-time teacher's salary.

On her first day, the parents closed their doors in her face when she sought permission to teach their children. There were about 70 children on the site, aged up to 16, and most of them could neither read nor write. But the parents slowly came around and allowed the younger children to attend the caravan school. The older ones, however, made teaching almost unbearable, as Rosemary told *Irish Press* journalist John McEntee in 1978:

I found finally a way of controlling the teenage boys, although I do not admire myself for doing it. I was at the end of my tether with their total defiance and aggression and physical pain of things being thrown at me so I threatened to go off and get their fathers, at which they immediately turned away from the scene of misdemeanour and meekly went away.

The teaching programme went from strength to strength and, within two years, several of Rosemary's students were attending local schools. 'Progress has been enormous from a caravan that used to be covered in excrement and urine to the point where they sweep up after a session,' she said. There were intractable issues, too, not least the ingrained discrimination in mainstream education. Rosemary was incensed:

They have experienced a lot of victimisation. Gypsies going to school are very often conspicuous and other children often chant, 'You're a gypsy, you're a gypsy,' in the playground. They still don't mix as much as they should. I had an enormous hassle with the local swimming pool people. They wouldn't let the Travellers use the pool but now they are allowed.

Some of them are very bright with great artistic talent. We should be able to tap their special talents. The boys like woodwork and metal work. They should be provided with alternative possibilities to tarmacadaming and scrap because they are trades that are dying out.

In the meantime, Rosemary and Andrew had become parents. The couple returned to Dublin to have their first child, Tamzin, in 1970, and Jason two years later. Initially, pregnancy came as a shock to a woman who feared motherhood might take the spontaneity out of life – but it was the perfect role for Rosemary, who raised her children to believe that anything was possible.

'Mum tried to teach us to embrace life, make the most of it and live each day as if it were the last,' says Tamzin. 'She taught us not to be afraid of anything or anyone, to ask questions, to believe that you can achieve anything you want, and to be kind and generous to others.'

'She believed anything was possible and that you could do anything if you put your mind to it,' adds Jason. 'She also brought me up very much feeling that there was nothing a man could do that a woman couldn't. I didn't see any difference between men and women. If anything, women are generally better communicators and more intelligent; she instilled and demonstrated that.'

Both of them, however, were acutely embarrassed when, aged 42, their mum decided to become a clown. She signed up to learn the basics of knife-throwing, mime, fire-eating, juggling and walking on glass and was soon performing to a less-than-enthused public. As Rosemary recalled later: 'I used to go into the centre [by then, the family had moved from London to Brighton] and lie on the broken glass – and I thought, "Wow! Everyone's going to fall for this." But that's not what happened. Pedestrians were just staring at me and my kids were going, "Oh, look at mum," but I kept at it.'

Jason recalls with horror being put in a little waistcoat, aged about seven, and included in the act. Both he and Tamzin say it was also really difficult at school when their classmates teased them for 'begging' in town, although begging might have been more lucrative. The first week's takings amounted to the princely sum of 7½p. The following week, things improved. The collection almost doubled – to 13p – and Rosemary, ever-determined, continued on.

It wasn't long before the plaudits came and a few years later, once again, she was front-page news, this time making it on to the cover of *Time Out* magazine as 'Rosy the Clown', the magazine's Street Magician of the Year. She said she discovered the essence of clowning while performing in Italy, when she realised that it was possible to communicate very well without language:

> When I began I didn't know what clowning was all about. It isn't about impressing people, it's about truthfulness, being vulnerable. It's about sharing your happiness, unhappiness, successes or failures with your audience. There are very few things that really matter in life and, most of all, it doesn't matter what people think. That's what I try and express in my show.

That ability to express herself without words also had another unexpected benefit; it meant she was able to reach people when others couldn't. 'When I did my show,' Rosemary explained, 'I found people who had never spoken before started talking, and people who were catatonic responded. I think it's because they saw me making a fool of myself and they weren't afraid to express themselves. Some of these people showed a remarkable sense of humour.'

She began to look for sponsorship to allow her to perform for children with special needs and sent flyers to every business she could think of. 'I even wrote to local funeral parlours, which I suppose was in bad taste, and sauna baths who thought I was a pervert,' she told journalist Peter Marriott in 1985. In a 15-year career in clowning, she entertained hundreds of thousands of children but, recalled Pat Williams, she would happily perform to an audience of one:

> I once saw her making herself quite invisible behind a very small pink glove puppet, tenderly coaxing a desperately ill child at Great Ormond Street Hospital to respond to its gentle advances. Another time, while she was performing at an autistic home in Philadelphia, a shout of laughter erupted from a child whom the staff had that morning decided was unreachable and would have to leave the home: they called Gibb's work that day 'a miracle'.

Rosemary Gibb made a natural clown with her flower-festooned bowler hat, her patched baggy trousers and the enduring athleticism that allowed her to ride upside down on a motorbike, but she began to delve more deeply into the magic that had always been a part of her act. She tested the waters at her local magic shop in Brighton, where they stared at her as if she had two heads – 'it was because I was a woman' – but she didn't let that put her off.

In the same way that she had practised juggling at home, she now turned her hand to magic and spent hours in the garage perfecting her tricks. As Tamzin recalls:

> Mum was forever practising her magic on whoever walked through the door, on whoever looked like they needed

cheering up in the street. Her spontaneity was endless, envi-
able and unnerving at times. We would often come home
to find an extra person sitting with us for dinner, someone
mum had got talking to in the street, someone in more need
than us, a dog lost or unwanted – everyone was welcome in
our house.

Having an open house had its drawbacks too. Sometimes
things went missing – their grandfather's watch on one occasion – but Rosemary had an endless faith in people and
continued to 'collect waifs and strays' as her father once put it.

She could be outrageous and wild and unpredictable – all
the things teenagers can find hard to take. 'I just wanted a mum
who was at home and made cakes, who wore a bra and shaved
her armpits,' says Tamzin. But looking back on it now, both she
and Jason consider their childhood an incredibly enriching
and enlightening time.

One of the ways she reached out to teenage Jason was to
suggest they take scuba-diving lessons together. They started
in a local swimming pool and had several adventures together
all over the world. They were incredibly close, Jason says,
adding that he is gutted she never had an opportunity to get to
know his three children (Rosie, Sorrel and Mako) or Tamzin's
son and daughter (Louis and Lola). She would have made a
wonderful grandmother, he adds.

She did, however, grasp every opportunity to forge
wonderful friendships. Rosy, as she was known then, met
Alida Schieffelin-Gersie in the 1980s and they became very
close friends. As they got to know one another, Alida felt she
had already sensed Rosy's presence in the world before they

had even met. As a child growing up in the Netherlands, one of Alida's favourite books featured an adventurous girl called Rosemary. The fictional girl had a doctor father, loved horse riding and had once even saved a dog from a freezing river. It's the kind of coincidence that stretches credulity – or brings you out in goosebumps.

'We had a great connection,' Alida says. 'It was very special. We had a wonderful time in all the years we knew each other and we talked virtually daily.' She recalls a person who worked 'her butt off to bring delight and interest to the world'. On one of those occasions, she and Rosy were walking on a street in Islington at about 10 pm when they looked through the window of a restaurant and saw about four or five ladies at a table looking distinctly bored with each other. Rosy went inside and started to practise table magic with cards as the women looked on in awe. Then, as quickly as she had appeared, she left them:

> She might do something similar on the bus, on the street; if there was an opportunity to delight people or give them some intrigue or give them a bit of a challenge, that is really what she loved to do. She was an amazing being in the world, but sometimes that generosity of spirit could be difficult for others. It isn't necessarily easy to stand on the street for 10 minutes while Rosy is practising magic in some restaurant. But that was who she was – a unique being.

Rosy lived life very intensely, which Alida says came at a cost:

> The depth of her connection with people and animals and the world also generated a lot of pain in her and she could

get very upset by that. She hoped that she could do more than any of us are able to do. She could cry very intensely at the sorrows in the world and the sorrow in herself about the sorrow in the world. And then she would return to joy and laugh. Her laughter was deep and infectious.

Despite the pain it occasionally caused her, she was always looking for new projects and new ways to engage with the world. Rosy the Clown soon gave way to Rosy the Magician and it wasn't long before she gained a new following. She was already well established when she performed for the invited studio audience on *The Late Late Show*, one of the most-watched programmes on Irish television. Her father had been invited to speak on the show and she was asked to warm up the audience. Dr Jack Gibson was a well-known surgeon who had successfully used hypnosis to perform over 4000 procedures without anaesthetic. He also treated thousands of people who suffered from addictions, phobias and psychosomatic diseases.

Before the show went on air, Rosy took to the stage. She asked a member of the audience to tear a piece from a newspaper before setting the remaining fragment alight and putting it in a kettle. She then cajoled the show's celebrated host, Gay Byrne, into dancing around the kettle while chanting a magic word. He duly obliged while she juggled oranges and threw them into the audience. She asked for one to be returned and when she peeled it, there was the piece of torn paper that the audience thought they had seen burning in the kettle. It fitted perfectly with the volunteer's torn half.

Soon there were invitations from the British Council, the UK's international cultural and educational organisation. Rosy adopted the stage name Champagne and brought her show to audiences all around the world, from Brazil and Peru to Madras and Bahrain.

—

In 1995 she became the first Irish woman to be admitted to the International Magic Circle, an old boys' club with a membership of some 1400 men but just 24 women. To gain admittance, she had to perform in front of a jury of her peers. On the day it all went a bit Tommy Cooper but, like the bumbling but brilliant magician, she succeeded in pulling it out of the hat – 'Just like that,' as he used to say – when it really mattered.

The following year she was awarded the Craig Trophy by the International Brotherhood of Magicians. At the time, she told journalist Ed Power in the *Irish Examiner*: 'The Craig Award is an absolutely massive competition and my victory will do a great deal for women who are trying to break into the magic profession.'

She continued to perform and to travel into her fifties but arrived home after one trip feeling completely flattened by what she thought was a severe case of anaemia. She knew something was very wrong when she had difficulty jumping on her horse at her holiday home in Spain. It came as a blow, however, to discover she had stomach cancer, which had spread to the rest of her body. She had one serious operation and a second, even more complicated intervention was planned.

'When she came home after surgery, the first thing she did was cook us a huge stew, even though she couldn't eat it herself,' her daughter recalls.

Jason too remembers her strength and determination. A few days after having her stomach removed, she wanted to go for walks and talked about going up and down several flights of stairs to regain her strength.

Facing into her second operation, she and her father worked on a hypnosis script to offset the risk of severe blood loss. For weeks beforehand, she kept repeating to herself that her blood vessels would come under her mind's control, they would contract and stop bleeding. The anaesthetist even repeated the phrase while she was undergoing the operation. She didn't lose any blood and the operation lasted six hours instead of the anticipated eight.

Rosy came through the operation and remained positive, although still very ill and in hospital. Her daughter, who had just got her dream job working as a stage manager at the reopened Globe Theatre in London, visited her mother after work every evening. It was a very special time, Tamzin recalls: 'She brought out the best in me and the worst in me, but during that time together we put everything right. She became very dignified in her illness and very calm.'

She died after a five-month illness on 13 July 1997. Shortly after that Tamzin met Queen Elizabeth II at the Globe Theatre and remembered that her mother had said she would never curtsy if she met the queen as she is no more important than anyone else: 'I am ashamed to this day that I did in fact curtsy, but I did get my own back. When speaking to Prince Charles about the weight of the wooden doors going onto stage, I said to him: "We're all very strong, feel my muscles." He did, to the utter horror of my colleagues. That was definitely mum's defiance shining through.'

Her family mark her anniversary annually, paying tribute to a woman who flouted convention and who, like her father, delighted in proving that anything was possible. She was a woman who loved a lot, gave a lot, wept when she was happy, wept when she was sad and, muses her husband, would certainly have gone on to reinvent herself again had she lived.

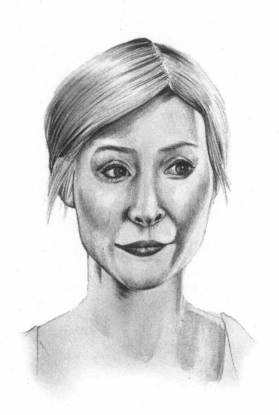

Jemma Redmond

GROUNDBREAKING BIOTECHNOLOGIST
WHO PRINTED LIVING TISSUE
(1978–2016)

We are pushing the boundaries of what is possible in tissue engineering. We print human tissue and potentially human organs. We make robots that make people.

Jemma Redmond, CEO, Ourobotics

Jemma Redmond had a vision. She believed she could find a way to 3D print human organs so that she could heal herself – along with millions of others facing a range of health issues from infertility to organ failure. It sounds like science fiction. She said so herself but, crucially, she added the qualifier: 'It's sci-fi – *for now*.' In her lifetime she made more progress than anybody thought possible. She designed and developed a bioprinter that could 3D print cells and keep them alive. It was pioneering work that attracted global attention.

And she wasn't going to stop there. She believed it was possible not only to print human organs for transplant but to improve on nature's design, essentially making stronger, more resilient human beings. She saw health as an engineering problem and she believed 3D printing could deliver far-reaching medical solutions to human problems.

In part, she was looking for a solution to her own medical problem. When she found out she was infertile, she wanted to 'fix it' and set about finding a way to 3D print ovaries and a uterus. As she explained in an interview in 2015:

> There are a number of reasons I got into the field, but – I found out I couldn't have children – I was trying to find solutions to the problem. I was trying to see if I could actually fix things or re-generate tissue. And that's kind of how I got into bioprinting. I came across this field, and it was like 'Wow, you can actually grow tissue.'

She started to build early prototypes at her own kitchen table using everyday appliances: a cooker, a heater, an air compressor from a car, anything that was to hand. When things got too hot in the kitchen – which they did – she used the extractor hood to get rid of the fumes. 'It was quite dangerous, actually,' she said. 'It was pretty wacky.'

There was nothing new in that, though, as she had always been 'dabbling with stuff' growing up in Tallaght, Dublin. She was born on 16 March 1978, the eldest of Lorraine and Christy Cahill's three children. Her first brother Bryan was born in 1981, followed by Philip in 1984. Jemma took her grandmother's surname, Redmond, as they were particularly close.

As a child she was always making and taking things apart to see how they worked. But more than that, when she went to put them together again, she wanted to see how she might improve the design. She also had a deep interest in health and when she heard that a neighbour had cancer, she said she would go about finding a cure, her mother Lorraine says.

'She had a brilliant mind,' her father Christy says. And it was constantly whirring, her mother chips in. 'Her mind was going twenty to the dozen. She never stopped. She'd forget to eat; she'd be sitting at her laptop and fall asleep over it and then she'd wake up and start working again.'

There was always time for a good pun, though. Jemma, her dad and brother Philip were committed punsters, turning mealtimes into quick-witted bantering sessions. Her mother throws her eyes up to heaven at the thought of it but smiles when recalling her daughter's dry sense of humour.

That wry outlook on the world shines through her presentations, her social media posts and the interviews she gave to numerous magazines interested in her work. But there was a more serious side too. She spoke and wrote often about the difficulties of being born intersex, or to quote the Transgender Equality Network Ireland definition, being born with characteristics that do not strictly belong to male or female categories. Jemma Redmond, who identified as a woman, was more straightforward. She simply said: 'I have some differences in my body.'

Those differences, she later explained, went on to shape and inform every aspect of her life. After studying electronic engineering in Dublin, she went to Robert Gordon University in Aberdeen in 2000 to study applied physics. It was there that she developed her interest in the biology side of things because, as she said, 'I have some personal interest in that area.'

In the years that followed, she refined her vision and gathered the educational qualifications and experience she needed to make it a reality. By 2014 she had amassed a certificate in electronic engineering, a degree in applied physics, a diploma in project management and a master's in nanobioscience. At that stage she knew exactly what she wanted to achieve and was working as a research assistant at University College Dublin, testing and developing bioprinters, which she hoped could eventually print human tissue and organs.

The following year she set up her own bioprinting company, Ourobotics. Dr Tony Herbert, CEO of Irish Precision Optics, was sufficiently impressed by her as a scientist and an entrepreneur to offer her laboratory space in an incubator unit. Jemma's company was one of five operating out of Summerhill North in Cork city. She jumped at the opportunity and when she moved in, she posted on Twitter: 'It's alive! Well not quite … it's my lab. Mine!'

She posted regularly on social media, everything from her favoured puns to developments in bioprinting and comments on discrimination. When she died suddenly, aged just 38, her friends kept her Facebook page open as a tribute to a woman who believed that she could make the impossible happen. And she did, as she noted with an admirable measure of glee in November 2015: 'Someone told me something couldn't be done … but lateral thinking and taking apart software has worked again. Hooray for me!'

Back in the lab, she put that lateral thinking to work. One of her first projects was working to 3D print an ear. She outlined her progress in puns on Twitter: 'Someone said we "hear" you printed an ear – but it's 'ear'ly days, I said.'

Shortly after that, Duncan Turner, a general partner at SOSV, gave her the opportunity to take part in the HAX accelerator programme to work on a prototype 3D bioprinter in Shenzhen in China. Bill Liao, another general partner at SOSV (the venture capital firm runs the programme) remembers Jemma as an intellectual and visionary who wanted to make a real difference in the world: 'She saw health as an engineering problem, which honestly it is. A lot of healthcare she saw as little better than voodoo or butchery as opposed to well-refined engineering. She was very smart and very technically capable and she had ambitions to print a working set of ovaries and a womb.'

Over four intense months in China, Jemma and her team produced a number of prototypes before developing a 10-material bioprinter, the first of its kind. Revolution, as she called the printer, was capable of printing complex tissues and keeping them alive. And it was, literally, revolutionary. It was also very heavy – and fragile – so she and her colleagues travelled with it, dragging it through a number of international airports before finally touching down in San Francisco to give a demonstration on how it worked. Then, as Jemma light-heartedly told a conference some time later, this happened:

We had the machine on top of the table for demo day and I was so exhausted that I leaned back on the table and the table tilted and the machine fell on the floor and smashed to pieces and the room went silent. We continued on … I just kicked the machine under the table … it was grand. We came back to Cork and built another machine and went a bit further.

That was typical of her, says business associate Alexandra Whelan:

> She was extraordinary. Nothing stopped her. If there was an issue, or a problem, or something didn't work out, she went straight on to the next thing. She was a dynamo. She applied for everything under the sun and worked morning, noon and night. She got into a plane in the same way some people get into a car, getting a cheap flight online to go off somewhere to meet someone. She was working to get funding and backing.

She was also getting noticed. In January 2016 Ourobotics came first out of 200 entrants to win the inaugural Silicon Valley Open Doors Europe start-up competition. A month later she told a conference in Cork that she hoped to produce low-cost bioprinters that had the potential to cut transplant waiting lists, significantly reduce health costs and end the need to test on animals. As she explained to delegates at SynBio Future 2016 Conference:

> Often surgery is not enough. We don't have enough tissue; we don't have enough donors. We [Ourobotics] print human tissue and potentially human organs. We are pushing the boundaries of what is possible in tissue engineering. We make robots that make people. People are waiting for [transplants] for four years. There are ways to fix this. We can use 3D bioprinters to create tissues from donors or from the patient's own cells. Over 100,000 transplants are done per year – and there could be a lot more if there was more tissue available.

She believed she could print organs that could be ready for transplant in three months. And she could do so for a fraction of the cost that it takes to procure them at the moment. Jemma also saw a way of making affordable bioprinters that might realistically be in hospitals within 10 to 20 years. She hoped to cut tens of thousands of euro off the price, making them available for just €12,500:

I have noted in the past that devices like the microwave only started to become mainstream when they became cheaper and that was because certain components had become cheaper. If we can use hybrid 3D bioprinting technology to do this, it means we can make a wide range of more expensive elaborate machines cheaper and simpler.

Jemma Redmond's vision wasn't sci-fi any more. She was talking to professionals all over the world about printing organs and limbs. 'There is a literal "arms" race going on,' she said with her trademark humour.

She told delegates she hadn't yet looked at how she would transplant the printed organs into the body but she believed it was possible to grow tissue and insert it into the body where it would grow itself: 'It will happen – and we are the ones who will make it happen.' She also thought she could improve on nature's design: 'As a physicist, why do exactly what nature is doing, why not make it better? Why can't we make better organs – add in some sensors? You could do anything really.'

And she could do anything. Jemma's friends and colleagues say she was a true innovator who saw possibilities where others didn't, but she faced many battles too – for funding, for investment, for recognition. For instance, when she was once asked at a conference why she had started by printing a middle finger, she said it was meant as a joke. Or more accurately, it was a bioprinted hand gesture to her superiors at the time who had cut her funding.

Later, she tweeted that she couldn't believe she had told that story in public. She was shy and often said the thought of speaking in public was a nightmare because she was an introvert. But, in a sense, that was the least of it. Although she didn't talk much about the nature of her work, her parents had the impression she was often hitting her head against a brick wall trying to get support in Ireland. She would have had a better chance if she had stayed in China, or in Australia, where she lived for a year, or in the US, her father says.

It was a point she made strongly herself and criticised 'conservative' Ireland for not supporting breakthroughs in research, such as bioprinting:

It's harder to get approval to do certain things [in Ireland], whereas it would be a lot easier to do in China and the US. There's a certain level of conservatism here, they don't like new technology in Ireland in my opinion. We're more prone to supporting software companies and shying away from bioprinting.

She also thought that she faced an uphill struggle because she was a woman:

You feel like you're talking sometimes, and no one is paying attention to you. And suddenly the ideas are circulated again by somebody else, and then, 'Wait a second, I said that. Like, two weeks ago. Hello.' That happens a lot. That's kind of hard, not being taken seriously. There's a bias there that you can't seem to shake off. So you have to work a lot harder to get noticed and to build credibility.

Yet she was getting noticed and many of her peers greatly admired her work. In April 2016 she was selected by Google Ireland to take part in its Adopt A Startup programme. Alexandra Whelan, a business innovation specialist, worked with her on the programme. International interest in her work was growing. 'She was beyond cutting edge. She was a whirlwind; it was impossible to keep up. She really wanted to help as many people as possible but at times she needed gravity boots,' she says.

Colleague and friend Tony Herbert in Cork tells a similar story of a woman whose 'remorseless logic, all-encompassing knowledge, expertise and superb confidence in her mission' impressed so many. He says Jemma was a helium balloon while he was the lead ballast. She was constantly innovating and moving from project to project, while he was counting how much each project might cost and how the company might get it to market:

She was a triumph of hope over reality. Her work was very inspiring. In criticism, she was a bit like a butterfly going from flower to flower. It was hard to get her to settle down and focus on something commercial. She knew perfectly well the exigencies of being commercial but she leapt ahead of reality. A concept formed in her mind but the gap between that and the marketplace was colossal.

At the same time, had she been spared, he says, he believes Jemma Redmond was the kind of truly creative, driven and successful entrepreneur who moves mountains and creates the Apples and Microsofts of this world: 'She was a remarkable person. I don't know I can do justice to her. She was a very independent individual. She found it very difficult to accede to anybody – that was both a strength and a weakness. She had difficulty taking advice – this was annoying, entertaining and refreshing. She was a woman of vision and creativity.'

Friend and backer Bill Liao echoes that, saying Jemma was a leading light. 'She was also a tremendously good person and supportive of many others,' he says. 'She was a member of the transgender community. There is still a lot of prejudice against LGBT (lesbian, gay, bisexual, transgender) people and she encountered that headlong.'

She posted about street harassment; being verbally abused, taunted, touched, even punched. Some people passed remarks; thoughtless comments based on a kneejerk reaction to subtle physical differences. It cut Jemma to the quick, her parents recall now, with deep sadness. She was very sensitive, although Lorraine says she also kept everything bottled up. Yet she made a stand, writing about public ignorance and ongoing discrimination faced by intersex people.

In 2015 she commented on an article that denounced the practice of 'normalising' intersex children at birth. It pointed out that many countries imposed a sex on children at an early age, through surgery and hormone treatments, but two major European agencies saw that as an infringement of human rights. They recommended that birth certificates should allow for gender to be registered as 'sex neutral'.

'This is good,' she wrote, and continued:

> The treatment of intersex people is one in which we are
> shamed into keeping silent by know-nothing doctors … who
> are afraid of what society will say. At least people are aware
> that this is a huge human rights issue. First up, as someone
> with a dsd (disorders of sexual development)/intersex varia-
> tion) these surgeries don't just happen to you as a baby they
> happen to you as a child, a teenager, even an adult.

She went on to say that surgeries, hormones and not being
told the truth about your situation by 'uneducated doctors' was
likely to lead to mental trauma and lifelong medical problems.
While there was an overlap between trans rights and intersex
rights, they were still quite different as most intersex people
stay with the gender they were raised with. Intersex people
want to make decisions about their own bodies and not have
them made by doctors, parents or society:

> I've observed parents with intersex children get really upset,
> blame themselves, blame the child, this pressure I feel comes
> from society and its unhealthy obsession with other people's
> genitals. Then doctors/surgeons/butchers come along and
> also try to convince the parents to perform surgery on the
> child. Now not all doctors will do this but most will unfor-
> tunately … they honestly believe that they are helping these
> kids. Raising children in some stupid binary way is harmful
> in general anyway, children should just be allowed to be
> themselves. They know who they are.

She said medical students and doctors in Ireland – and indeed in most countries – needed to be educated about intersex variations, as they were not as uncommon as people are led to believe: 'I also want to point out that an intersex person can vary in appearance; not everyone looks ambiguous but can be different with regards to chromosomes or subtle variations in their anatomy.'

When Intersex Awareness Day came around that October, she drolly posted: 'Today is intersex awareness day, so there now you're aware! Hooray.' She went on to say that she felt 98 per cent of people didn't know or understand what intersex meant. 'Most people who are intersex in Ireland keep it really secret. Won't tell anyone … and because of that no one understands.'

Back in her lab in Cork, she continued to refine her printers. In 2016 she went to Germany with Alexandra Whelan to show-case her work at a MedTech innovation event. She had attached a video to her bioprinter in the lab in Cork and dialled in through her mobile phone so that she could show people how it worked. She also gave them a takeaway reminder of what she planned to do – a test tube containing a heart-shaped sweet. 'Print your heart out,' she used to say.

Ironically, in April 2019, scientists in Israel produced the world's first 3D printed heart using human tissue. Researchers at Tel Aviv University made a miniature heart from a patient's cells and it was photographed in a test tube, just as Jemma had fore-seen. Those scientists, like Jemma, predicted that there could be organ printers in hospitals within a decade using a technology that could save the lives of hundreds awaiting transplant.

It was hard for Jemma's associates to keep track of her process. As Bill recalls: 'Her lab looked like as if somebody had taken a whole lot of different pieces of electronics and a couple of sticks of dynamite and exploded them. She had tidied up certain areas so that it was workable.' She made references to her own untidiness herself and joked that she would develop a robot who could put order on the lab.

She had exceptional clarity when it came to what she wanted to achieve though, and no doubt whatsoever that she would achieve it. When she died suddenly on 16 August 2016, it came as an unspeakable shock. Her parents Lorraine and Christy still don't have words to describe the depth of their loss. They do, however, want to say loud and clear that it's time for the Irish government and its agencies to fund and support the country's young entrepreneurs. 'It makes me mad that they don't support them when they are alive and then when they are dead, they are full of praise,' says Lorraine.

The tributes poured in from all around the world for a woman who, in the words of writer and publishing expert David Worlock, encapsulated the spirit of the age. 'Jemma's ability to drive learning into business development and pitch at goals that stretch the range of human aspiration should be what we mean when we talk about the spirit of our age,' he wrote.

He also noted that she had done much to increase awareness of the issues faced by intersex people: 'In our world, which struggles to increase diversity, reduce gender barriers and allow each of us the full range of opportunity to match our skills and ambitions, this fact [of being intersex], set against her achievements, should alone mark her out as one of the special people who should stand for these troubled but ever hopeful times.'

It's a theme that is taken up by her friend and associate Bill Liao. The Cork-based entrepreneur and CoderDojo co-founder says he plans to campaign about discrimination, of all hues, in the months and years ahead. He too has personal experience of prejudice, in particular growing up in Australia where he was singled out because he was half Chinese.

In terms of her work, Bill Liao describes Jemma Redmond as a world leader in her field who got quite a long way towards achieving her aim. Others are now following in her footsteps. She didn't leave a functioning company behind but other scientists are turning her futuristic dream into a reality. Ourobotics, her company, was named after the ouroboros, the ancient symbol of a serpent eating its own tail. It is said to signify infinity or the cycle of birth and death. Jemma might be glad to see that what she created is continuing elsewhere.

Before her sudden death, she told her business associate Alexandra Whelan that she had taken up running again. She was a keen athlete and liked mountain biking, martial arts and swimming. At university in Aberdeen, she captained the fencing team and the ju-jitsu team. She planned now to get back into running and said that she was even thinking about taking Saturdays off.

She didn't get to do that. Her untimely death was a great loss to the world, as her large circle of friends in the tech and LGBT communities said in messages of condolence to her parents after her death in 2016.

One of those messages sums up the enduring legacy of an extraordinary woman. 'Jemma', wrote one friend and associate, 'demonstrated that if you really wanted something, you could make a plan to get there. She was full of plans to create new ways that had value not just for herself but for other people.'

In one of her last interviews, she was asked what advice she would give to women thinking of entering a similar field. This is what she said:

I would say have faith in yourself. Don't get pushed around so much. Show confidence. I also think women should be more supportive of each other, instead of being derogatory towards each other, because that's a big problem. It erodes confidence. It's just better to build everybody else's confidence up, because you can build your own that way. So I'd say be confident, and try not to be nasty to other people, because it will always come back at you. It's kind of like karma, right?

Bibliographical Notes

Chapter 1: Woman of the Burren

The content for this chapter draws heavily on the report of excavations at Poulnabrone tomb published in 2014, as well as the findings of recent analysis of ancient DNA carried out at Trinity College Dublin.

The portrait of the Woman of the Burren is constructed from the detailed findings outlined in Dr Ann Lynch's *Poulnabrone: An Early Neolithic Portal Tomb in Ireland*, Archaeological Monograph Series: 9, 2014. I am very grateful to Dr Barra O'Donnabhain, author of the chapter on the bioarchaeology of human remains with Dr Mara Tesorieri, for sharing his many insights with me.

I am also very grateful to Dr Lara M. Cassidy who spoke about her research in ancient DNA. Her findings are outlined in 'Neolithic and Bronze Age migration to Ireland and the establishment of the insular Atlantic genome', Lara M. Cassidy, Rui Martiniano, Eileen M. Murphy, Matthew D. Teasdale, James Mallory, Barrie Hartwell and Daniel G. Bradley, *Proceedings of the National Academy of Sciences*, USA, September 2015; 'Scientists Sequence First Ancient Irish Human Genomes', tcd.ie, 28 December 2015.

The notes on Ötzi come from South Tyrol Museum of Archaeology http://www.iceman.it/en/clothing/.

Chapter 2: Macha

I am very grateful to Damien Houlahan and the staff at Navan Centre and Fort in Armagh for showing me around this singular site and explaining its many aspects.

Thank you too to Kate Fitzpatrick, whom I met there, for taking the time to explain her work with Celtic myth. It is outlined in beautifully written detail in her book, cited below.

The story of Macha was drawn from the version told at Navan Centre and Fort and the one recounted by Kate Fitzpatrick.

Works cited:

Fitzpatrick, Kate, *Macha's Twins: A Spiritual Journey with the Celtic Horse Goddess* (Imran Publishing, 2017).

Lynn, Chris, *Navan Fort: Archaeology and Myth* (Wordwell, 2003).

Lynn, Chris, McSparron, Cormac, and Moore, Peter, *Excavations at Navan Fort*, Data Structure Report: Navan Fort, Co. Armagh, Centre of Archaeological Fieldwork, School of Archaeology and Palaeoecology, Queen's University Belfast, 2002.

Mallory, J.P., and Stockman, G. (eds), *Ulidia*, Proceedings of the First International Conference on the Ulster Cycle of Tales, Belfast and Emain Macha (December Publications, 1994).

Raftery, Barry, *Pagan Celtic Ireland, The Enigma of the Irish Iron Age* (Thames & Hudson, 1994).

Waddell, John, *Archaeology and Celtic Myth* (Four Courts Press, 2015).

Waterman, D.M., *Excavations at Navan Fort, County Armagh 1961–71*, completed and edited by C.J. Lynn; general editor Ann Hamlin (The Stationery Office, Belfast, 1997).

Warner, Richard B., 'Ptolemy's Isamnion Promontory: Rehabilitation and Identification', *Emania* 21, 2013.

Articles and online sources:

An Trumpa Creda, *Archaeology Ireland*, Winter 2000, Vol. 14, No. 4, Issue No. 54, also at Ancient Music Ireland, http://ancientmusicireland.com/page/papers-articles.html.

Lönze, Holger, 'Exploring the Alchemy of Sound', *Archaeology Ireland*, Winter 2018, Vol. 32, No. 4, Issue No. 126.

Moriarty, Colm, and Corless, Adrienne, 'A Barbary Ape Skull from Navan Fort, Co Armagh', irisharchaeology.ie.

Táin Bó Cúailnge, recension 1, https://celt.ucc.ie//published/T301012/text001.html.

Chapter 3: St Dahalin

I owe a great deal to historian and author Bryan MacMahon who shared his research and very many insights into the history and archaeology of Kerry Head.

Sincere thanks are also due to Dr Elva Johnston, Associate Professor at the School of History, University College Dublin, who was so generous with her time and offered suggestions based on her extensive research on Irish saints and early medieval Ireland. She also explained the etymology of Dahalin's name.

I'm indebted to local people Joe Slattery, the Gentleman family (Billy, Amanda and Patrick), Dr Maurice O'Halloran and Ciaran Walsh, who told me about the well's history and its enduring legacy.

Details of what sixth-century religious, daily and political life might have been like were drawn from the following archaeological and historical sources:

Harney, Lorcan, 'Christianising pagan worlds in conversion-era Ireland: archaeological evidence for the origins of Irish ecclesiastical sites', *Proceedings of the Royal Irish Academy*, Vol. 117C (Royal Irish Academy, 2017).

Johnston, Elva, 'The Saints of Kerry in the Early Middle Ages', forthcoming.

O'Sullivan, Aidan, and Nicholl, Tríona, 'Early medieval settlement enclosures in Ireland; dwellings, daily life and social identity', *Proceedings of the Royal Irish Academy*, Vol. 111C (Royal Irish Academy, 2010).

O'Sullivan, Muiris, and Downey, Liam, 'Early Churches – Agriculture and Food', *Archaeology Ireland*, Vol. 31, No. 1 (Spring 2017), pp. 18–21.

During a tour, Annie Birney at the National Museum of Ireland opened a fascinating window into the period by explaining the relevance of some of the artefacts that survive from early medieval Ireland.

Other works cited include:

Johnston, Elva, 'The "pagan" and "Christian" identities of the Irish female saint' in Mark Atherton (ed.), *Celts and Christians: New Approaches to the Religious Traditions of Britain and Ireland* (University of Wales Press, 2002); 'Powerful women or patriarchal weapons? Two medieval Irish saints', *Peritia*, 15. pp. 302–10 (Brepols, 2001).

Johnson, Máire, 'In the Bursting of an Eye: Blinding and Blindness in Ireland's Medieval Hagiography', in 'Wounds and Wound Repair in Medieval Culture', *Explorations in Medieval Culture*, Volume: BRILL (2015).

MacMahon, Bryan (ed.), *Our Christian Heritage* (Ballyheigue Parish History and Heritage Group, 2012).

MacMahon, Bryan, *The Story of Ballyheigue* (Oidhreacht, 1994).

O Donovan, J., *The antiquities of the county of Kerry* (Royal Carberry Books Ltd, 1841), pp. 46–7.

Ó Riain, Pádraig, *A Dictionary of Irish Saints* (Four Courts Press, 2011).

Tarrant, Bernadette, *Exploring the Rich Heritage of the North Kerry Landscape* (Listowel Archaeological and Historical Committee, 1990).

Toal, Caroline, *North Kerry Archaeological Survey* (Brandon, 1995).

Stokes, Whitley (ed.), *Lives of Saints from the Book of Lismore* (Oxford, 1890), pp. 72–3, lines 2431–7, details the exchange between Canir and Senán. Available online: https://archive.org/details/LivesOfSaintsFromTheBookOfLismore/page/n5. Translation courtesy of Dr Elva Johnston.

Journals and newspapers:

Bitel, Lisa M., 'Women's monastic enclosures in early Ireland: a study of female spirituality and male monastic mentalities', *Journal of Medieval History* Vol. 12 (1986) pp. 15–36.

Cogitosus, 'Life of St Brigit', Sean Connolly and J.M. Picard, *The Journal of the Royal Society of Antiquaries of Ireland*, Vol. 117 (1987), pp. 5–27.

'The Danes in Ireland', report of a talk by The Very Rev. T. Lee to Cork Young Men's Society, *Cork Examiner*, 9 December 1897, which contains the description of the Vikings.

O'Shea, Rev. Kieran, 'Bishop Davis Moriarty's Diary, 1856', extracts in *Journal of the Kerry Archaeological and Historical Society*, No. 17, 1984, pp. 113–26.

The testimony from Michael Godley, Dromatoor, Co. Kerry, and collected by Eily Godley is part of the National Folklore Collection UCD, www.duchas.ie.

Chapter 4: Gormlaith

I am very grateful to Dr Catherine Swift, Lecturer in History at Mary Immaculate College Limerick.

Works cited:

Clarke, Howard B., 'Sitriuc Silkbeard (Sitric, Sigtryggr Ólafsson Silkiskeggi)', *Dictionary of Irish Biography* (Cambridge University Press, 2009).

Cusack, M.F., *Illustrated History of Ireland, from the Earliest Period* (Longmans, Green, & Co., 1871).

Duffy, Sean, *Brian Boru and the Battle of Clontarf* (Gill & Macmillan, 2013).

Mac Shamhráin, Ailbhe, 'Gormlaith', *Dictionary of Irish Biography* (Cambridge University Press, 2009).

Ní Bhrolcháin, Muireann, 'Who was Gormlaith's mother? A detective story' in *Lost and Found II – Rediscovering Ireland's past* (2009), pp. 83–94.

Ni Dhonnchadha, Maire & Bourke, Angela (eds), 'Gormlaith and her Sisters c. 750–1400', *The Field Day Anthology of Irish Writing, vol. IV: Irish women's writing and traditions*, p. 188, (Cork University Press, 2002).

Swift, Catherine, 'Gormlaith ingen Murchada ben Briain, Brian's evil nemesis – female trouble-maker', Brian Boru Lecture Series, 2014.

Ua Clerigh, Arthur, *The History of Ireland to the Coming of Henry II*, Vol. 1, (T. Fisher-Unwin, 1910).

Articles and online sources:

Swift, Catherine, 'St Flannan and St Rícenn: labouring kings and literate mothers in medieval Clare', *The Other Clare* 37, 2013, pp. 35–8.

Cosgrave, Art, 'Marriage in Medieval Ireland', *History Ireland*, Issue 3 (Autumn 1994).

Downham, Clare, 'The Battle of Clontarf in Irish history and legend', *History Ireland*, Vol. 13, Issue 5 (Sept/Oct 2005).

Ní Mhaonaigh, Máire, 'Tales of Three Gormlaiths in Medieval Irish Literature', *Ériu*, Vol. 52, Royal Irish Academy (2002), pp. 1–24.

'Battle of Clontarf', podcast by Dr Elva Johnson, http://historyhub.
ie/1014-brian-Boru-battle-of-clontarf.

'Queen Gormlaith, Brian Boru and The Northmen of Dublin', lecture
by Dr Howard Clarke, 2014, http://www.dublincity.ie/story/
queen-gormlaith-brian-Boru-and-northmen-dublin-transcript.

Cogadh Gáedhel re Gallaibh https://archive.org/details/
cogadhgaedhelregootodd/page/n14.

Chapter 5: Aoife MacMurrough

I am very grateful to Dr Linda Doran at the School of Irish, Celtic Studies
and Folklore at University College Dublin for sharing many insights on the
role of women in twelfth-century Ireland.

Thank you too to Eamonn McEneaney, director of Waterford Treasures
museum, for helping me to imagine Aoife's wedding day in Waterford in
1170.

Many thanks are due also to archaeologist and architectural historian
Ben Murtagh for sketching an evocative picture of what daily life inside a
noble's castle in the 1100s might have been like. He also read a draft of this
chapter and made many excellent suggestions.

Also, a special note of thanks to archaeologist Catherine McLoughlin
Stafford for her feedback and encouragement.

Works cited:

Bradley, J., and Murtagh, B., 'William Marshal's Charter to Kilkenny,
1207: background, dating and witnesses', in J. Bradley, C. O Drisceoil
and M. Potterton, *William Marshal and Ireland*, 201–48 (2016).

Doyle, Maureen, 'Dress and ornament in early medieval Ireland –
exploring the evidence' in *Fragments of Lives Past: archaeological
objects from Irish road schemes*, Bernice Kelly, Niall Roycroft and
Michael Stanley (eds), *Archaeology and the National Roads Authority,
Monograph Series No. 11* (National Roads Authority, 2014).

Dictionary of Irish Biography, entries for 'Aífe' by Marie Therese
Flanagan; 'Clare, Richard de ('Richard fitz Gilbert', 'Strongbow')' by
David Beresford; 'Isabella Marshal' by David Beresford; 'William

Marshal' by Ronan Mackay and David Beresford (Cambridge University Press, 2009).

Duffy, Sean (ed.), *Medieval Ireland: An Encyclopedia*, (Routledge Revivals, 2005).

Flanagan, Marie Therese, *Irish Society, Anglo-Norman Settlers, Angevin Kingship: Interactions in Ireland in the Late Twelfth Century* (Clarendon Press, 1989).

Sheehy, Jeanne, *The Rediscovery of Ireland's Past: The Celtic Revival 1830–1930* (Thames & Hudson, 1980).

Orpen, Goddard Henry, *Ireland under the Normans 1169–1216*, Volume I (Oxford, 1911).

Vincent Nicholas, 'Angevin Ireland' in *The Cambridge History of Ireland, Volume I, 600–1550*, Brendan Smith (ed.), (Cambridge University Press, 2018).

Otway-Ruthven, J., *Liber Primus Kilkenniensis, The Kilkenny Journal* (1961).

Newspapers/journals:

A Medieval 'Power Couple', *History Ireland*, https://www.historyireland. com/medieval-history-pre-1500/a-medieval-power-couple.

'English Heritage gives Dover Castle a Medieval Makeover', https://www.theguardian.com/artanddesign/gallery/2009/jul/31/ english-heritage-dover-castle.

Online sources:

Geraldis Cambrensis, *The Conquest of Ireland*, http://www.yorku.ca/ inpar/conquest_ireland.pdf.

The Song of Dermot and the Earl or The Deeds of the Normans in Ireland, https://archive.org/stream/songdermotandeaooregagoog/ songdermotandeaooregagoog_djvu.txt.

'William Marshal, Earl of Pembroke (1147–1219), Crusader, Templar, Kingmaker'. The reference to Goodrich Castle comes from this piece: http://www.turtlebunbury.com/history/history_heroes/hist_hero_ wmarshall.htm.

Chapter 6: Roesia de Verdun

My thanks to Dr Gillian Kenny, who shared her research on Roesia and the women of medieval Ireland.

I am also grateful to Professor Tadhg O'Keeffe who first introduced me to Roesia de Verdun.

Works cited:

Barry, T.B., *The Archaeology of Medieval Ireland* (Routledge, 1987).

Curtis, Edward, 'The spoken languages of medieval Ireland', from *Government, War and Society in Medieval Ireland. Essays by Edmund Curtis, A.J. Otway-Ruthven and James Lydon*, Peter Crooks (ed.), (Four Courts Press, 2008).

De Pizan, Christine, *The Treasure of the City of Ladies,* translated by Sarah Lawson (Penguin, 1985).

Dugdale, William, *The Baronage of England* (London: printed by Tho. Newcomb for Abel Roper, John Martin and Henry Herringman, 1675–6).

Johns, Susan M., *Noblewomen, Aristocracy and Power in the Twelfth-Century Anglo-Norman Realm* (Manchester University Press, 2003).

Kenny, Gillian, 'Roesia de Verdun, Norman femme sole', Women's Museum of Ireland.

Kenny, Gillian, 'The wife's tale: Isabel Marshal and Ireland' in Bradley, John, Ó Drisceoil, Cóilín, & Potterton, Michael, *William Marshal and Ireland* (Four Courts Press, 2017).

Lawrence, Hugh (ed.), *The Letters of Adam Marsh, Volume 1.*

Mackay, Ronan, 'De VERDUN (de Verdon), Roesia (Rohese, Rose)', *Dictionary of Irish Biography* (Cambridge University Press, 2009).

McNeill, T., *Castles in Ireland. Feudal Power in a Gaelic World* (Routledge, 1997).

Tanner, Heather J. (ed.), *Medieval Elite Women and the Exercise of Power, 1100–1400: Moving Beyond the Exceptionalist Debate* (Palgrave Macmillan, 2019).

Vincent, Nicholas, 'Angevin Ireland' in *The Cambridge History of Ireland, Vol. I, 600–1550*, Brendan Smith (ed.), (Cambridge University Press, 2018).

Journals and online sources:

Kenny, Gillian, 'The Women of County Louth in the Later Medieval
   Period, 1170–1540', *Journal of the County Louth Archaeological and
   Historical Society*, Vol. 26, No. 4, 2008, 579–94.

'The Wife's Tale: Women's lives in medieval Tipperary', podcast by Dr
   Gillian Kenny.

O'Keeffe, Tadhg, 'Roesia de Verdun and the building of Castleroche, Co.
   Louth', *The Castle Studies Group Journal* No. 28, 2014–15.

'House of Augustinian nuns: The priory of Grace Dieu', *A History of
   the County of Leicestershire*, Vol. 2 (1954), 27–8, https://www.british-
   history.ac.uk/vch/leics/vol2/pp27-28.

'The de Verdun family of England, Normandy & Ireland', http://www.
   de-verdon.uk/.

'Towns of Anglo-Norman origin', Royal Irish Academy.

Calendar of documents relating to Ireland presented in Her Majesty's
   Public Record Office, London, 1171–1251, H.S. Sweetman (ed.),
   (Longman, 1875), Nos. 2276; 2334; 2446; 2544; 2588.

The description of the construction of the castle is based on experi-
mental archaeology at Château de Guédelon in France, which is being
reconstructed using thirteenth-century tools and techniques.

The description of weapons and tableware at the lord's table are based
on finds at the National Museum of Ireland.

The legend of Roesia de Verdun, or at least one version of it, comes
from Rev. A.W. Atkins' account in 1938, Duchas.ie.

Chapter 7: Margaret O'Carroll

I am very grateful to Dr Bernadette Cunningham, deputy librarian of the
Royal Irish Academy in Dublin. I have drawn extensively from her book
Medieval Irish Pilgrims to Santiago de Compostela for the descriptions of
pilgrimage to north-west Spain in the fifteenth century.

Works cited:

Blackburne, Elizabeth Owens, *Illustrious Irishwomen*, Vol. I, (Tinsley Brothers, 1877).

Cunningham, Bernadette, *Medieval Irish Pilgrims to Santiago de Compostela* (Four Courts Press, 2018).

Duffy, Sean, (ed.), *Medieval Ireland, An Encyclopedia* (Routledge, 2005).

Kenny, Gillian, *Anglo-Irish and Gaelic Women in Ireland c. 1170–1540* (Dublin, 2007).

McCrait, L.M., *The Romance of Irish Heroines* (Dublin, 1913).

Meek, C.E. & Simms, M.K. (eds), *The Fragility of her Sex? Medieval Irish Women in their European Context* (Four Courts Press, 1996).

O'Byrne, Emmett, 'O'Carroll (Ní Chearbhaill), Mairghréag', *Dictionary of Irish Biography*, (Cambridge University Press, 2009).

O'Byrne, Emmett, 'O'Carroll (Ó Cearbhaill), Tadhg Ailbhe', *Dictionary of Irish Biography*, (Cambridge University Press, 2009).

Simms, Katharine, 'Guesting and Feasting in Gaelic Ireland', *Journal of the Royal Society of Antiquaries of Ireland*, Vol. 108 (1978), pp. 67–95.

Simms, Katharine, 'Gaelic Culture and Society' from *The Cambridge History of Ireland: Volume 1, 600–1550*, Brendan Smith (ed.), (Cambridge University Press, 2018).

Simms, Katharine, 'Ní Chearbhaill, Mairgréag [Margaret O'Carroll] (d. 1451), celebrated hostess', *Oxford Dictionary of National Biography* (Oxford University Press, 2004).

The Annals of Connacht, 1433.2 at https://celt.ucc.ie/.

Journals:

Edel Bhreathnach, 'The Tech Midchúarta, "The House of the Mead-Circuit: Feasting, Royal Circuits and the King's Court in Early Ireland"', *Archaeology Ireland*, Vol. 12. No. 4, Winter 1998.

The Irish Ecclesiastical Record, Series III, Vol. V (Dublin, 1884), https://archive.org/stream/irishecclesiasto1recogoog#page/n307/mode/2up/search/clyn.

Chapter 8: Katherine Fitzgerald

My sincere thanks to Dr Clodagh Tait, senior lecturer in history at Mary Immaculate College, Limerick, for sharing her research on the Old Countess of Desmond.

Many thanks too to Dr Aoibheann Nic Dhonnchadha, medical manuscripts expert and Assistant Professor at the Dublin Institute for Advanced Studies, who very kindly outlined the medical knowledge of the day.

Other works cited:

Chambers, Anne, *Eleanor, Countess of Desmond* (Gill & Macmillian, 2011).

Clavin, Terry, 'Fitzgerald (Butler), Eleanor', *Dictionary of Irish Biography* (Cambridge University Press, 2009).

Crooks, Peter and Duffy, Seán, (eds), *The Geraldines and Medieval Ireland: The Making of a Myth*, Medieval Ireland Series 1 (Four Courts Press, 2016).

Demaitre, Luke, *Medieval Medicine: The Art of Healing, from Head to Toe* (Praeger, 2013).

Flavin, Susan, *Consumption and Culture in Sixteenth-Century Ireland: Saffron, Stockings and Silk*, Irish Historical Monographs (Boydell Press, 2014).

Gernon, Luke, *A discourse of Ireland*, 1620, https://celt.ucc.ie//published/ E620001/.

Lennon, Colm, *Sixteenth Century Ireland*, New Gill History of Ireland (Gill, 1994, 2005).

MacCurtain, Margaret, and O'Dowd, Mary (eds), *Women in Early Modern Ireland* (Edinburgh University Press, 1991).

MacCurtain, Margaret, et al., 'An Agenda for Women's History in Ireland, 1500–1900', *Irish Historical Studies*, Vol. 28, No. 109, 1992, pp. 1–37.

McCormack, Anthony, 'Fitzgerald, Katherine, Countess of Desmond (d. 1604)', *Oxford Dictionary of National Biography* (Oxford, 2004).

Moore, Thomas, 'The Fudge Family In Paris Letter X. From Miss Biddy Fudge To Miss Dorothy ----' online at http://poetspoetry.com /thomas-moore/fudge-family-in-paris-letter-x-from-miss-biddy -fudge-to-miss-dorothy-27359.

O'Dowd, Mary, *A History of Women in Ireland, 1500–1800* (Pearson Education Limited, 2005).

Sainthill, Richard, *The Old Countess of Desmond: An Inquiry* (University Press, M.H. Gill, 1861).

Spenser, Edmund, *A View of the State of Ireland*, https://celt.ucc.ie//published/E500000-001/.

Wincott Heckett, Elizabeth, 'The Apparel oft Proclaims the Man', *Northern Archaeological Textiles: NESAT VII*: Textile Symposium in Edinburgh, Frances Pritchard and John Peter Wild (eds), Oxbow Books, 1999.

Articles and online sources:

Gaelic Medical Manuscripts from the Academy Collections, Royal Irish Academy, https://www.ria.ie/gaelic-medical-manuscripts-academy-collections.

Hardinge W.H., 'On the old countess of Desmond', *Proceedings of the Royal Irish Academy (1836–1869)*, Vol. 8 (1861–1864), pp. 477–83.

Dorney, John, The Desmond Rebellions Part I & II, www.theirishstory.com.

'Historical celebrities connected with Youghal', *Cork Constitution*, 7, 21 and 28 November 1885.

Parr's Pills reference from the caption on the portrait of 'Countess of Desmond: Engraved from a Painting in the Collection At Dublin Castle' (London, 1861).

Tait, Clodagh, 'The Old Countess, the Geraldine knight and the lady antiquarian: a conspiracy theory revisited', *History Ireland*, Vol. 21, May/June 2013.

Chapter 9: Katherine Jones

I owe a great debt of gratitude to Dr Evan Bourke, who very generously shared so many of the insights he gained into the life and work of Lady Ranelagh while researching his doctoral project, 'A godly Sybilla, an erudite wife and burdensome sister: the formation and representation of women's reputations within the Hartlib Circle 1641–1661' (NUI Galway, 2018).

I am also very grateful to Dr Harman Murtagh who was able to flesh out the details of the siege of Athlone in such vivid detail. I drew on his expertise and the references in his seminal book on the history of Athlone, *Athlone: History and Settlement to 1800* (The Old Athlone Society, 2000).

Many thanks too to Therese Grennan at Athlone Castle for helping to fill in that part of the picture.

I have quoted from some of Lady Ranelagh's letters, copies of which were very kindly given to me by Dr Evan Bourke. They are:

Katherine Jones, Lady Ranelagh, to Richard Boyle, First Earl Cork, 26 December 1642, Dublin. From holograph in National Library of Ireland, MS 43266/20, 4°.

Katherine Jones, Lady Ranelagh, to Richard Boyle, First Earl of Burlington, February 1659, London. From holograph in Chatsworth House, Cork Mss, Vol. 30. Letter 95, 2°.

Katherine Jones, Lady Ranelagh, to Margaret Boyle, Countess of Orrery, 1689, London. From holograph in West Sussex Record Office, Petworth House, Orrery MS 13219, 8°.

Katherine Jones, Lady Ranelagh, to Anne Hamilton, Duchess of Hamilton, 6 August 1690, London. From holograph in National Records of Scotland, Edinburgh, GD406/1/3797, 8°.

Katherine Jones, Lady Ranelagh, to Anne Hamilton, Duchess of Hamilton, 28 August 1690, London. From holograph in National Records of Scotland, Edinburgh, GD45/14/237/3, 8°.

I have also drawn on the letters of Sir John Leeke in *Memoirs of the Verney Family*, https://bit.ly/2E8VaxP.

Other works cited:
Bourke, Evan, *Female Involvement, Membership, and Centrality: A Social Network Analysis of the Hartlib Circle.* Literature Compass (John Wiley and Sons, 2017).

Bourke, Evan: Herstory profile of Katherine Jones: www.herstory.ie/news/2017/7/4/katherine-jones-viscountess-ranelagh

Canney, Nicholas, *Making Ireland British 1580–1650* (Oxford University Press, 2001).

Connolly, Ruth, 'Viscountess Ranelagh and the Authorisation of Women's Knowledge in the Hartlib Circle' in J. Harris and E. Scott-Baumann (eds), *The Intellectual Culture of Puritan Women*, 1558–1680 (2010).

Darcy, Eamon, *The Irish Rebellion of 1641 and the Wars of the Three Kingdoms*, Royal Historical Society (Boydell Press, 2013).

DiMeo, Michelle, *Katherine Jones, Lady Ranelagh (1615–91)*, thesis (University of Warwick Publications, 2009).

DiMeo, Michelle, 'Lady Ranelagh's Medical Authority' in *Women and Epistolary Agency in Early Modern Culture, 1450–1690*, James Daybell and Andrew Gordon (eds), Routledge, 2016.

MacCurtain, Margaret, and O'Dowd, Mary (eds), *Women in Early Modern Ireland* (Edinburgh, 1991), p. 95.

Ohlmeyer, Jane, *Making Ireland English: The Irish Aristocracy in the Seventeenth Century* (Yale University Press, 2012), p. 204.

Pal, Carol, *Republic of Women: Rethinking the Republic of Letters in the Seventeenth Century* (Cambridge University Press, 2010).

Lamb, Edel, *Reading Children in Early Modern Culture*, Early Modern Literature in History (Palgrave Macmillan, 2018).

Sherlock, Rory, *Athlone Castle: An introduction to the history and architecture of Athlone Castle* (Westmeath County Council, 2016).

Taylor Fitzsimon, Betsey, 'Jones, Lady Katherine Viscountess Ranelagh Boyle' in James McGuire and James Quinn (eds), *Dictionary of Irish Biography* (Cambridge University Press, 2009).

Chapter 10: Ellen Hutchins

I am deeply indebted to Madeline Hutchins who gave me many of Ellen's letters along with other relevant material. She also very graciously commented on a draft of this chapter, offering many clarifications and improvements. Her research is available on https://www.ellenhutchins.com/.

I have drawn extensively from the 'Memoir of Ellen Hutchins', written by Ellen's niece Alicia Hutchins some decades after her death. It gives an evocative account of Ellen's life and work, and quotes from some of her letters. The chapter was fleshed out by the works cited below:

Abarta Heritage audio, The Ellen Hutchins Trail, https://www. abartaheritage.ie/product/ellen-hutchins-trail/.

Connolly, S. 'Family, Love and Marriage: Some Evidence from the Early Eighteenth Century', in M. MacCurtain and M. O'Dowd (eds), *Women in Early Modern Ireland* (Edinburgh, 1991).

Dutton, Sarah, 'Ellen Hutchins – Ireland's First Female Botanist', The New York Botanical Garden's Talk Science Blog (2015).

Hume, Robert, 'Ballylickey's famous botanist was among world's finest plant experts', *Southern Star*, 2015.

Lucey, John and Hutchins, Madeline, *Ellen Hutchins (1785-1815): Botanist and Artist,* paper on the provenance and background of Alicia Hutchins' Memoir (2016). Available online at https://www.ellenhutchins.com/links-resources/.

Lunney, Linde, 'Hutchins, Ellen (1785–1815), *Dictionary of Irish Biography* (Cambridge University Press, 2009).

'Memoir of Ellen Hutchins', Representative Church Body Library, Dublin, MS 47, reproduced in Lucey/Hutchins paper.

Mitchell, M.E. (ed.,) *Early Observations on the Flora of Southwest Ireland. Selected letters of Ellen Hutchins and Dawson Turner 1807–1814,* National Botanic Gardens, Glasnevin, Dublin, Occasional Papers XII, 1999.

Salter-Townshend, 'Ellen Hutchins (1785–1815) – Ireland's first female botanist', Women's museum of Ireland (2015), http://womensmuseumofireland.ie/articles/ellen-hutchins-1785-1815.

Secord, Anne, 'Hutchins, Ellen (1785–1815)', *Oxford Dictionary of National Biography* (Oxford University Press, 2004).

Chapter 11: Lady Sligo

Very many thanks to Sheelyn Browne, who first introduced me to her great-great-great-grandmother Lady Sligo in 2014.

Thank you too to Famine scholar Professor Christine Kinealy, who first put Lady Sligo's letters on exhibition at Ireland's Great Hunger Institute at Quinnipiac University of Hamden, Connecticut, and spoke to me about the woman who wrote them.

I'm also hugely grateful to Biddy Hughes, general manager and head of commercial development at Westport House, who showed me around the house on many occasions and explained its fascinating and multilayered history.

Works cited:

Chambers, Anne, *The Great Leviathan* (New Island Press, 2017). Details from Lord Sligo's diary come from this definitive biography.

Gannon, Caroline, 'The Women of Westport House', thesis submitted to the Galway-Mayo Institute of Technology.

Kinealy, Christine, King, Jason and Reilly, Ciarán (eds), *Women and the Great Hunger* (Quinnipiac University Press, 2016).

Letters:

Marchioness of Sligo to Dowager Marchioness of Sligo, 3 March 1817, MS40911/4, Westport House Estate papers, National Library of Ireland, refers to the family nicknames.

Sligo to Dowager Marchioness of Sligo, 2 May 1817, Sligo Papers, No. 47, TCD, mentions 'Kitten', the couple's first child, Louisa.

Sligo to Dowager Marchioness of Sligo, 28 March 1817, Sligo Papers, No. 56, TCD, refers to Catherine's reluctance to have two wet nurses in the house at the same time.

Sligo to Dowager Marchioness of Sligo, 1 May 1817, Sligo Papers, No. 60, TCD, includes the SOS for a housekeeper.

Sligo to George Caldwell, 31 January 1816, Sligo Papers, No. 39, TCD refers to his being more in love with his wife-to-be each day.

The details of the compensation paid to the Brownes comes from 'Legacies of British slave ownership', University College London, Department of History, 2015.

Newspapers:

Tuam Herald, 31 October 1857.

Freeman's Journal, 2 Sept 1853.

'Education in Ireland, Lord and Lady Sligo', *Dublin Morning Register*,
    23 May 1829.

Mayo Constitution, 19 January 1847.

The Weekly Chronicle, 6 January 1850.

Belfast Morning News, 24 February 1865.

'Journey to Freedom', *The Gleaner*, 4 August 2012.

'Sligoville – Jamaica's First Free Village Established To Prepare For
    Emancipation', *The Gleaner*, 16 August 2014.

Dublin Evening Packet and Correspondent, 13 June 1844.

'History of Highgate House, Jamaica', *The Gleaner*, 7 August 2007.

Chapter 12: Jo Hiffernan

This chapter is based largely on the correspondence in the James McNeill
Whistler archive at the University of Glasgow: *The Correspondence of
James McNeill Whistler, 1855–1903*, Margaret F. MacDonald, Patricia de
Montfort and Nigel Thorp (eds), University of Glasgow, 2003–10, online
edition, https://www.whistler.arts.gla.ac.uk/.

Letters cited include:

695: Gustave Courbet to J.W. [James Whistler] about their time in
    Trouville.

8042: J.W. to Henri Fantin-Latour.

11977 and 13149: J.W. on *The Girl in White*.

9186: Jo's comments on *The Girl in White*.

11483, 11480 & 12127: J.W. gives Jo power of attorney.

1954: J.W. writes to his son from Venice.

6527: J.W.'s mother says she will pray for Jo.

11844: Jo to solicitor asking for money.

12812: Jo's sister Bridget Agnes' marriage certificate, which names their
    father.

Works cited include:

Clive Emsley, Tim Hitchcock & Robert Shoemaker, 'Irish London, The Proceedings at the Old Bailey' at www.oldbaileyonline.org.

Havemeyer, Louisine, *Sixteen to Sixty: Memoirs of a Collector* (Ursus Press, 1993).

Pearson, Hesketh, *The Man Whistler* (House of Stratus, 2015).

Sutherland, Daniel E., *Whistler: A Life for Art's Sake* (Yale University Press, 2014).

The Young George du Maurier, A Selection of his Letters, 1860–67, edited by Daphne du Maurier (Doubleday Inc., 1952).

Shortall, Eithne, 'Joanna Hiffernan ruled out as origin of Courbet's *L'Origine du Monde* painting', *The Sunday Times*, 30 September 2018.

'Le modèle de «L'Origine du monde» enfin identifié', *Libération*, 25 September 2018.

Chapter 13: Jennie Hodgers

My sincere thanks to documentary-maker Fiona Ní Eidhin for telling me about Jennie Hodgers/Albert Cashier. Fiona produced the TG4 documentary *Jennie Hodgers – Saighdiúr Lincoln* (Jennie Hodgers – Lincoln's Soldier), which is available here: https://youtu.be/szfsg0x37K0?.

When writing about Albert Cashier, I have used the pronoun 'he' – as he did during his lifetime – and when writing about Jennie Hodgers, I have used 'she'.

Other works cited:

Conklin, Michael, 'Walk Like a Man: The Jennie Hodgers Story', Michael Conklin, *History Magazine*, December/January 2010, available online at http://www.jcs-group.com/military/war1861people/women.html.

Davis, William, *History of the 104th Pennsylvania Regiment* (Applewood Books, Massachusetts, 1866), p. 123.

Shiels, Damian, http://irishamericancivilwar.com/2011/08/17/jennie-hodgers-the-irishwoman-who-fought-as-a-man-in-the-union-army/.

Wood, Wales W., *A history of the Ninety-fifth regiment, Illinois infantry volunteers : from its organization in the fall of 1862,*

until its final discharge from the United States service, in 1865,
Chicago Tribune company's book and job printing office, 1865.
Available at https://archive.org/stream/ninetyfifthregoowoodrich/
ninetyfifthregoowoodrich_djvu.txt.

Newspapers:
The Hartford Republican, Hartford, Kentucky, 6 June 1913, https://www
.newspapers.com/clip/15598766/hartford_republican_hartford_ky/.
'BRAVE WOMAN'S SECRET', *Anglo-Celt*, 13 December 1913.
'MASQUERADED AS A MAN. Served in Gen Grant's army', *Sunday
Independent*, 12 April 1914.
'Gutsy Jennie Hodgers', Iris Nelson, *Herald Whig*, 25 May 2013.

Websites:
http://www.jcs-group.com/military/war1861people/women.html
https://americancivilwar.com/women/
https://quod.lib.umich.edu/c/clementsmss/umich-wcl-M
-2422bus?view=text

Chapter 14: Lizzie Le Blond

This chapter is based almost entirely on Lizzie Le Blond's memoir, *Day in,
Day out* (The Bodley Head Ltd, 1928). With special thanks to Rosemary
Raughter.

Other works cited include:
Le Blond, Mrs Aubrey, *True Tales of Mountain Adventure*, e-book.
Raughter, Rosemary, 'Elizabeth Hawkins-Whitshed of Killincarrick: a
Victorian lady in the High Alps', www.countywicklowheritage.org.
Raughter, Rosemary, 'A Wicklow Woman's War',
www.countywicklowheritage.org.
Morning Post, 26 June 1879.
Morning Post, 14 June 1900.
Tatler, 7 January 1953.

Chapter 15: Clotilde Graves

I am extremely grateful to Dr Jenny Bloodworth who has done extensive work on Clotilde Graves and is an authority on her life and work. She very generously spoke to me about her research. She has written a master's dissertation as well as a doctoral thesis on Clotilde Graves and it was she who pointed me in the direction of the archive of the Royal Literary Fund. The personal details about Clotilde's life and her experience of working late into the night and later suffering from brain fever are all gleaned from the letters she wrote to them.

I'm very grateful too to Eileen Gunn at the Royal Literary Fund who granted permission to allow the British Library to make digital copies of letters from Loan 96 RLF1/2692 and forward them to me.

Sincere thanks to Frank Trimm of the Buttevant Heritage Group who graciously shared his extensive research on the barracks at Buttevant.

Kieran Wyse, Reference and Local Studies, at Cork Library, was also very helpful.

Works cited:

Bloodworth, Jenny, *Clotilde Graves: Journalist, Dramatist and Novelist*, PhD
     thesis submitted to the School of English, University of Leicester (2012).
Graves, Clotilde Inez Mary, *The Dop Doctor* (Project Gutenberg e-book).
Shelley, Lorna, 'Female Journalists and Journalism in fin-de-siècle
     Magazine Stories', *Nineteenth-Century Gender Studies*, Issue 5.2
     (Summer 2009).
Whyte, Frederic, *William Heinemann: A Memoir* (Jonathan Cape, 1928).
Letters from the Royal Literary Fund archive (Loan 96 RLF1/2692).
Letter from Clotilde Inez Mary Graves [Richard Dehan] to Malcolm
     Watson, discussing a four-act romantic comedy, 6 January 1903,
     National Library of Ireland.

Newspapers and journals:

Editor's comments on her being 'quite one of us' come from 'Flashes
     from the Footlights', *The Licensed Victualler's Mirror* (29 April 1890).
The Era, 25 July 1885, review of *The Babes* in the Gaiety Theatre, Dublin.

The Era, 5 November 1887, Review of *Nitocris*.

Irish Press, 5 December 1932.

Richard Dehan obituary, *New Zealand Evening Post*, Volume CXV, issue 11, 14 January 1933, www.natlib.govt.nz.

Irish Press crossword, 11 November 1971.

Cork Examiner, obituary, 6 December 1932.

Roscommon Weekly Messenger, 18 April 1908.

'A Lady Journalist', *Sheffield Evening Telegraph*, 28 August 1888.

The Sketch, 27 April 1896.

Chapter 16: Sr Concepta Lynch

My sincere thanks to Sr Frances Lally who was an invaluable source of information and shared her extensive archive with me. The details of the students and many of the personal details about Sr Concepta come from her.

I am deeply grateful to artists Veronica Heywood and Jo Callanan, who showed me around the oratory. They also allowed me to consult their extensive archives. (Interviews conducted on 24 May 2018.)

My thanks too to Fr Myles Healy who shared his memories of his mother's schooldays and Sr Concepta with me.

Many thanks to Síghle Bhreathnach-Lynch who answered many questions and very kindly read and commented on a draft of this chapter.

Nigel Curtin, Local Studies librarian at the Lexicon in Dun Laoghaire, went out of his way to provide archive material on Sr Concepta.

Many thanks to James O'Sullivan, Dun Laoghaire–Rathdown County Council, who very kindly arranged access to the oratory.

Thank you too to the National Gallery of Ireland and the Centre of Irish Studies.

Works cited:

A Shrine of Celtic art: The Art of Sr. M. Concepta Lynch O.P., introduced by Etienne Rynne, published by the Irish Dominican Sisters, Dun Laoghaire.

Arnold, Bruce, *Irish Art: A Concise History* (Thames & Hudson, 1969).

Bhreathnach-Lynch, Síghle, 'Sr Concepta Lynch OP (1874–1939): a unique contribution to Irish art' in O'Connor, Éimear (ed.), *Irish Women Artists, 1800–2009: Familiar but Unknown* (Four Courts, 2010).

Kipling, Rudyard, *Delphi Collected Works of Rudyard Kipling (Illustrated)*, Kindle edition.

Lally, Sr Frances OP, 'Sacred Heart', *Word* magazine, May 2008.

Little, George A., 'An Oratory and Its Eloquent Art', in the *Irish Rosary*, Jan–Feb 1961, pp. 21–8.

Sheehy, Jeanne, *The Rediscovery of Ireland's Past: The Celtic Revival 1830–1930* (Thames & Hudson, 1980).

Snoddy, Theo, *Dictionary of Irish Artists: 20th Century* (Wolfhound Press, 1996).

Memories of a Dun Laoghaire Dominican Convent primary school, 1848–1998, published by the Dominican sisters, 1998, an invaluable source for many of the details of Sr Concepta's teaching life.

Newspapers and online sources:

'Dorothy Ward and Shaun Glenville: A Pantomime Partnership', http://www.its-behind-you.com/wardglenville.html.

The Art Journal, June 1880.

'Hidden Treasure', *Irish Press*, 9 February 1961.

The Irishman column, *The Irish Times*, 5 February 1881.

'Magical shrine to Celtic art part of Open House weekend', *The Irish Times*, 16 October 2018.

Lally, Sr Frances, 'Kingfisher in Flight', in *Weavings*, a magazine celebrating Dominican women.

Chapter 17: The Overend Sisters

I am very grateful to Barbara Carney for sharing her memories of life at Airfield House in the mid-1980s and early '90s. Many thanks too to Genevieve Whitfield, heritage and events manager at Airfield, for the tour of the house and gardens. I couldn't have assessed the Overend letters without help from Nicola Kelly, archivist at the OPW-Maynooth University Archive and Research Centre at Castletown, Celbridge, Co. Kildare.

The letters quoted in the text are:
PP/AIR 833: Letter from Naomi on the German takeover of Austria.
PP/AIR 909: Letter from soldier J.A. MacMunn.
PP/AIR 911: Letter from soldier Arthur Verschoyle.
PP/AIR 912: Humphrey Butler's letter to his cousin Lily Overend.
PP/AIR 725: Letter from Lily's mother Letitia M. Butler about settling into the farm in Airfield.
PP/AIR 784: Trevor Overend's letter to Lily dated 24 June 1879.
PP/AIR 1082: Lily's letter to Letitia from Switzerland.
PP/AIR 1082: Lily's letter to Letitia from Paris.
PP/AIR 1841: Trevor's first letter to Naomi.
PP/AIR 1020: Letitia's diary entry about her Uncle Tommy.
PP/AIR 1022: Letitia on the Easter Rising.
PP/AIR 74: Aunt Fanny on the Easter Rising.
PP/AIR 2701: Letter from Dr Ella Webb to Letitia.
PP/AIR 1043: Letitia diary entry about Skellig Rock.
PP/AIR 3324/3325/3326: Letitia on her world tour with the British Medical Association.
PP/AIR 1033: Letitia's diary entry on Dr Bethel Solomons' Caesarean section operation.

Works cited:
Kelly, Laura, *Irish women in medicine, c.1880s–1920s: Origins, Education and Careers* (Manchester University Press, 2012).

Newspapers, journals and articles:
Larkin, Bernadette, 'Overend Women: Independent women of the 1900s', Women's Museum of Ireland https://womensmuseumofireland.ie/articles/the-overend-women.
Montgomery, Bob, 'The 1903 Irish Gordon Bennett Cup Race', http://www.gordonbennettroute.com/1903race.html.

O'Dwyer, Rory, 'On show to the world: the Eucharistic Congress, 1932',
 History Ireland, Issue 6 (Nov/Dec 2007), Volume 15.

'Jubilee Nurse – the forgotten heroine of Ireland's public health service',
 Kildare History Journal, electronic version, posted July 2013.

'Treatment of Rickets. New Dublin Institution', *The Irish Times*, 5 June 1924.

'Overends stay put …' Jim Farrelly, *Evening Herald*, 28 March 1973.

'Coveney reopens Airfield urban farm after €11m revamp', Alison Healy,
 The Irish Times, 10 April 2014.

Chapter 18: Mabel Colhoun

I am deeply grateful to Mabel Colhoun's niece Kyleen Clarke and her husband Richard Clarke who spoke about Mabel and welcomed me into their home to view the family archive.

Many thanks to Karine Bigand, who first told me about Mabel and put me in touch with Denise Henry, who has done extensive research on her life and work. Denise very generously shared her research and offered guidance and introductions. Her 2012 dissertation, *Mabel Remington Colhoun: The making of an Archaeologist (1905–1992)*, offers unrivalled insights into the life and times of Mabel Colhoun.

Many thanks too to Brian Lacey and Roy Hamilton who graciously shared their many memories of Mabel.

Works cited:

Colhoun, Mabel R., *The Heritage of Inishowen: Its Archaeology, History and Folklore* (North West Archaeological and Historical Society, Coleraine, 1995).

The Clarke Archive, which contains newspaper clippings, photographs and family letters and postcards written by Mabel from 1920s to the 1990s.

Early Medieval Ireland: Archaeological Excavations 1930–2004, Early Medieval Archaeology Project (EMAP) Report 2.1 Report to INSTAR 2008, UCD School of Archaeology/School of Geography, Palaeoecology and Archaeology, QUB/CRDS/ACS, December 2008.

Newspapers and journals:

'The pioneer of nursery education', *The Northern Constitution*, 17 June 1978, the Clarke archive.

Gormley, Kathleen, 'A Tribute to No Ordinary Woman Miss Mabel Remington Colhoun', *Ulster Local Studies*, Vol. 14 No. 2, Winter 1992, pp. 83–3.

Kelly, Owen, 'Moving spirit behind the archiving of a peninsula', *The Irish News*, 30 March 1996.

Dooher, J., Review of *The Heritage of Inishowen*, *Ulster Local Studies*, Vol. 18, No. 1, Summer 1996, pp 112–15.

Londonderry High School Old Girls' Association Magazine 1957 and 1958, which include Mabel's reports when she was Chairman of the Londonderry Nursery School Management Committee.

Chapter 19: Rosemary Gibb

I am exceptionally grateful to Rosemary's family – Andrew, Tamzin and Jason – for sharing their memories of a wife and mother. I have drawn extensively from their reminiscences, given so generously and openly, as well as from Rosemary's father's memoir, detailed below.

Sincere thanks too to Senator David Norris for recalling his 30-year friendship with Rosemary Gibb. I also want to thank Rosemary's close friends Katherine Cohen and Alida Schieffelin-Gersie for sharing their memories of Rosemary.

Works and articles cited:

Gibson, Jack, *Memoirs of an Irish Surgeon: An Enchanted Life* (2000).

Dictionary of Irish Biography (Cambridge University Press, 2009).

'Medal for girl who saved dog', *Irish Press*, 29 March 1963.

'Jumped into Liffey to save pigeon', *Irish Independent*, 1 July 1965.

'Naas girl rescues crippled pigeon', *Nationalist and Leinster Times*, 9 July 1965.

McEntee, John, 'Educating the children … for what sort of future?' *Irish Press*, 23 May 1978.

Marriott, Peter, 'Rosemary just loves clowning', *Irish Press*, 20 November 1985.

'Rosy Magic', *Evening Herald*, February 1996.

Obituary by Pat Williams, *The Independent*, 22 July 1997.

Obituary, *Sunday Tribune*, 27 July 1997.

Appreciation by David Norris, *The Irish Times*, 5 August 1997.

Chapter 20: Jemma Redmond

My sincere thanks to Jemma Redmond's parents Lorraine and Christy who welcomed me into their home and shared memories of Jemma.

Thank you too to Bill Liao, Tony Herbert and Alexandra Whelan who spoke about a friend and colleague.

I have quoted from Jemma Redmond's address to the SynBio Future 2016 Conference in Cork to explain her work and vision in her own words. The story about the printed finger is also contained in this clip. It is online at https://www.labtube.tv/video/ourobotics-the-future-of-bioprinting#.

Her comments on the treatment of intersex people in Ireland were posted under the article 'Practice of "normalising" intersex children at birth denounced by Europe', thejournal.ie, 13 May 2015.

Other articles and websites cited:

Human rights and intersex people, issue paper published by the Council of Europe Commissioner for Human Rights, Council of Europe, 2015.

'Inspirational Ourobotics founder Jemma Redmond dies unexpectedly', Gordon Hunt, siliconrepublic.com.

'Female Founder Spotlight: Jemma Redmond of Ourobotics', Kayla Liederbach, SOSV, 18 September 2015.

'This start-up says conservative Ireland is afraid to fund world-changing biotech', Killian Woods, 21 February 2016, Fora.ie.

'The spirit of our age,' David Worlock, davidworlock.com.